AF564688

CORROSION AND ENVIRONMENT

CORROSION
AND
ENVIRONMENT

By

Dr. Khalid Sulaiman Khalyl Khairou

Chairman/Professor
Dept. of Chemistry
Faculty of Applied Sciences
Umm-Al-Qura University
Makkah Al-Mukarramah
Saudi-Arabia

&

Dr. Ishaq Zaafarany

M.Sc., Ph.D.
Associate Professor
Dept. of Chemistry
Umm-Al-Qura University
Makkah Al-Mukarramah
Saudi-Arabia

DISCOVERY PUBLISHING HOUSE PVT. LTD.
NEW DELHI-110 002

Published by:
Tilak Wasan
DISCOVERY PUBLISHING HOUSE PVT. LTD.
4383/4B, Ansari Road, Darya Ganj
New Delhi-110 002 (India)
Phone : +91-11-23279245, 43596064-65
Fax : +91-11-23253475
E-mail : discoverypublishinghouse@gmail.com
sales@discoverypublishinggroup.com
parul.wasan@gmail.com
web : www.discoverypublishinggroup.com

First Edition: **2013**

ISBN: 978-93-5056-245-1

Corrosion and Environment

Printed at:
Aditi Fine Art Press
Delhi

Preface

Environment is the sum of all social, cultural, biological, physical and chemical factors which constitute the surroundings of human beings, who are both creator and molders of their environment. Environment is never constant; it is continuously changing, slowly by nature, rapidly and drastically by all living beings, especially man.

Corrosion and destruction of metal and building materials is a very burning topic of environmental effects. Today, its chemistry is very interesting.

I congratulate the author professor Dr. Khalid Khairo chairman and Dr. Ishaq Zaafarany (co-author) of the department of chemistry, Umm-Al-Qura University, Makkah Al-Mukarramah, K.S.A, who have floated a book entitled **"Corrosion & Environment"** which was badly needed to support and enlighten the students of Saudi Arabian Universities with current knowledge of corrosion, due to which world is facing a loss of millions of crore dollars every year.

The language of book is simple and lucid, understandable and informative, and equally useful to students and common literate person.

–Authors

Contents

Preface

1. **Introduction** 1

Corrosion.

2. **Literature Survey and Scope of the Work** 4

Survey of the Earlier Work—Scope of the Work.

3. **Consequence of Corrosion** 13

The Consequences of Corrosion—Importance of Corrosion Studies—The Corrosion Challenge—Nature and Extent of The Corrosion Problem—Hazard Symbol—Types of Hazard Symbols—Radioactive Sign—Current Trefoil Symbol—The Early Radioactive Trefoil (1946)—The New ISO 21482 Radiation Symbol—Biohazard Symbol used since 1966—Drawing—Tattoos—Poison Sign—Skull and Crossbones—Warning Sign—German Road Warning Sign—Chemical Hazard—European Hazard Symbols—Non-standard Warning Signs.

4. **Types of Corrosion** 22

Uniform Corrosion—Galvanic Corrosion—Concentration Cell Corrosion—Soil Corrosion—Pitting Corrosion—Intergranuiar Corrosion—Water line Corrosion—Stress Corrosion—Corrosion of Plastic and Elastomers—Erosion Corrosion and Fretting—Electrochemical Theory of Corrosion—Electrochemical Kinetics—Kinetics of Electrochemical Reaction—Linear Polarization Resistance and the Stern-Geary Equation—Losses Due to Corrosion.

5. **Metallic Corrosion** 48

Tribocorrosion—Phenomena in Different Engineering Fields—Biotribocorrosion—Passive Metals—Stress Corrosion Cracking—Metals Attacked—Polymers Attacked—Crack Growth—Prevention—Examples—Bacterial Anaerobic Corrosion—Anaerobic Corrosion—Transformation of Ferrous Hydroxide into Magnetic—Nominally

Anaerobic Corrosion of Carbon Steel in Near-Neutral pH Saline Environments—Iron Bacteria—Bacteria Known to Feed on Iron ore Thiobacillus Ferrooxidans and Leptospirillum Ferrooxidans—Habitat—Possible Indicators—Prevention—Control—Shock Chlorination—Copper Band Corrosion—Cooper—Characteristics—Physical—Chemical—Isotopes—Main Article: Isotopes of Copper—Occurrence—Production—Reserves—Methods—Recycling—Binary Compounds—Organocopper Chemistry—Copper(III) and Copper(IV)—Erosion Corrosion of Copper Water Tubes—Occurrence—Zinc Pest—Environmental Stress Fracture—Stress Corrosion Cracking—Hydrogen Embrittlement—Case Studies—Fracture—What is a Stress Fracture?—How is a Stress Fracture Diagnosed?—Why Did I get a Stress Fracture?—What is the Treatment for a Stress Fracture?—Concrete—Electrical Resistivity Measurement of Concrete—Method—Transformer Method—Standards—Application.

6. Corrosion in Non-metals **76**

Corrosion of Glasses—Glass Corrosion Tests—See Also—Corrosion—Galvanic Corrosion—Galvanic Series—Corrosion Removal—Intrinsic Chemistry—Passivation—Corrosion in Passivated Materials—Pitting Corrosion—Weld Decay and Knifeline Attack—Crevice Corrosion—Microbial Corrosion—High Temperature Corrosion—Methods of Protection from Corrosion—Reactive Coatings—Anodization—Biofilm Coatings—Controlled Permeability Formwork—Cathodic Protection—Sacrificial Protection—Impressed Current Cathodic Protection—Anodic Protection—Economic Impact—References.

7. Theories of Corrosion **88**

Heterogeneous Theory—Homogeneous Theory—Expressions for Corrosion Rate—Corrosion Monitoring Techniques—Non-Electrochemical Methods—Electrochemical Methods—D.C. Methods—A.C. Methods.

8. Theory of Atmospheric Corrosion **95**

Experimental Procedure—Inhibitors (VCI)—Samples and their Composition—Corrosion Rate Expressions—Weight Loss Studies—Results and Discussion—Meteorological and Pollution Data—Mild Steel (MS)—Aluminium—Zinc—Copper—Weight Loss Measurements—Conclusion.

9. Methods of Corrosion Control **107**

Methods of Corrosion Control—Modification of Metal—Cathodic Protection—Anodic Protection—Corrosion Inhibitors—Classification of Inhibitors—Alkaline and Neutral Neutral Inhibitors—Adsorption and Its Influence on Inhibition of Corrosion—Electrostatic Adsorption—Chemisorption and p-Orbital Adsorption—Physical or Van Der Wall's Type of Adsorption—Correlation between Adsorption and Inhibition of Corrosion—Adsorption Isotherms—Methods of Evaluation of Inhibitors—Non-Electrochemical Methods—Electrochemical Methods—Polarisation Method—Impedance Method—Other Methods—Mechanism of Inhibition.

10. **Inhibitors** **121**

Classification of Inhibitors—Anodic Inhibitor—Cathodic Inhibitor—Mixed Inhibitor—Enzyme Inhibitor—Inhibitor in Acid Solution—Interaction between Organic Inhibitor and metal surface—Physical Adsorption Mode—Chemisorptions—Effect of Adsorption Inhibitors on Cathodic and Anodic Partial Processes—Thermodynamic and Corrosion Kinetics in the Presence of Inhibitors—Adsorption Isotherm—Langmuir's Adsorption Isotherm.

11. **Synthesis of Inhibitors** **132**

Techniques Adopted—Weight Loss Measurements—Weight Loss Measurements at Different Temperatures—Synergistic Effect—Gasometric Studies—Potentodynamic Polarisation Studies—Impedance Measurements—Statistical Analysis—Surface Examinations—References.

12. **Corrosion Testing** **147**

Base Case—Coated Case—Lessons Learned-Review Questions—Material Issues—Design Issues—Processing Issues—Testing/Environmental Exposure Issues—References.

13. **Sample Research Work on Corrosion** **155**

K.S. Khairou and I. Zaafarany—Some sulphated water soluble natural polymer (carrageenans) compounds as corrosion inhibitors for dissolution of iron in hydrochloride acid solution.

K.S. Khairou and I. Zaafarany—Pitting corrosion of pure iron electrode in OH/CL solutions and its inhibitions by sulphated water soluble natural polymer.

K.S. Khairou and I. Zaafarany—Potential-modulated reflectance study of the iron in alkaline solution.

I. Zaafarany—Cyclic voltammetric behaviour of iron electrode in sodium hydroxide solution.

I. Zaafarany—Electrochemical behaviour of iron electrode in sodium sulphide solutions.

I. Zaafarany and H. Boller—Cyclic Voltammeteric behaviour of copper electrode in sodium sulfide solutions.

I. Zaafarany and K.S. Khairo—Electrochemical behaviour of iron electrode in NaOH solutions.

Wequar Ahmad Siddiqi, Vishwa Mohan Chaubey and M. Sharif Ahmad—Inhibiting effect of cytosine derivative on the corrosion of mild steel in acidic medium.

Wequar Ahmad Siddiqi, Vishwa Mohan Chaubey and M. Sharif Ahmad—Inhibiting of acid corrosion on mild steel with agar in hydrochloric acid medium at different temperatures.

Jitendra Singh Chauhan and D.K. Gupta—Corrosion inhibition of copper in sulphuric acid using different surfactants.

Index 239

1

Introduction

The word 'corrosion' is derived from the Latin word *corrosus* which means eaten away or consumed by degrees; an unpleasant word for an unpleasant process. Corrosion is defined as the destruction of materials caused by chemical or electrochemical action of the surrounding environment. This phenomenon is experienced in day-to-day living. The most common examples of corrosion include rusting, discolouration and tarnishing. Corrosion is an ever occurring material disease. It can only be reduced. It cannot be prevented because thermodynamically it is a spontaneous phenomenon.

In fact, economy of any country would be drastically changed if there were no corrosion. For example, automobiles, ships, underground pipelines and household appliances would not require coatings. The stainless steel industry would disappear and copper would be used for electrical applications. Although corrosion is inevitable, its cost could be reduced. Corrosion can be fast or slow. Sensitized 18-8 stainless steel is badly attacked in hours by polythionic acid. Railroad tracks usually show slight rusting not sufficient to affect their performance over many years. The famous iron pillar in Delhi (India) was made almost 2000 years ago and is almost as good as new. Its height is 32 feet and dia 2 feet. It should be noted however, that it has been exposed mostly to arid conditions.

Metal exists in nature in the form of oxides, sulphides, sulphates and carbonates. These chemically combined states of metal known as "ore" have "low energy and this thermodynamically stable state of metal". Metals are extracted from their ores. These extracted metals in isolated form have higher energy and thus are thermodynamically in unstable state. Thus, it is a natural tendency of metal to go back to thermodynamically stable state. With a few exceptions, metals are unstable in ordinary aqueous environment, but tend to revert the compounds which are more stable; the process is called corrosion. Metals generally acquire thermodynamically stable state by interacting chemically or electrochemically with its environment to form surface compounds and undergo corrosion. Corrosion is the primary means by which metals deteriorate hence corrosion may be defined as gradual destruction of material's surface usually by solution. Metals also corroded when exposed to gaseous materials like acid vapours, formaldehyde gas ammonia gas and sulphur containing gases.

Corrosion

Corrosion generally refers to any process involving the deterioration or degradation of metal component. The best known case is rusting of iron. Rusting is a term reversed for steel and iron corrosion, although many other metals form their oxides when corrosion occurs. Corrosion processes are usually electrochemical in nature, having the essential features of battery. When metal atoms are exposed to an environment containing water molecule, they can give up electrons becoming positively charged ions so that an electrical circuit can be completed. This effect can be concentrated locally to form a pit or sometimes a crack or it can extend across a wide area to produce general wastage. Due to corrosion useful properties of metals such as malleability, ductility and electrical conductivity are lost.

India: It is almost 32 years since the first corrosion map of India was brought out. Over a span of these years, lots of environmental changes have occurred due to industrialization, population growth and enormous vehicle population. Durability data clearly indicated that non-ferrous via galvanized steel and aluminium have better durability factors. However, the factors vary from location to location. If durability factor and cost factor are taken together it can be clearly seen that aluminium has appreciable cost benefit ratio. At certain locations galvanized steel may prove to be a cost effective material. Vashi *et al.* [1971] reports the corrosion rate of aluminium as well as the sulphation rate was determined under outdoor exposure at Ankleswar, South Gujarat, India representing an industrial atmosphere. Monthly corrosion rate of aluminium vary from 4 to 30 (1 to 5 μm/y) mg/sq. dm. The values for yearly rates being 65 to 126 (1 to 15 μm/y) mg/sq.dm. Aluminium or aluminium coated sheets would, therefore, give better performance in comparison with mild steel or zinc.

The corrosion rate of aluminium in rainy months (22.7 mg/sq.dm.) was higher than the rate in winter months (6.5 mg/sq.dm.) and summer months (10.5 mg/sq. dm). Odnevall *et al.* summarized the results from an extensive field exposure programme implemented to study possible seasonal dependencies of copper corrosion rates and runoff rates. Two-year exposures in one urban and one rural environment were performed at four different starting seasons. An extensive multi-analytical approach was undertaken of all exposed samples. Seasonal differences in corrosion product formation were observed during the first month of exposure and attributed mainly to differences in relative humidity conditions. Seasonal differences in corrosion rate at the rural site could be discerned throughout the whole two-year exposure, again, mainly attributed to differences in relative humidity. No seasonal effect could be observed at the urban site indicating that other parameters influenced the corrosion kinetics at this site. While corrosion rates exhibit a continuous decrease with exposure time, the yearly runoff rates are independent of time. Depending on starting months the yearly copper runoff rates ranged from 1.1 to 1.7 g 2y^{1} for the urban site, and from 0.6 to 1.0 g 2y^{1} for the rural site. These seasonal variations were primarily attributed to differences in precipitation quantity and environmental characteristics. Runoff rates are significantly lower than corrosion rates as long as the adhering copper patina is growing with exposure time. The results obtained in the MICAT project for carbon steel specimens exposed for 1 to 4 years in 22 rural and urban atmospheres in the Ibero-American region. Test site characterization, chemical and morphological determination of the steel corrosion product layers (SCPLs) contributed to understanding the corrosion phenomena involved. It was observed how some climatological factors could affect steel corrosion rates and SCPL properties. Although the studied atmospheres were classified into different ISO groups, steel corrosion rates did not differ significantly.

2

Literature Survey and Scope of the Work

Mild steel is one of the important construction materials which is extensively used in chemical and allied industries for the handling of acid, alkali and salt solutions. It gets corroded when the acid is kept in it for a long time, during acid pickling, descaling of boilers and oil-well acidisation. Therefore, the study of the corrosion control of mild steel in acid media is of both academic and industrial concern. The use of inhibitors is one of the most practical methods for protection of metals against corrosion, especially in acid media. The technology of corrosion inhibition through the use of inhibitors involves mostly adsorptive film formation. The inhibitors form protective films on the surface of the metals. These protective films slow down the corrosion process by getting adsorbed all over the metal surface.

Many organic compounds with at least one polar atom like nitrogen, oxygen, sulphur and phosphorous are found to have wide applications as corrosion inhibitors. In general, the polar function is regarded as the centre for the establishment of chemisorption process. Phosphorous containing compounds such as phosphates, phosphonates and phosphonium salts are suggested as effective additives for neutral and acidic electrolytes. A review of the literature on this subject is presented below.

Survey of the Earlier Work

Many onium salts, particularly nitrogen compounds, have been tried as corrosion inhibitors, especially in acid media. Similarly phosphonium, sulphonium and arsenium derivatives have also been tried in various media. Von L. Horner *et al.* have attempted some of the quaternary phosphonium salts for the corrosion of iron in HCl in the absence of oxygen. Their attempt to find a relationship between the reduction potential and inhibition efficiency has shown that there is no significant relationship between the reduction potential and their inhibition efficiency. Saveant *et al.* and Horner *et al.* have studied and found that salts with complicated ligands have been reported to be more effective inhibitors than those with smaller groups.

Troquet *et al.* have studied phosphonium compounds for the corrosion inhibition of zinc and iron in 1 N HCl and 6 N H_2SO_4 respectively and arrived at the conclusion that the complexity of the mechanism of zinc corrosion inhibition is due to a process of secondary inhibition caused by electro-splitting. However these compounds, when used as inhibitors in 6 N H_2SO_4 for the corrosion inhibition of iron, offer protection through good primary inhibition combining electrostatic adsorption and chemisorption. Chemisorption has been shown to take place by adsorption of π-bond orbital from aromatic rings. Veres *et al.* have reported the chemical passivation of ferrous materials in presence of salts of phosphonic acids.

Hernias *et al.* have made an extensive study on the inhibiting effect of propyltriphenylphosphonium bromide on stainless steel corrosion in 1 M sulphuric acid. Said *et al.* have made an attempt to study the effects of addition of $Ph_3P^+I^-$ on the corrosion behaviour of nickel in 1 M sulphuric acid medium. A study on the corrosion inhibition of mild steel by benzotriazole derivatives in acid medium has been carried out Tamil Selvi *et al*. Corrosion inhibition of carbon steel in HCl medium by organic compounds containing hetero atoms has been studied by Athar *et al.*

Muralidharan *et al.* have studied the effect of piperidones on corrosion inhibition of mild steel in acid solutions. An extensive work on the inhibition of mild steel in HCl medium in the presence of thiocarbamides has been carried out by Stoyanora *et al.* They have studied the effect of concentration and temperature of the corrosion medium on the protection of the compounds. The inhibition effects of some mercapto-triazole derivatives on the corrosion of mild steel in 1 M HCl have been studied by Wang *et al.* Pingo Mutombo and Norman Hackerman have studied the effect of some organophosphorous compounds in the corrosion behaviour of iron in 6 M HCl. They have tried with tetraphenylphosphonium chloride, 3-chloro-methyltriphenylphosphonium chloride and 4-benzyltriphenyl phosphonium chloride. They have reported that all these compounds have inhibition efficiency greater than 90 per cent in the concentration of 10^{-3}–10^{-4} M. They have concluded that the inhibitors are of mixed type.

A study on tetraphenylphosphonium chloride as a novel molecular probe for imaging tumours has been carried out by Jung-Jun Min *et al.* They have arrived that the sensitive tumour accumulation of ^{3}H-TPP with less propensity for inflammatory regions warrants further investigation of radio labelled phosphonium analogs for tumour imaging in living system.

A study has been carried out by Hluchan *et al.* using amino acids as corrosion inhibitors of mild steel in hydrochloric acid solutions. Bartos and Hackerman have studied the inhibition actions of propargyl alcohol during anodic-dissolution of iron in hydrochloric acid.

Batidas *et al.* have studied the influence of the substituent butyl group in n-butylamine which has been used as a mild steel corrosion inhibitor in hydrochloric acid medium. The corrosion inhibition of mild steel in acid media by a new triazole derivative has been extensively studied by Bentiss *et al.*

Landvay-Gyrik *et al.* have made an attempt to study the impedance diagram obtained in the case of iron dissolution in dilute H_2SO_4 solution. Elkadi *et al.* have studied the inhibition action of some tetrazine derivatives on the corrosion of mild steel in acid media.

Bentiss *et al.* have used the substituted 1,3,4-oxadiazoles as corrosion inhibitors of mild steel in acid media. The electrochemical study on the inhibiting action of some organic phosphonium compounds on the corrosion of mild steel in a aerated acid solutions has been studied by Morad *et al.*

The corrosion inhibition characteristics of isomers of phenylenediamine, toluene and nitroaniline have been studied on mild steel in 1 N HCl and 1 N H_2SO_4 media. They have predicted that the compounds obey Temkin adsorption isotherm.

Fatty acid oxadiazoles have been studied as acid corrosion inhibitors for mild Mohammed Ajmal *et al.* A new class of thiadiazole derivatives has been as corrosion inhibitors of mild steel in acid media by El Azhar *et al.* A study on the application of AC resistmetry to monitor the localised corrosion of iron has been done by Kazuhisa Azumi *et al.* Santana Rodrguez *et al.* have studied the mathematical and electrochemical characterization of the layer of corrosion products on carbon steel in various environments.

Arshadi *et al.* have studied the inhibition effects of mild steel in hydrochloric and sulphuric acid solutions. Wang Huilong *et al.* used some bisquaternary ammonium salts for the inhibition of corrosion of carbon steel in HCl solution. AC and DC study of the temperature effect on mild steel corrosion in acid media in the presence of benzimidazole derivatives has been carried out by Popova *et al.* Kardas has studied the inhibition effect of 2-thiobarbituric acid on the corrosion performance of low-carbon steel in 0.5 M HCl solution, Abdel Rahim *et al.* has conducted the study of the concentration and temperature effects by using aliphatic amino acids as corrosion inhibitors for mild steel in sulphuric acid medium.

Khaled has made an extensive study in the inhibition of iron by some organic phosphonium chloride derivatives in acid media. Ozcan *et al.* have attempted to find the relationship between inhibition efficiency and chemical structure by using organic sulphur containing compounds as corrosion inhibitors for mild steel in acid media. Harek and Larabi have studied the corrosion inhibition of mild steel in 1 M HCl by N-phenylhy-drazide and N-phenylthiosemicarbazide. Khaled *et al.* have studied piperidines corrosion inhibitors for iron in HCl medium. Bouklah *et al.* have tried some new derivatives as corrosion inhibitors of steel in HCl solution.

Durnie *et al.* have studied the influence of various inhibitors on the corrosion rate of mild steel in brine electrolyte under carbon dioxide conditions. They have attempted to predict the adsorption properties of carbon dioxide corrosion inhibitors structure-activity relationship. The protection of surface of steel from corrosion in acidic solution by the introduction of thioflavin sulphur has been studied by Nada F. Atta.

The inhibition effect of 2-thiobarbituric acid on the corrosion performance of mild steel in HCl medium has been studied by Kardas. An investigation of the inhibitive effect of ortho-substituted anilines on corrosion of iron in 1 M HCl solution and 0.5 M H_2SO_4 solution has been made by Khaled and Hackerman.

Babic-Samardzija *et al.* have studied the corrosion inhibition of N-heterocyclic amine and their derivatives for iron in perchloric acid medium. They have also made an attempt to study the inhibition of N-dithiocarbamato (1, 4, 8, ll-tetrazacyclotetradecane) cobalt(III) complex on the corrosion of iron in $HClO_4$ acid. The theoretical study of the structural effects of polymethylene amines on corrosion inhibition of iron in acid solutions has also been carried out by them.

The inhibitive properties, adsorption and surface study of butynol and pentynol as corrosion inhibitors for iron in HCl solution have been carried out by Babic-Samardzija *et al.* A group of hetrocyclic diazoles has been used as inhibitors by Babic-Samardzija *et al.* An extensive study on the inhibitive properties and surface morphology of the compounds has been carried out by them.

Some triazole derivatives have been tried as corrosion inhibitors for iron in acidic media by Babic-Samardzija and Hackerman. Bentiss *et al.* have studies the inhibition adsorption process in mild steel using substituted thiazoles as inhibitors in HCl system.

Tafel extrapolation method has been usually applied to measure the corrosion rates. A study on the validation of corrosion rates measured by

Tafel extrapolation method has been carried out by Me Cafferty. Wang used some triazole derivatives as corrosion inhibitors for mild steel corrosion in phosphoric acid medium. Lebrini *et al.* have tried to correlate the structure of the compounds with corrosion inhibition activity using some thiadiazole derivaties for mild steel corrosion in acid solutions.

Babic-Samardzija and Hackerman have studied the iron corrosion inhibition with dihydrobis-and hydrotris-(1-pyrazolyl) borates. Turcio Ortetga *et al.* have studied the interaction of imidazoline compounds with Fe as a model for corrosion inhibition. A study on the corrosion inhibition and adsorption behaviour of methionine on mild steel in sulphuric acid and synergistic effect of iodide ion has been carried out by Oguzie *et al.* and Benabdullah *et al.* have carried out an extensive work on the role of phosphonate derivatives on the corrosion inhibition of steel in HCl medium.

Scope of the Work

Eventhough much work has been carried out in the field of corrosion control continuous search is being made for the identification of better inhibitors to meet the needs of industries. The effect of temperature on the inhibition process is also of great industrial importance. Effective inhibitors are expected to perform under a wide range of conditions. Corrosion is more severe during the pickling and cleaning of metals and alloys using acid solutions; hence special attention must be paid for the selection of inhibitors for such practical applications.

The selection of appropriate inhibitors mainly depends on the type of acid, its concentration, temperature and velocity of flow, the presence of dissolved inorganic or organic substances, even in minor amount and, of course, on the type of material exposed to the action of acidic solutions. Considering the technical process of pickling, good inhibitors must meet quite number of requirements, such as effective inhibition of metal dissolution, effective pickling in the presence of higher valency cations, effective at low concentration and higher temperatures, thermally and chemically stable, effective inhibition of hydrogen up-take by the metal, good surfactant characteristics and good foaming characteristics.

To meet the above requirements, it is aimed to synthesise a series of organic phosphonium compounds and carry out a systematic study which can explore the potentiality of the compounds as corrosion inhibitors. The inhibition performance shown by organic phosphonium compounds may depend mainly on the interaction between the phosphorous and the metal surface. The electron density on the organic functional group facilitates the formation of adsorption bond. The strength of the bond depends on the properties of both the adsorbed phosphonium moieties and the metal surface. In these phosphonium compounds the phosphorous atom is considered as the reaction centre for the chemisorption process. The review of literature cited above shows that phosphonium compounds can be used very well to control corrosion of metals, but very limited studies have been made with these compounds as corrosion inhibitors and hence the present study.

A family of organic phosphonium compounds given below has been selected for the corrosion inhibition studies of mild steel in HCl and H_2SO_4 media:

1. (4-Aminophenyl) triphenylphosphonium chloride (ATP)
2. (4-Hydroxyphenyl) triphenylphosphonium chloride (HTP)
3. (4-Propylphenyl) triphenylphosphonium chloride (PTP)
4. (4-Ethylphenyl) triphenylphosphonium chloride (ETP)
5. Tetraphenylphosphonium chloride (TP)
6. (4-Acetamidophenyl) triphenylphosphonium chloride (AmTP)
7. (4-Chlorophenyl) triphenyl phosphonium chloride (CTP)
8. (3-Formyl-4-chlorophenyl) triphenylphosphonium chloride (ACTP)
9. (4-Nitrophenyl) triphenylphosphonium chloride (NTP).

The choice of these compounds has been primarily based on the idea to have a clear picture of the role of electron donating as well as electron withdrawing nature of the substituting groups in one of the phenyl rings of the organic phosphonium compounds that chiefly govern the electrostatic interaction and chemisorption which decide the inhibition performance of the compounds.

The usual weight loss studies, gasometric, potentiodynamic polarisation and impedance studies form the methodology of the experimental approach. The weight loss technique studied at room temperature and at elevated temperatures and gasometric studies will be useful in determining the inhibition efficiency of the compounds. The polarisation studies are intended to evaluate the corrosion potential, corrosion current and no Tafel slopes which will help to propose a suitable mechanism of inhibition. The charge transfer resistance and double layer capacity values are to be calculated through impedance measurement. The surface coverage values calculated therefrom will help to propose a suitable adsorption isotherm that characterises the adsorption process which is primarily responsible for the inhibition process.

The surface examination of the metal specimen both under corroded and inhibited conditions is to be made through Scanning Electron Microscopic

(SEM) studies. The performance of each compound is to be identified based on the above experimental results and correlated to the structural and the electronic effects of the substituents. This will help us to have a clear insight into the process of inhibition and performance of the compounds which may culminate in the identification of some potential pickling inhibitors.

REFERENCES

Abdel Rahim, M.A., B. Hanaa, Hassan and M.W. Khalil, *Material und werks.,* 28, 198 (2004).

Abdel-Aal, M.S., A.A. El Miligy, G. Reiners and W.J. Lorenz, *Proc. Fourth European Symposium on Corrosion Inhibitors*, Ferrara 1975, University of Ferrara, 364-368 (1975).

Ajmal, Mohammed and Danish Jamal, *Anti-Corrosion Methods and Materials,* 47(2), 77 (2000).

Al-Mayof, A.M., A.K. Al-Ammery and A.A. Suhybani, *Corrosion,* 57, 614 (2001).

Antropov, L.I., I.S. Pogreboa and G.I. Dremova, *Zashch. Met.,* 3, 10 (1971).

Arshadi, M.R., M.G. Hosseini and M. Ghorbani, *Br. Corros. J.,* 37, 76 (2002).

Athar, M., H. Ali and M.A. Quraishi, *Br. Corros. J.,* 37, 155 (2000).

Azumi, Kazuhisa, Kei Lokibe, Tomohiro Ueno and Masahiro Seo, *Corros. Set.,* 44(6), 1329 (2002).

Babic-Samardzija, K. and N. Hackerman, *Anti-Corrosion Methods and Materials.,* 53(1), 19 (2006).

Babic-Samardzija, K. and N. Hackerman, *J. Solid State Electrochem.,* 9(7), 483 (2005).

Babic-Samardzija, K., C. Lupu, N. Hackerman and AR. Barron, *J.Mat. Chem.,* 15(19), 1908 (2005).

Babic-Samardzija, K., K.F. Khaled and N. Hackerman, *Applied Surface Science,* 240(1), 327 (2005).

Bartos, M. and N. Hackerman, 1992 *J. Electrochem. Soc.,* 139(12), 3428 (1992).

Batidas, J.M., J.D. Damborenea and A.J. Zquez, *J. Appl. Electrochem.,* 27, 345 (1997)

Benabdellah, M., A. Dafali, B. Hammouti, A. Aouniti, M. Rhomari, A. Raada, O.Senhaji and J.J. Robin, *Chem. Engg. Com.,* 194(10), 1938 (2007).

Bentiss, F., M. Lagrenee, J.C. Traisnel and Hornez, *Corros. Sci.,* 41(4), 789 (1999).

Bentiss, F., M. Lebrini and M. Legrenee, *Corros. Sci.* 47(12), 2815 (2005).

Bentiss, F., M. Traisnel and M. Lagrencee, *Br. Corros. J.,* 35(4), 315 (2000).

Bentiss, F., M. Traisnel and M. Lagrencee, *Corros. Sci.,* 42, 127 (2000).

Bentiss, F., M. Traisnel and M. Lagrenee, *Corros. Sci.,* 42(1), 127 (2000).

Bouklah, M., B. Hammouti, M. Benkaddour, A. Attatyibat and S. Radi, *Pigments and Resin Technology,* 34(4), 197 (2005).

Driver, R. and R.J. Meakins, *Br. Corros. J.,* 15(3), 128 (1980).

Durnie, W., R. De Marco, B. Kinseklla, A. Jefferson and B. Pejci, *J. Electrochem. Soc.,* 152(1), 81 (2005).

El Azhar, M., B. Mernari, M. Traisnel, F. Bentiss and M. Lagranee, *Corros. Sci.,* 43(12), 2229 (2001).

Elkadi, L., B. Mernari, M. Traisnel, F. Bentiss and M. Lagrenee, *Corros. Sci.*, 42(4), 703 (2000).

Ertel, H. and L. Horner, *Proc. Second European Symposium on Corrosion Inhibitors*, Ferrara 1965, University of Ferrara, 71 (1966).

Frignani, A., G. Travanellt, F. Zucchi and M. Zucchini, *Proc. Fifth European Symposium on Corrosion Inhibitors*, Ferrara 1980, Univ. of Ferrara, 1185 (1980).

Gardner, G., *Corrosion Inhibitors*, NACE, Houston (Texas), 158 (1973).

Grigore'ev, V.P. and V.V. Kuznetsov, *Zashch. Met.*, 4(2), 203 (1968).

Harek, Y. and L. Larabi, *Kem. Ind.*, 53, 55 (2004).

Hermas, A.A., M.S. Morad, and M.H. Wahdan, *J.Appl. Electrochem.*, 34, 95 (2004).

Hluchan, V., B.L. Wheeler and N. Hackerman, *Werkastoffe und Korrosion.*, 39(11), 512 (1988).

Horner, L. and F. Rottger, *Korrosion*, 16,57(1963).

Horner, L. and K. Meisel, *Werkst. Korros.*, 29, 654 (1978).

Horner, L. and K. Rottger, *Werkst. Korros*, 15, 228 (1964).

Huilong, Wang, Zheng Jiashen and Liu Jing, *Anti-Corrosion Methods and Materials*, 49, 127 (2002).

Kardas, G., *Fizyko Khimichna Mekhanika Materialliv*, 41, 51 (2005).

Kardas, G., *Materials Science*, 41(3), 337 (2005).

Khaled, K.F. and N. Hackerman, *Materials Chemistry and Physics*, 82(3), 949 (2003).

Khaled, K.F., *Applied Surface Science*, 23, 230 (2004).

Khaled, K.F., K. Babic-Samardzija and N. Hackerman, *J. Appl. Electrochem.*, 34 (7), 697 (2004).

Lebrini, M., F. Bentiss, H. Vezin and M. Lagrenee, *Corros. Sci.*, 48(5), 1279 (2006).

Lendvay-Gyrik, G., Meszaros, G. Meszaros and B. Lengyel, *Corros. Sci.*, 42(1), 79(2000).

Lorenz, J.W. and H. Fischer, *Proc. Second European Symposium on Corrosion* Inhibitors, Ferrara 1965, University of Ferrara, 81 (1966).

Mc Cafferty, E., Corros. *Sci.*, 47(12), 3202 (2005).

Meakins, R.J., *J. Appl. Chem.*, 13, 339 (1963).

Min, Jung-Jun, Sandip Biswal, Christopher Depose and Sanjiv Gambir, *J.Nuc. Med.*, 45, 636 (2004).

Morad, M.S., *Corros. Sci.*, 42(8), 1307 (2000).

Muralidharan, S., R. Chandrasekharan and S.V. Lyer, Proceedings of the Indian Academy Sciences (Chemical Science), 112, 127 (2000).

Mutombo, Pingo and Norman Hackerman, *Anti-Corrosion Methods and Materials*, 45, 413 (1998).

Nada Atta, F., *Euro. Poly. J.*, 41(12), 3018 (2005).

Oguzie, E.E., Y. Li and F.H. Wang, *J. Colloid and Interface Sci.*, 310(1), 90 (2007).

Ozcan, M., I. Dehri and M. Erbil, *Applied Surface Science*, 236, 155 (2004).

Petrenko, A.T. and L.I. Antropov, Committee on Corrosion and Protection of Metals, All-Union Council of the Scientific-Technical Society, No. 2., 82 (1957).

Popova, A., E.Sokolova, S.Raicheva and M. Christov, *Corros. Sci.*, 45(1), 33 (2003).

Quraishi, M.A. and Danish Jamal, *Anti-Corrosion Methods and Materials*, 47, 233 (2000).

Ramesh Babu, B. and R. Holze, *Br. Corros. J.*, 35, 204 (2000).

Reshetnikov, S.M., *Zh. Prikl. Khim.,* 54(3), 590 (1981).

Reshotnikov, S.M., *Zashch. Met.,* 16(5), 623 (1980).

Riggs, O.L. and R.L. Every, *Corrosion,* 18(7) 262 (1962).

Riggs, O.L., Jr., *Corrosion Inhibitors*, NACE, Houston (Texas), 26 (1973).

Rodrguez, J.J Santana, F.J. Santana Hernandez, and Gonzalez Gonzalez, *Corros. Sci.*, 44(11), 2597 (2002).

Said, F., N. Souissi, A. Dermaj, N. Hajjaji, E. Triki and A. Srhiri, *Materials and Corrosion,* 56, 619 (2005).

Sanyal, B. and Kumkum Srivastav, *Br. Corros. J.,* 2, 103 (1974).

Sastry, T.P. and V.V. Rao, *J. Electrochem, Soc.,* 30, 289 (1981).

Saveant, J.M. and Sukhac Binh, *J. Org. Chem.,* 42, 124 (1977).

Schmitt, G., Br. *Corros. J.,* 19, 165 (1984).

Stoyanora, A.E., E.I. Sukolova and S.N. Ravicheva, *Corros. Sci.,* 39, 1595 (1997).

Tamil Selvi, S., V. Raman and N. Rajendran, *J. Appl. Chem.,* 33, 1175 (2003).

Trabanelli, G. and V. Garassiti, *Advances in Corrosion Science and Technology*, Vol. 1, Plenum, New York-London (1970).

Troquet, M., B. Lavessiere, J.P. Labbe and J. Pagetti, *Proc. Fifth European Symposium on Corrosion Inhibitors*, Ferrara 1980, University of Ferrara, 941 (1980).

Turcio-Ortega, D., T. Pandiyan, J. Cruz and E. Garcia-Ochoa, *J. Phys. Chem.,* 11(27), 9853 (2007).

Veres, A., G. Reinhard, and E. Kalman, *Br. Corros.* J., 27, 147 (1992).

Wang, H., R.Liu and J. Xin, *Corros. Sci.*, 46, 2455 (2004).

Wang, L., *Corros. Sci.,* 48(3), 608 (2006).

3

Consequence of Corrosion

The Consequences of Corrosion

The consequences of corrosion are many and varied and the effects of them on the safe, reliable and efficient operation of equipment or structures are often more serious than the simple loss of a mass of metal. Failures of various kinds and the need for expensive replacements may occur eventhough the amount of metal destroyed is quite small. Some of the major harmful effects of corrosion can be summarized as follows:

(*i*) Reduction in thickness of metal leading to loss of mechanical strength and structural failure or breakdown. When the metal is lost in localized zones so as to give a crack-like structure, considerable weakening may result from quite a small amount of metal loss.

(*ii*) Hazards or injuries to people arising from structural failure or breakdown (*e.g.* bridges, aircraft, cars, etc.)

(*iii*) Loss of time in availability of profile-making industrial equipment.

(*v*) Reduced value of goods due to deterioration of appearance.

(*v*) Contamination of fluids in vessels and pipes.

(*vi*) Perforation of vessels and pipes allowing escape of their contents can cause harm to the surroundings. For example a leaky domestic radiator can cause expensive damage to carpets and decorations, while corrosive sea water may enter the boilers of a power station if the condenser tubes perforate.

(*vii*) Loss of technically important surface properties of a metallic compound. These could include frictional and bearing properties, ease of fluid flow over a pipe surface, electrical conductivity of contacts, surface reflectivity or heat transfer across a surface.

(*viii*) Mechanical damage to valves, pumps, etc.

(*ix*) Blockage of pipes by solid corrosion products.

(*x*) Added complexity and expense of equipment which needs to be designed to withstand a certain amount of corrosion and to allow corroded components to be conveniently replaced.

Importance of Corrosion Studies

It is now-a-days necessary to pay more attention to metallic corrosion studies than that was done earlier due to:

(*i*) Increasing use of metals in the field of science and technology.

(*ii*) Use of rare and expensive metals whose protection requires special precautions.

(*iii*) Use of new high strength alloys which are usually more susceptible to certain type of corrosive attack.

(*iv*) Increasing pollution of air and water resulting in a more corrosive environment.

(*v*) Strict safety standards of operation equipment which may fail in a catastrophic manner due to corrosion.

The Corrosion Challenge

Some of the figures and facts which illustrate the importance of corrosion studies are highlighted below:

(*i*) The annual economic losses in Europe due to corrosion damage are estimated at 4 to 5 per cent of the Gross Domestic Product (GDP) of each member state; the direct cost of corrosion in the U.S. is a staggering amount of $276 billion accounting to approximately 3.1 per cent of its GDP.

(*ii*) About 25 per cent of the damage could be prevented just by applying already well established knowledge, namely, choosing the appropriate corrosion protection and making the correct choice of materials.

(*iii*) In chemical and other process industries such as power generation, material production and petrochemistry—where equipment reliability and durability have a vast influence on almost every industrial operation, it is estimated that over 60 per cent of all mechanical failures are effectively due to corrosion.

Nature and Extent of the Corrosion Problem

Sensational figures have been published with regard to the annual cost of corrosion and protection against corrosion. One estimate places this loss at over 6 billion dollars. An accurate estimate is, of course, impossible but it is not difficult to perceive that the cost is enormous when we consider that corrosion occurs, with varying degrees of severity, in practically all cases where metals and alloys are used. Everyone is familiar with the rapid rate at which iron and steel corrode or rust when exposed to atmosphere and rain.

Some of the fluids which cause corrosion that pose difficulties serious enough to warrant actual investigations are the following: Fresh, distilled, salt, and mine water; rural, urban, and industrial atmospheres, steam and other gases such as chlorine, ammonia, oxygen, carbon disulphide, sulphur dioxide, and fuel gases; mineral acids such as nitric, sulphuric, and hydrochloric, organic acids such as acetic, formic, and citric; alkalis such as caustic and ammonium hydroxide, soil, solvents such as alcohols and dry cleaning materials; vegetable and petroleum oils and a variety of food products. Two of the most common and most plentiful materials known, namely, air and water also cause corrosion and considerable effort and money have been spent to minimize their destructive effects.

Apart from the cost in dollars, corrosion is a serious problem because it directly and definitely contributes to the depletion of our natural resources. For example, steel is made from iron ore and our reserves of iron ore are diminishing. In addition, approximately four tonnes of coal are required to produce 1 tonne of steel. Our copper reserves are dwindling, and copper is one of the principal elements used in the production of corrosion-resistant alloys. In addition chemists and chemical engineers have other vital interests in the corrosion problem. Some of the reasons for their concern are described below:

(*i*) **Higher temperature and pressure:** The trend, conspicuous during recent years, in the chemical industry towards higher temperatures and pressures have made possible new processes or improvements in old processes—for example, better yields, greater speed, or lower cost of production. Higher temperature and pressure usually pose more severe corrosive conditions. Many of the present day operations would not have been possible or economical without the use of corrosion-resistant materials. The annual tonnage of stainless steel purchased by the chemical industry today is many times more than that purchased some ten years ago.

(*ii*) **Reduction in maintenance costs**: Substantial savings can be obtained in most types of chemical plants through the use of corrosion-resistant materials of construction. One example is classic in this respect. A plant effected an annual saving of more than 10,000 dollars merely by changing the bolt material on some equipment from one alloy to another more resistant to the conditions involved.

(*iii*) **Contamination of product**: In many cases the market value of a chemical plant product, is directly related to its purity and quality. Freedom from contaminations is also a vital factor in the manufacture of transparent plastics, food products and drugs. In some instances contamination causes adverse catalytic effects which are noticeable-for example, in the manufacture and transport of hydrogen peroxide.

(*iv*) **Plant shutdowns:** Far too often plants are shutdown or portions of the process stopped because of unexpected corrosion failures. Sometimes these shutdowns are caused by corrosion involving no change in process conditions, but often they are caused by changes in operating procedures regarded as incapable of increasing the severity of the corrosive conditions. Sudden and rapid corrosion of stainless steel equipment caused is an example of plant shutdown.

(*v*) **Valuable chemicals:** Particularly during recent years, the products or intermediates handled in a chemical plant are often expensive. Substantial production losses of these materials to the sewer because of corrosion failures are, of course, to be avoided.

(*vi*) **Safety:** The handling of chemicals at high temperatures and pressures, explosive materials, and acids such as hydrochloric acid and concentrated sulphuric acid demand materials of construction which minimize corrosion failures if severe injury or loss of life are to be avoided. Corroding equipment is known to have caused fairly harmless compounds to become explosive. Economizing on materials of construction is generally not desirable if safety is risked.

Hazard Symbols

Hazard symbols are recognizable *symbols* designed to warn about hazardous materials or locations. The use of hazard symbols is often regulated by law and directed by *standards organizations*. Hazard symbols may appear with different colors, backgrounds, borders and supplemental information in order to signify the type of hazard.

Types of Hazard Symbols

Name	Symbol	Unicode	Image
Toxic/Poisonous sign	☠	U+2620	
Caution sizn	☡	U+2621	
Radioactive sign	☢	U+2622	
Ionizing radiation sign	?	?	
Non-ionizing radiation sign	?	?	
Biohazard sign	☣	U+2623	
Warning sign	□	U+26A0	
High voltage sign	□	U+26A1	
Magnetic Field symbol	?	?	
Chemical weapon symbol	?	?	
Laser hazard sign	?	?	
Optical radiation	?	?	
Tsunami hazard sign	?	?	

The Early Radioactive Trefoil (1946)

The international radiation symbol (also known as *trefoil*) first appeared in 1946, at the *University of California*, Berkeley Radiation Laboratory. At the time, it was rendered as magenta, and was set on a blue background. The modern version is black against a yellow background, and it is drawn with a central circle of radius *R*, an internal radius of 1.5*R* and an external radius of 5*R* for the blades, which are separated from each other by 60°.

The New ISO 21482 Radiation Symbol

On February 15, 2007, the *IAEA* and the *ISO* announced a new *ionizing radiation* symbol to supplement the traditional trefoil symbol. The new symbol is aimed at alerting anyone, anywhere to the potential dangers of being close to a large source of ionizing radiation. Experts have felt that the trefoil symbol had little intuitive value and was less likely to be recognized by those not educated in its significance. According to the IAEA, in a survey conducted at an international school, many children mistook the trefoil for a non-threatening propeller. Hence, the Agency, along with the *International Organization for Standardization* has devised this symbol for sealed radiation sources. It depicts, on a red background, a black colored trefoil radiating waves, a skull and crossbones, and a person running away from the scene.

The radiating trefoil suggests the presence of radiation and the red background and skull and crossbones warn of the danger. The person running away from the scene suggests the action of avoiding the labelled material. The symbol had been tested in countries with different population of varying groups, ages, and educational backgrounds to ensure that it clearly conveys the message "danger: stay away". The new symbol is not intended to be generally visible, but appear on device internals housing radiation sources so that if someone attempts to disassemble a device it provides an explicit warning not to proceed any further.

Biohazard Symbol used since 1966

Biohazard sign

Developed by the *Dow Chemical Company* in 1966 for their containment products.

According to Charles Baldwin, an environmental-health engineer who contributed to its development: "We wanted something that was memorable but meaningless, so we could educate people as to what it means." In an article in *Science* in 1967, the symbol was presented as the new standard for all biological hazards ("biohazards"). The article explained that over 40 symbols were drawn up by Dow artists, and all of the symbols investigated had to meet a number of criteria:

(*i*) striking in form in order to draw immediate attention;

(*ii*) unique and unambiguous, in order not to be confused with symbols used for other purposes;

(*iii*) quickly recognizable and easily recalled;

(*iv*) easily stenciled;

(*v*) symmetrical, in order to appear identical from all angles of approach; and (*vi*) acceptable to groups of varying ethnic backgrounds." The chosen scored the best on nationwide testing for memorability.

It is used in the labelling of biological materials that carry a significant health risk, including viral samples and used *hypodermic needles*.

Drawing

All parts of the biohazard sign can be drawn with a compass and straightedge. The basic outline of the symbol is a plain trefoil which is three circles overlapping each other equally like in a triple venn diagram with the overlapping parts erased. The diameter of the overlapping part is equal to half the radius of the three circles. Then three inner circles are drawn in with 2/3 radius of the original circles so that it is tangent to the outside three overlapping circles. A tiny circle in center has a diameter 1/2 of the radius of the three inner circle, and arcs are erased at 90°, 210°, 330°. The arcs of the inner circles and the tiny circle are connected by a line. Finally, the ring under is drawn from the distance to the perimeter of the equilateral triangle that forms between the centers of the three intersecting circles. An outer circle of the ring under is drawn and finally enclosed with the arcs from the center of the inner circles with a shorter radius from the inner circles.

Tattoos

A tattoo of the biohazard sign is recognized within the gay community to indicate the wearer is living with HIV. The origins for this practice aren't clear, but they range from a response to William F. Bucklev's call for the tattooing of HIV positive individuals to a few activists within ACT UP.

Poison Sign

Skull and Crossbones

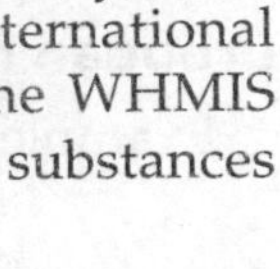

The skull-and-crossbones symbol, consisting of a human skull and two bones crossed together under the skull, is today generally used as a warning of danger, particularly in regard to poisonous substances.

The symbol, or some variation thereof, specifically with the bones (or swords) below the skull, was also featured on the Jolly Roger, the traditional flag of European and American pirates. It is also used by Skull and Bones, a secret society at Yale University, as well as the international male collegiate fraternity Phi Kappa Sigma. It is also part of the WHMIS home symbols placed on containers to inform that the contents are substances are poisonous.

In the United States, due to concerns that the skull and bones symbol's association with pirates encourages children to play with toxic materials, the Mr. Yuk symbol is also used to denote poison.

Warning Sign

On warning signs, an exclamation mark is often used to draw attention to a warning of danger, hazards, and the unexpected. In Europe, this type of sign is used if there are no other appropriate signs to denote a hazard. When used in traffic signs a plate describing the hazard must be present'. On an upright sign it is usually mounted under the exclamation mark.

Chemical Hazard

NFPA 704 standard hazard sticker or *placard*.

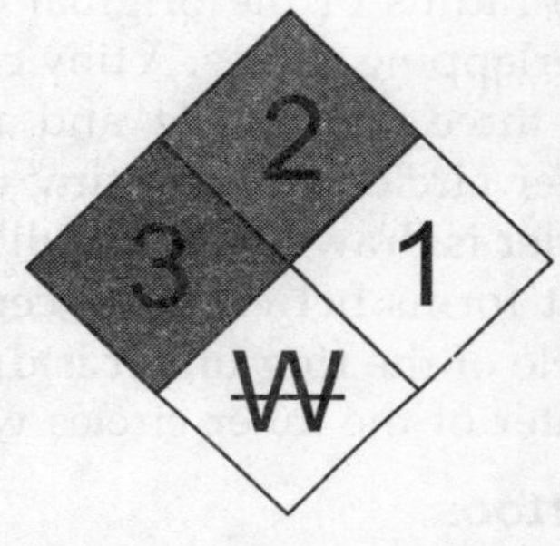

European hazard sign, meaning highly inflammable (33)–gasoline (1203)

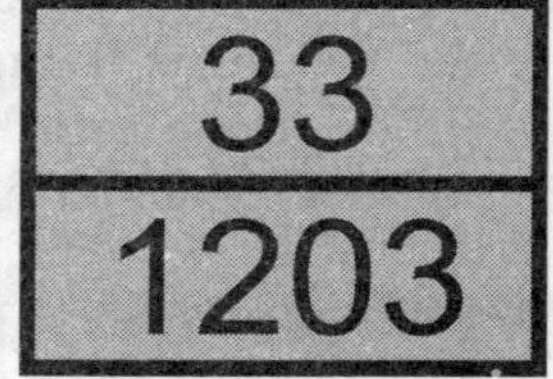

A chemical hazard label is a pictogram applied to containers of dangerous chemical compounds to licate the specific risk, and thus the required precautions. There are several systems of labels.

The U.S.-based National Fire Protection Association (NFPA) has a standard NFPA 704 using a diamond with four colored sections each with a number indicating severity 0—4 (0 for no hazard, 4 indicates a severe hazard). The red section denotes flammability. The blue section denotes health risks. Yellow represents reactivity (tendency to explode). The white section denotes special hazard information. This is used primarily in the USA.

In Europe, another standard is used, as fixed in the European Agreement concerning the International carriage of Dangerous Goods by Road. Vehicles carrying dangerous goods have to be fitted with orange signs, where the lower number identifies the substance, while the upper number is a key for the threat it ly pose. These symbols cannot be readily interpreted without the aid of a key.

European Hazard Symbols

Example of European warning for flammable substances:

Non-standard Warning Signs

High voltage sign on a fence around the Beromünster Reserve Broadcasting Tower. *English:* When you climb over the fence, you are in danger of death! The tower and the cables are high voltage!

A large number of warning signs of non-standard designs, such as the one on the right at the Beromünster Reserve Broadcasting Tower, are in use around the world.

4

Types of Corrosion

Introduction and Definition of Basic Corrosion Conditions

The Auto/Steel Partnership (A/SP) is an innovative international association that includes DaimlerChrysler Corporation, Ford Motor Company General Motors Corporation and twelve North American sheet steel producers. The Partnership was formed in 1987 to leverage the resources of the automotive and steel industries to pursue research projects leading to excellence in the application of sheet steels in the design and manufacture of vehicles. The Partnership has established project teams that examine issues related to steel properties including strength, dent resistance, surface texture and coating weights, as well as manufacturing methods including stamping, welding and design improvements.

The Light Truck Frame Project Team was established to address mass reduction initiatives associated with light truck frames and includes representatives from Daimler Chrysler, Ford, General Motors, frame manufacturers, and the producers of frame component steels.

Reducing the steel thickness of the components in a frame would reduce the mass of a frame. However, doing so may not satisfy all of the frame stiffness requirements. Judicious use of thinner, higher strength steel enables designers to achieve a degree of mass reduction and satisfy many of the engineering and performance criteria. If significant corrosion occurs, one critical performance parameter that could suffer as material thickness decreases is structural strength. Given the same corrosion rate, a thinner steel component will reach the critical thickness at which structural failure occurs sooner than a thicker component. Therefore, if steel thickness is reduced to decrease mass, then additional measures may have to be taken to control corrosion in order to maintain the same structural performance of the frame over time.

Bare steel, in the presence of oxygen and moisture, corrodes. To mitigate corrosion, frame engineers select design characteristics that prevent poultices and water entrapment. In addition frames are often coated after fabrication to improve corrosion resistance. Corrosion protection is the result of the combination of the material, design, post-coating and the manufacturing processes selected.

Recognizing the importance of corrosion resistance, particularly with the use of thinner, higher strength steel underbody components, the Light Truck Frame Project Team developed this Guide. Focusing on the elements of protecting underbody structural components against corrosion, this Guide is aimed at automotive underbody component engineers who are responsible for design, process, product, material selection or corrosion performance. The relative importance of the various options within each of the corrosion protection factors (material, design, post-coating and manufacturing processes) is outlined. It is intended to assist designers in addressing the issue of corrosion protection.

Definition of Basic Corrosion Conditions

In automotive applications, there are five types of steel corrosion: uniform corrosion, crevice corrosion, pitting corrosion, galvanic corrosion and cosmetic corrosion.

The most familiar type of corrosion is termed uniform corrosion. It tends to proceed evenly over the entire exposed surface of any uncoated part and eventually causes a general thinning of the metal. While best known, it is the least damaging. In automotive applications, uniform corrosion is not related to perforation or structural damage, and therefore, it is not addressed further in this publication.

Crevice corrosion is often associated with small volumes of stagnant solution or electrolyte trapped in crevices of joints, or in surface deposits and poultices. Pitting corrosion is a localized attack, usually caused by chlorides. Pits form resulting in a roughened surface. Crevice-corrosion and pitting corrosion result in an accelerated attack on the metal. In some instances, the attack is severe enough to lead to premature, and often catastrophic, functional failures. For example, structural requirements may be compromised or a body panel may be perforated.

Galvanic corrosion occurs when dissimilar metals are in contact with one another in the presence of an electrolyte. It can be detrimental or beneficial. For example, an aluminium component in contact with a steel component may corrode in order to protect the steel. This situation is injurious to the aluminium component. On the other hand, steel is often given a metallic zinc coating. The zinc sacrifices itself, thereby prolonging the life of the component made from the zinc coated steel. Corrosion that initiates on a visible surface of a vehicle, usually at nicks or scratches in a post-coating, is called cosmetic corrosion. Of primary concern is poor appearance due to red rust, stain and paint blisters.

Crevice Corrosion

Crevice corrosion is a damaging type of corrosion because it is sharply focused on localized areas, usually invisible in its early stages. The attack is swift, often resulting in unexpected or premature failure. Crevice corrosion is often associated with small volumes of stagnant solution or electrolyte trapped in holes, on gasket surfaces, at joints (Figure 4.1 and 4.2), under fasteners, and in surface deposits or poultices (Figure 4.3).

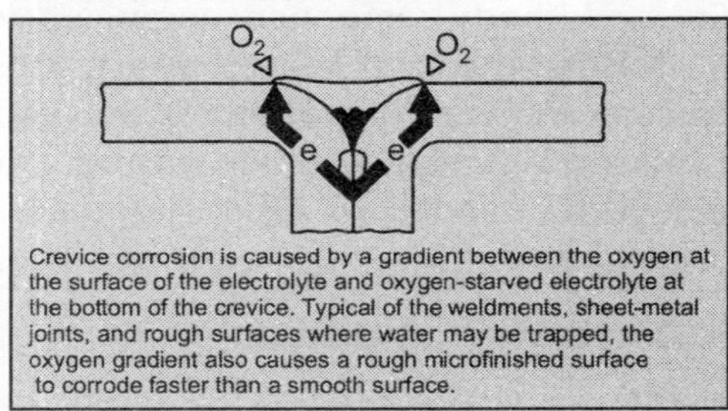

Fig. 4.1 : Crevice corrosion at weld joint.

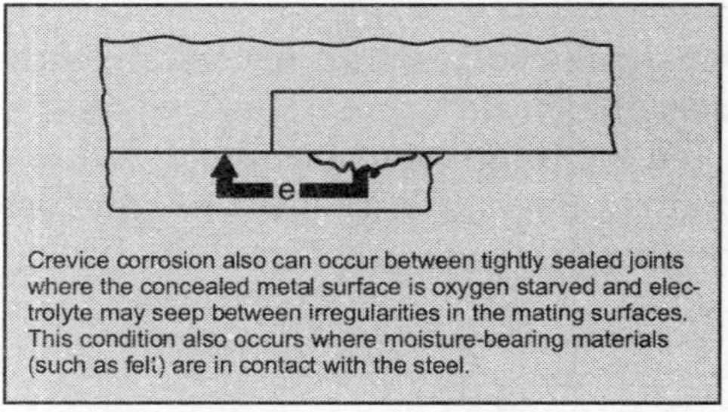

Fig. 4.2 : Crevice corrosion at lap joint.

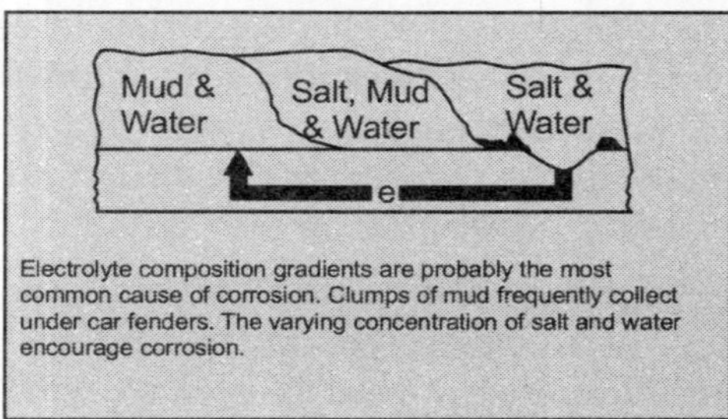

Fig. 4.3 : Crevice corrosion under poultice.

There is disagreement among researchers regarding the mechanism governing crevice corrosion. One school of thought believes crevice corrosion is the result of differences in the metal ion or oxygen concentration within the crevice and on surrounding surfaces. Often, crevice corrosion is described as oxygen concentration cell corrosion, caused by oxygen availability at the surface of the electrolyte and oxygen starvation at the surface of the metal.

Other studies have shown that although metal ion and oxygen concentration differences exist, the corrosion mechanism is more complex and can be explained by acid formation within the crevice. Although oxygen is depleted in the crevice, metal dissolution continues because the excess of positively charged metal ions is balanced by the migration of anions (especially chloride ions) from the bulk solution into the crevice (Figure 4.4). The metal chloride concentration in the crevice increases. Hydrolysis of the metal chloride follows and the pH falls within the crevice, resulting in an autocatalytic anodic process.

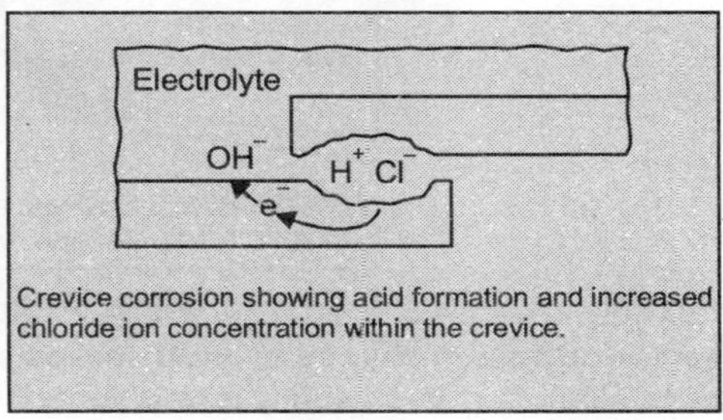

Crevice corrosion showing acid formation and increased chloride ion concentration within the crevice.

Fig. 4.4 : Crevice corrosion at lap joint.

Crevice corrosion remains a major problem because current vehicles have a multitude of box sections and joints. It is virtually impossible to eliminate the minute gaps between joined surfaces, which are the prime sites for crevice attack. The severity of crevice corrosion is evidenced by perforation of body panels and chassis components.

Much of the crevice corrosion problem is due to road debris trapped in pockets, corners, ledges, and on some vertical surfaces (Figure 4.5). These poultices hold salty electrolyte or moisture in intimate contact with the metal. The lack of run-off and thorough air-drying of the metal explains why vertical and upper surfaces (such as on fenders) frequently corrode.

Plugging of drain holes is another cause of crevice corrosion. A damp poultice builds up in the lower interior of doors, rocker panels and tailgates, and perforation results.

Some metals or alloys that rely on passive layers or oxide films for corrosion protection, for example, some aluminium and stainless steel alloys, are particularly susceptible to crevice attack in chloride media. The high concentration of chloride or hydrogen ions destroys the films, resulting in increased metal dissolution rates. Aluminium and stainless steel can be specially alloyed to improve their crevice corrosion resistance.

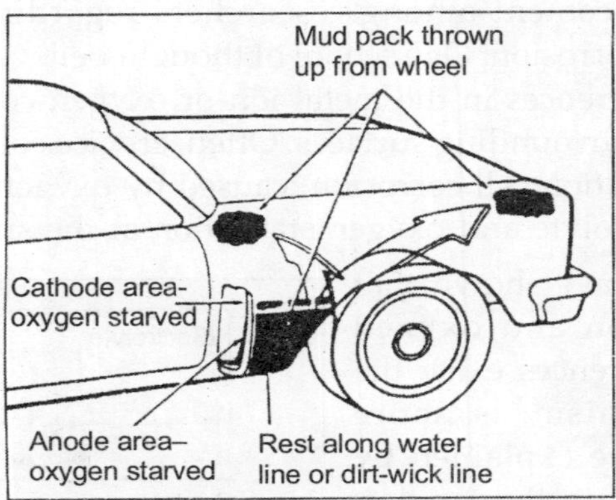

Fig. 4.5 : Mud packs.

Crevice corrosion caused by mud, leaves and other road debris packed against the under-side offenders usually is undetected until perforation takes place. This form of corrosion also can occur along the upper edge of mud packs on vertical fender surfaces.

An effective way to combat crevice corrosion is to minimize or eliminate crevices during the design stage. Once a vehicle is in service, proper maintenance to keep surfaces clean also helps control crevice corrosion.

Pitting Corrosion

Pitting corrosion is a localized attack, usually caused by chlorides. The mechanism governing pit growth is similar to that of crevice corrosion. In fact, pits are "mini" crevices which usually have diameters equal to their depth. They can occur so closely spaced that they give the appearance of a roughened surface. Pitting corrosion is a self-initiating form of crevice corrosion, in that the corrosion process creates the pit or crevice, which propagates at an accelerated rate and eventually perforates the metal. Initiation of pits usually results from non-homogeneity in the metal, breaks in protective films, surface deposits, defects or imperfections (Figure 4.6).

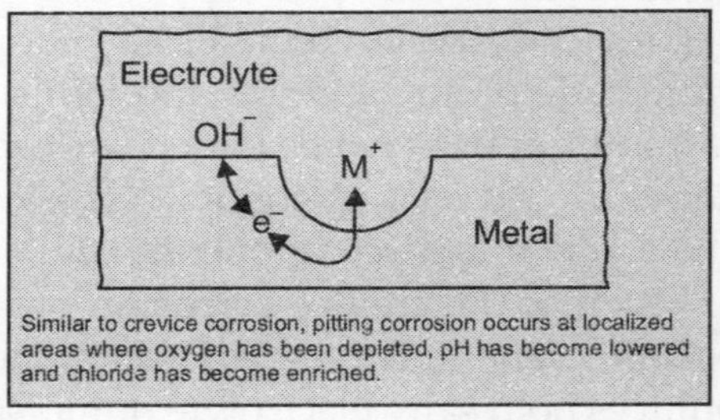

Similar to crevice corrosion, pitting corrosion occurs at localized areas where oxygen has been depleted, pH has become lowered and chloride has become enriched.

Fig. 4.6 : Pitting corrosion.

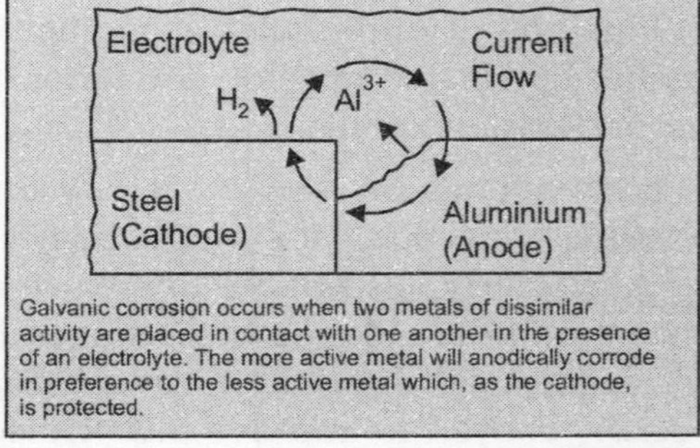

Galvanic corrosion occurs when two metals of dissimilar activity are placed in contact with one another in the presence of an electrolyte. The more active metal will anodically corrode in preference to the less active metal which, as the cathode, is protected.

Fig. 4.7 : Galvanic or bimetallic Corrosion.

Galvanic Corrosion

Galvanic corrosion, also referred to as two-metal or bimetalic corrosion, occurs when dissimilar metals are in contact in the presence of an electrolyte. The more active, or anodic, metal corrodes rapidly while the more noble, or cathodic, metal is not damaged. On the galvanic scale, aluminium and zinc are more active than steel and, in the presence of a chloride-containing electrolyte, will corrode preferentially when in contact with steel (Figure 4.7).

If an aluminium automotive part is in direct contact with a steel part, the aluminium part will corrode. To prevent the galvanic corrosion of the aluminium, the aluminium and steel parts should be electrically separated by a non-conductive spacer or sealer.

The galvanic corrosion mechanism can be used beneficially. It is widely employed as the primary protection system for steel. A thin coating of zinc on steel will corrode preferentially, and this sacrificial action provides long-term protection for the steel substrate.

Cosmetic Corrosion

Corrosion that initiates on a visible surface of a vehicle, usually at nicks or scratches in the post-coating is called cosmetic corrosion. Figure 4.8 shows some of the factors involved during the corrosion of painted cold rolled, zinc or zinc-alloy coated sheet steel at areas of localized paint damage.

In the case of cold rolled sheet steel, exposure to wet conditions leads to anodic dissolution of the steel at the exposed area with the formation of unsightly red rust. Because water, oxygen and ions migrate through and under the paint film, a cathodic reaction takes place beneath the paint adjacent to the damaged region. Electrons flow through the steel to balance the separated anodic and cathodic reactions. The high pH solution that is developed at the steel/paint interface causes a loss of paint adhesion, which is termed cathodic disbonding. Depending upon the types of paint system, pre-treatment and substrate, cathodic disbonding can proceed by one or more of several possible mechanisms, including: (1) saponification of the paint resin, which is a degradation of the polymer by hydroxyl ions; (2) dissolution of the phosphate layer; or (3) reduction of an oxide layer on the metal surface. During subsequent exposure to drying conditions, oxygen becomes available for increased cathodic activity at the area of initial damage. This oxygen allows anodic dissolution to spread into the delaminated region, and leads to further attack by anodic undermining. The formation of a rust layer beneath the film may lead to further damage due to mechanical wedging.

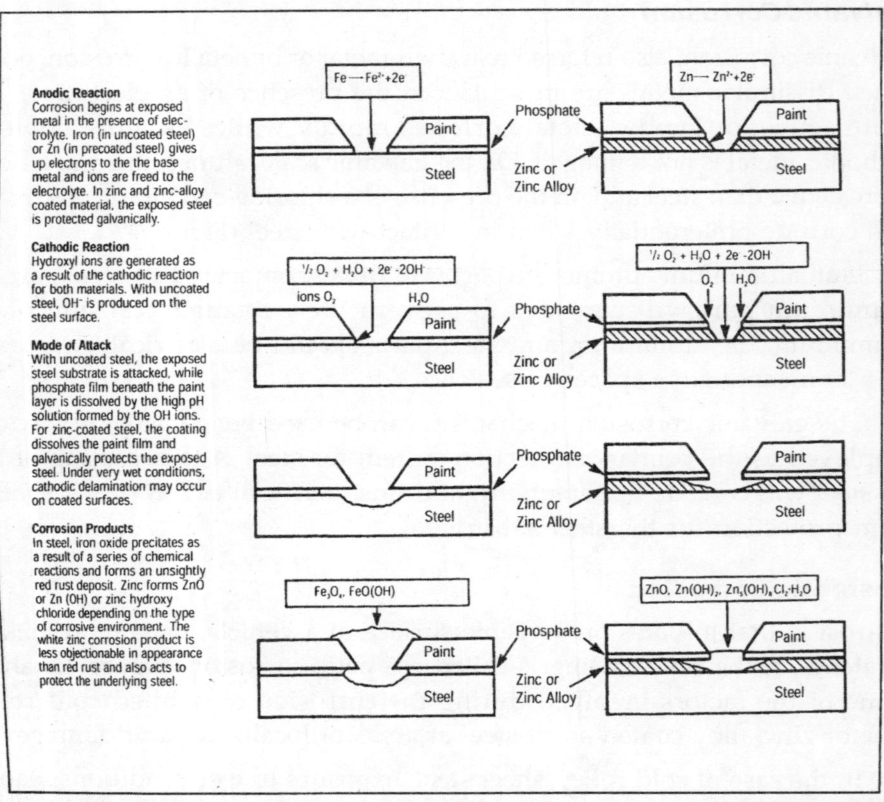

Fig. 4.8 : Corrosion processes at damaged paint site. Corrosion of steel at regions of paint damage is an electrochemical process. Metal is oxidized at anodic sites with the formation of electrons and ions. The electrons are transported through the metallic substrate to cathodic sites where they combine with water and oxygen to form hydroxyl ions. Zinc and zinc-alloy coated steels differ from uncoated steel in the locations of the anodic and cathodic sites, the mode of attack, and the corrosion products, as shown.

Repeated exposure to wetting and drying cyclesleads to a continuing attack on the steel substrate, formation of red corrosion products and a spreading loss of paint adhesion termed paint creepback. During initial stages of re-wetting, reduction of red corrosion products to magnetite [gamma-FeO(OH) $\rightarrow$ Fe_3O_4] may also contribute to the cathodic reaction. However, red rusting and paint creepback can usually be minimized by using a zinc or zinc-alloy coated steel substrate. For this reason, there has been widespread substitution in automotive bodies of zinc and zinc-alloy coated sheet steel for cold rolled sheet steel.

When a zinc or zinc-alloy coated sheet is used, the zinc coating corrodes preferentially as shown in Figure 4.8. In doing so, the coating acts as the anode in a galvanic couple and the exposed steel acts as the cathode. While the steel is thus protected, there is some loss of paint adhesion due to anodic undermining as the zinc coating is consumed. There may be further loss of adhesion in advance of the dissolution front due to cathodic disbonding.

Zinc ions, produced by dissolution of the coating, migrate to the exposed steel surface. There, they combine with hydroxyl ions from the cathodic reaction and form a white precipitate. The white precipitate is generally less objectionable in appearance than red rust. It also serves to inhibit the cathodic reaction in this region and slows the rate of zinc dissolution. Red rust will eventually develop on the exposed steel once the available zinc in the coating is consumed.

During intervals of dryness, both anodic and cathodic reactions are halted and the spread of paint damage is stopped. Thus, when dryness intervals are present, the degree of paint delamination for zinc and zinc-alloy coated steels exposed to actual service conditions is less than that for cold rolled steel. Further, with intervals of dryness, the oxides formed on coated steels are more protective in nature than the oxides formed on cold, rolled steel.

It should be noted that when coated steel and cold rolled steel are tested under conditions of continual wetness, such as in a salt-spray test, results opposite to those experienced in the real world, where intervals of dryness are present, can occur. For example, constant wetness tests would indicate cold rolled sheet experiences less paint delamination than coated sheet. Constant wetness tests also obliterate the superior protection offered by the oxides on a coated sheet. For these reasons, constant wetness tests, such as the salt-spray test, should not be used to evaluate the corrosion resistance of body panels.

Steel Materials

Flat rolled steels are versatile materials. They provide strength and stiffness with favourable mass to cost ratios, and they allow high speed fabrication. In addition, they exhibit excellent corrosion resistance when coated, high energy absorption capacity, good fatigue properties, high work hardening rates, aging capability, and excellent payability, which are required by automotive applications. These characteristics, plus the availability of high strength low alloy (HSLA) and alloy steels in a wide variety of sizes, strength levels, chemical compositions, surface finishes, with and without various organic and inorganic coatings, have made sheet steel the material of choice for the automotive industry.

Numerous steel grades, produced to precise specifications, offer the designer a wide range of mechanical properties. Low-carbon steels offer yield strengths up to 260 MPa (38 ksi), dent resistant steels offer yield strenghts up to 280 MPa (40 ksi), high-strength steels offer yield strengths up to 830 MPa (120 ksi) and ultra high-strength steels offer tensile strengths up to 1500 MPa (215 ksi). Low-carbon steels have excellent ductility. They are widely used for underbody structural components that are formed by stamping or roll forming sheet steel and by hydroforming steel tubes. High-strength steels usually have less ductility than low-carbon steels. However, they can be supplied with sufficient formability for the production of stamped or roll formed underbody structural components. Ultra high-strength steels have less formability than high-strength steels. However, they are suitable for roll formed sections and less severe stampings.

Manufacturers often select a steel grade based on minimum yield strength. For example, a frame manufacturer may select a hot rolled sheet with a minimum yield strength of 250 MPa (36 ksi). The frame manufacturer may also require that; the grade selected meet a desired chemical composition.

Current Method for Specifying Low-Carbon Steel

A relatively new SAE document, J2329, "Categorization and Properties of Low-Carbon Automotive Sheet Steels", is increasing in acceptance. SAE J2329 classifies low-carbon sheet by five grade-levels, with yield strength, tensile strength, elongation, r_m and n-value requirements. The intent is to assure that certain minimum levels of strength and formability exist for each grade. The system employs four characters. The first two alphabetic characters designate hot rolled (HR) or cold rolled (CR) method of manufacture. The third numeric character defines the grade level (one through five) based on yield strength range, minimum tensile strength, minimum per cent elongation, minimum r_m value, and minimum n-value. The fourth alphabetic character (E, U, R, F, N or M) classifies the steel type with regards to surface quality and/or aging character. An optional fifth character (C) may be used to restrict carbon content to a minimum of 0.015 per cent. If the steel sheet is a metallic-coated product, then the coating would be specified in accordance with the soon to be issued SAE J1562. An example of the above is HR2M 45A5AU, a hot rolled sheet, with Grade 2 mechanical properties and chemical composition, free of coil breaks and non-aging. It has an unexposed galvanneal coating on each side of 45g/m^2 (0.15 oz/ft^2).

Current Method for Specifying High-Strength and Ultra High-Strength Steel

High-strength steels were formerly specified in the automotive industry in accordance with SAE J1392. However, SAE J1392 will be replaced by SAE J2340 early in the year 2000. In SAE J1392, up to six characters are used. The first three characters denote the minimum yield strength in kips per square inch (ksi). One kip equals 1000 pounds force (4.45N). The fourth alphabetical character denotes general chemical composition, the fifth denotes general carbon level and the sixth alphabetic character denotes deoxidation/sulphide inclusion control practice. For example, 050XLK is a steel grade having a minimum yield strength of 50 ksi (345 MPa) and a minimum tensile strength of 60 ksi (414 MPa), an HSLA composition, a carbon content of 0.13 per cent maximum and it is produced to a killed (fine grain) practice. In addition to grade, it is necessary to specify whether the material is hot rolled sheet, cold rolled sheet, hot dip galvanized (hot rolled) sheet, hot dip galvanized (cold rolled) sheet, galvanneal (hot rolled) sheet, etc. For example, some full frames on light trucks have crossmembers made from 040XLK and 050XLK hot rolled sheets. Front rails on some passenger cars are made from 050XLF 45A45AU, which is a formable high-strength steel grade with an unexposed quality galvanneal coating of 45g/m^2 (0.15oz/ft^2) on each side.

At the present, there is no generally accepted standard for ultra high-strength steel grades. SAE J2340, which will be available early in the year 2000, will cover these grades. However, it is fairly common to specify ultra high-strength steel using numbers to express minimum yield or tensile strength and alphabetic characters to denote quality. For example, 120X is a microalloy steel having a minimum yield strength of 120 ksi (827 MPa). Grade HOT is dual phase steel with a minimum tensile strength of 140 ksi (965 MPa). The grade M130HT is a martensitic steel with a minimum tensile strength of 130 ksi (896 MPa). It should be noted that dual phase (T) and martensitic (M—HT) steels are specified using a minimum tensile strength (rather than a minimum yield strength, which is the prevalent practice steel).

Former Methods for Specifying Low-Carbon Steel

A quality descriptor is the traditional method employed to specify low-carbon steel. A descriptor such as CQ (commercial quality), DQ (drawing quality) or DQSK (drawing quality special killed) is used to ensure that the steel possesses the essential characteristics for the application/manufacturing process. A descriptor basically defines steelmaking practice, degree of chemical segregation, uniformity of properties, surface quality, internal soundness, etc. In other words, the quality descriptor is the steel grade. However, it is also necessary for the specifier to state the material required, *e.g.*, hot rolled sheet, cold rolled sheet, hot dip galvanized (hot rolled) sheet, hot dip galvanized (cold rolled sheet), galvanneal (hot rolled) sheet, etc. Many side rails and crossmembers in light truck frames are specified as CQ hot rolled sheet, DQ hot rolled sheet or DQSK hot rolled sheet. SAE J403 is another traditional method used to specify low-carbon steels.

SAE J403 uses a four-digit number to identify the chemical composition. The last two digits represent the nominal carbon content in hundredths of a per cent. For example, SAE 1010 has a 0.10 per cent nominal carbon content.

Although no mechanical properties are specified, the chemical composition is. For example, SAE 1010 hot rolled sheet, which is used for some components in full vehicle frames, must satisfy the following composition requirements:

Carbon	-	0.08 to 0.13 per cent by weight
Manganese	-	0.30 to 0.60 per cent by weight.
Phosphorous	-	0.040 per cent maximum by weight and
Sulphur	-	0.050 per cent maximum by weight.

Coatings

Underbody structural components are typically coated to provide a first line of defense against corrosion. For light truck frames, the two most common coatings are hot melt wax and electrocoat (E-coat). Paints are also used on current light truck frames. Conversion coatings enhance the adhesion of electrocoat or paint, land they are commonly used in conjunction with these two coating types. Many underbody structural components, such as front rails on passenger cars, are made from sheet steel pre-coated with a metallic coating, *e.g.*, galvanized or galvanneal sheet steel. Autophoretic and powder coatings are also used on underbody structural components.

Application Methods

The use of spray equipment to apply coatings is proven and well defined. Spray equipment acts upon a stream of coating (solvent or water borne particles) and by various means disperses the coating into a cloud of finely divided particles. The atomized particles are then deposited on the intended surface forming a protective or decorative coating.

Dip application is a method that involves dipping a part into a coating bath, draining the part, and force drying or baking the part. Dip coatings are often used for primer and one-coat applications.

Flow coating is an automatic coating operation in which the product to be coated is conveyed through a chamber equipped with low pressure nozzles that completely flood the product with a coating. The process does not involve any atomization. It is used for large articles that would require a dipping tank of impractical size and for articles with a shape that makes spray painting impractical.

Conversion Coatings

Phosphate conversion coatings are employed to enhance paint adhesion. By enhancing paint adhesion, they indirectly enhance corrosion resistance. There are several varieties of phosphate coatings, *e.g.*, iron, zinc or manganese.

Prior to the application of a conversion coating, the metal surfaces must be free of shop soils, oil, grease, lubricants and rust. The metal surfaces must be receptive to the formation of a uniform, adherent chemical film or coating. Surfaces may be cleaned by mechanical methods or, more commonly, by immersion or spray cleaner systems.

A phosphate coating is applied by immersing a clean metal part in a hot processing solution for 4-6 minutes, depending on the bath chemistry. The weight (thickness) of the conversion coating is dependent upon the manner in which the part is cleaned, the immersion time, the composition of the processing bath and the chemical composition of the metal itself.

Hot Melt Wax Coatings

Hot melt wax coatings are thermoplastic corrosion prevention compounds. They have a solvent or waterborne formulation. Since the 1970's, hot melt waxes have been used extensively on underbody structural components to provide corrosion protection and enhance vehicle durability. Hot melt waxes are usually applied through a dipping process. The wax is preheated to a temperature between 125 and 195°C (257 and 383°F). Following an alkali cleaning and water rinsing operation, parts are immersed in the molten wax. The thickness of the wax deposited on the parts is controlled through a preheat of the parts prior to dipping and the actual time of immersion in the hot melt wax. Following the immersion process, the coated parts are allowed to return to ambient temperature through a process that controls the uniformity and finish of the hot melt wax. Hot melt wax thickness is commonly specified as 75-125 micrometers (3-5 mils). Typically, hot melt wax coatings can withstand temperatures up to 143°C (290°F) without dripping.

Electrocoat (E-coat)

Electrophoretic deposition is a process in which electrically charged particles are deposited out of a water suspension to coat a conductive part. The process is more commonly known as electrocoating or E-coating. The idea of electrically discharging polymers to coat an object was first considered in the 1930's. Most of the basic research was conducted in Europe in the 1960s. North American companies began electrocoating in the late 1960s, and the process has been widely used for coating metal parts ranging from simple stampings to complex auto bodies.

The process requires a coating tank in which to immerse the part, as well as temperature control, filtering and circulation equipment. Electrocoating systems are known as anodic or cathodic depending upon whether the part is the anode or cathode in the electrochemical process. Cathodic systems are more common since they require less surface preparation and provide better corrosion resistance.

Electrocoating requires that the coating binder, pigment and additives be given an electrical charge. These charged materials, under the influence of an electric field, migrate through water to the part surface.

Once at the part, the charged materials give up their charge due to neutralization by electrochemically generated OH^- ions (cathodic process). Upon giving up their charge, the coating materials drop out of the water suspension and coalesce as a coating on the part surfaces. Electrocoat thickness typically ranges from 10 to 30 micrometers (0.4 to 1.2 mils).

Automotive parts that are electrocoated usually receive a zinc or iron phosphate treatment prior to deposition. This treatment enhances the application of the E-coat.

Metallic Coatings

Various types of metallic coatings can be applied to ferrous and non-ferrous substrates to inhibit corrosion and/or provide a decorative finish. The choice of a particular coating material is dependent upon, the severity of the corrosive environment, whether the part is subject to wear and abrasion, and the degree of visibility of the part in service.

Four common methods for applying metallic coatings are:

- ***Electroplating:*** The coating is deposited onto the substrate metal by applying an electrical potential between the substrate metal (cathode) and a suitable anode in the presence of an electrolyte. The electrolyte usually consists of a water solution containing salt of the metal to be deposited and various other additions that contribute to the plating process.
- ***Mechanical plating:*** Finely divided metal powder is cold welded to the substrate by tumbling the part, metal powder and a suitable media such as glass beads, in an aqueous solution containing additional agents. Mechanical plating is commonly used to apply zinc or cadmium to small parts such as fasteners.
- ***Electroless:*** In this non-electric plating system, a coating metal, such as cobalt or nickel, is deposited on a substrate via a chemical reaction in the presence of a catalyst.
- ***Hot dipping:*** A coating metal is deposited on a substrate by immersing the substrate in a molten bath of the coating metal.

Many underbody structural components are manufactured from sheet steel with a metallic coating. The steel mills supply hot or cold rolled sheet in coil form with metallic coatings applied by either electroplating or hot dipping. The most commonly supplied coatings include zinc, zinc-iron, zinc-nickel, aluminium, aluminium-zinc, tin and lead-tin.

Organic Coatings

The application of an organic coating, such as paint, is a cost effective corrosion protection method. Organic coatings act as a barrier to a corrosive solution or electrolyte. They prevent, or retard, the transfer of electrochemical charge from the corrosive solution to the metal underneath the organic coating.

An organic coating is a complex mixture of materials designed to protect the substrate and to enhance appearance. A coating is composed of binders, carriers, pigments and additives. Binders provide the major properties to the coating while the carriers (solvents and/or water) adjust the viscosity of the coating for application. Pigments impart specific properties to a coating such as corrosion resistance and color. Furthermore, when formulating a coating, the type of pigment and its volume are critical to the optimization of properties such as adhesion, permeability, resistance to blistering and gloss. Additives include thickeners, flow agents, catalysts and inhibitors.

Coating systems are often identified by the type of polymers employed. Commonly used organic coatings are:

- Alykd and epoxy ester coatings (air dried or baked to promote cross-link oxidation),
- Two-part coatings such as urethane coatings,
- Radiation curable coatings (acrylic and epoxy polymers),
- Latex coatings such as vinyl, acrylic or styrene polymer combinations,
- Water soluble coatings (versions of alkyd, epoxy ester or polyester coatings),
- High-solids coatings and
- Powder coatings (vinyl, polyester or epoxy polymers).

Autodeposition Coatings

Autodeposition is a waterborne process that depends on chemical reactions to achieve deposition. This process has been used commercially since 1973. The composition of an autodeposition bath includes a mildly acidic latex emulsion polymer, de-ionized water and proprietary ingredients. The chemical phenomenon consists of the mildly acidic bath attacking the steel parts being immersed and causing an immediate surface reaction that releases iron ions. These ions react with the latex in solution causing a depositon on the surface of the steel parts. The newly deposited organic film is adherent yet quite porous. Thus, the chemical activators can rapidly diffuse to reach the surface of the metal, allowing continued coating formation.

The coating thickness of the autodeposition film is time and temperature related. Initially, the deposition process is quite rapid, but slows down as the film begins to build or mature. As long as the part being coated is in the bath, the process will continue; however, the rate of deposition will decline. Typically, film thicknesses are controlled from 15 to 25 micrometers (0.6 to 0.8 mils).

Autodeposition will coat any metal the liquid touches. Parts that are tubular in shape, assembled parts or parts that have intricate designs can be coated by this process. Autodeposition does not require a phosphate stage and the coating is cured at a relatively low temperature.

Powder Coatings

In the powder coating process, a dry powder is applied to a clean surface. After application, the coated object is heated, fusing the powder into a smooth, continuous film. Powders are available in a wide range of chemical types, coating properties and colors. The most widely used types include acrylic, vinyl, epoxy, nylon, polyester and urethane. Modern application techniques for applying powders fall into four basic categories: fluidized bed process, electrostatic bed process, electrostatic spray process and plasma spray process.

The electrostatic spray process is the most commonly used method of applying powders. In this process, the electrically conductive and grounded object is sprayed with charged, non-conducting powder particles. The charged particles are attracted to the substrate and cling to it. Oven heat then fuses the particles into a smooth continuous film. Coating thicknesses in the range of 25 to 125 micrometers (1 to 5 mils) are obtained. Controlling a low film thickness is difficult. A booth and collection system can be used to collect overspray for re-use.

Corrosion, fire protection and fatigue failure of steel structure are some of the main concerns of an engineer involved in the design and construction of structural steel work and these aspects do warrant extra attention. A review of international literature and the state-of-the-art in steel construction would reassure the designer that many aspects of corrosion, fire and fatigue behaviour of structural steel work are no longer the major issues. For example the steel construction industry has developed excellent protective coatings that would retain service life even after 20 years without any attention! Similarly, the emergence of 'fire enginering of steel structures' as a specialised discipline has addressed many of the concerns regarding the safety of structural steel work under fire. In India 'Fire Resistant Steels (FRS)' are available which are quite effective in steelwork subjected to elevated temperatures. They are also cost effective compared to mild steel! Similarly, fatigue behaviour of steel structural systems has been researched extensively in the past few decades and has been covered excellently in the published literature. The revised Indian code IS 800 has introduced separate sections on each of the aspects pertaining to steel structures.

Corrosion is an electro-chemical process involving an anode, a cathode and an electrolyte. In the case of steel, when favourable condition for corrosion occurs, the ferrous ions go into solution from anodic areas. Electrons are then released from the anode and move through the cathode where they combine with water and oxygen to form hydroxyl ions. These react with the ferrous ions from anode to produce hydrated ferrous oxide, which further gets oxidised into ferric oxide, which is known as the 'red rust'.

From the above discussion, it is clear, that the main interest of the structural designers is to prevent the formation of these "corrosion batteries". For example, if we can wipe out the 'drop of water' shown in Fig. 4.11, the corrosion will not take place! Hence using the "eliminate the electrolyte" principle, wherever possible we need to device detailing and protection to surfaces of structural steel work to ensure that the combination of oxygen and water are avoided and hence the corrosion batteries are avoided. On the other hand, steel is anodic in the presence of stainless steel or brass and cathodic in the presence of zinc or aluminium and the second property can be used to protect it from corrosion.

The types of corrosion encountered in structural steel elements are:

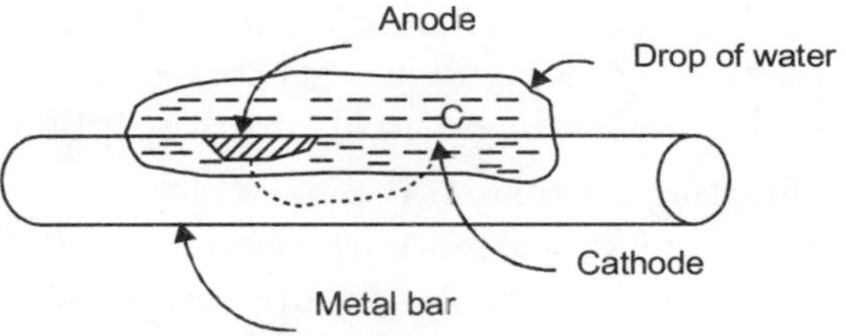

Fig. 4.11 : Mechanism of Corrosion in Steel.

Pitting corrosion

As shown in Fig. 4.11 the anodic areas form a corrosion pit. This can occur with mild steel immersed in water or soil. This common type of corrosion is essentially due to the presence of moisture aided by improper detailing or constant exposure to alternate wetting and drying. This form of corrosion could easily be tackled by encouraging rapid drainage by proper detailing and allowing free flow of air, which would dry out the surface.

Crevice corrosion

The principle of crevice corrosion is shown in Figure 1.12. The oxygen content of water trapped in a crevice is less than that of water which is exposed to air. Because of this the crevice becomes anodic with respect to surrounding metal and hence the corrosion starts inside the crevice.

Bimetallic corrosion

When two dissimilar metals (for *e.g.* Iron and Aluminium) are joined together in an electrolyte, an electrical current passes between them and the corrosion occurs. This is because, metals in general could be arranged, depending on their electric potential, into a table called the 'galvanic series'. The farther the metals in the galvanic series, the greater the potential differences between them causing the anodic metal to corrode. A common example is the use of steel screws in stainless steel members and also using steel bolts in aluminium members. Obviously such a contact between dissimilar metals should be avoided in detailing.

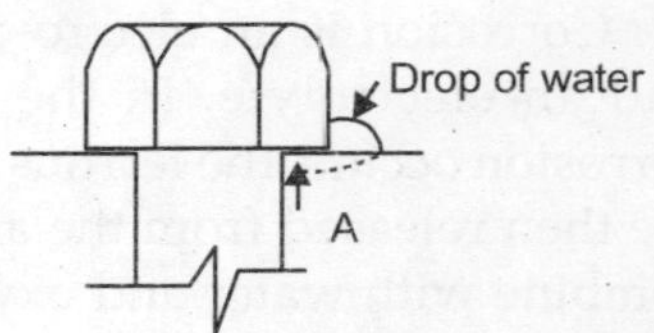

Fig. 4.12 : Mechanism of Crevice corrosion.

Stress Corrosion

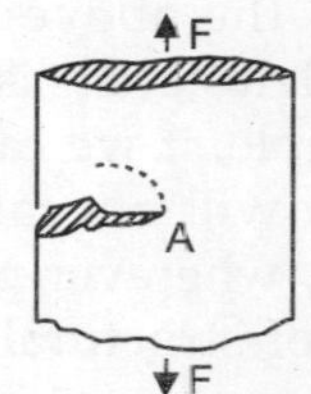

Fig. 4.13 : Mechanism of Stress corrosion.

This occurs under the simultaneous influence of a static tensile stress and a specific corrosive environment. Stress makes some spots in a body more anodic (especially the stress concentration zones) compared with the rest as shown in Fig. 4.13. The crack tip in Fig. 4.13 is the anodic part and it corrodes.
to make the crack wider. This corrosion is not common with ferrous metals though some stainless steels are susceptible to this.

Fretting corrosion: If two oxide coated films or rusted surfaces are rubbed together, the oxide film can be mechanically removed from high spots between the contacting surfaces as shown in Fig. 4.14. These exposed points become active anodes compared with the rest of the surfaces and initiate corrosion. This type corrosion is common in mechanical components.

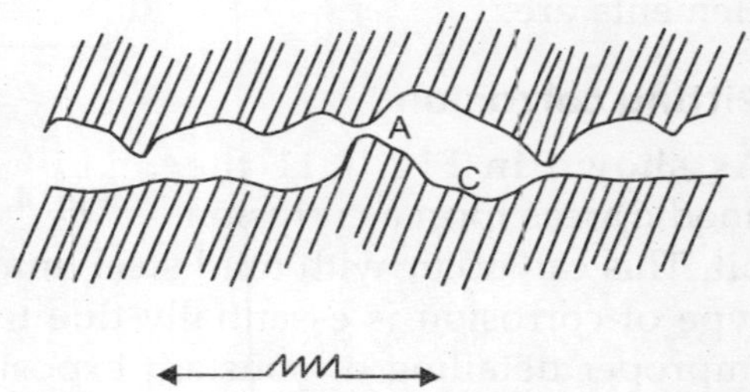

Fig. 4.14 : The Mechanism of Fretting corrosion.

Bacterial corrosion: This can occur in soils and water as a result of microbiological activity. Bacterial corrosion is most common in pipelines, buried structures and offshore structures.

Hydrogen embrittlement: This occurs mostly in fasteners and bolts. The atomic hydrogen may get absorbed into the surface of the fasteners. When tension is applied to these fasteners, hydrogen will tend to migrate to points of stress concentration. The pressure created by the hydrogen creates and/or extends a crack. The crack grows in subsequent stress cycles. Although hydrogen embrittlement is usually included in the discussion about corrosion, actually it is not really a corrosion phenomenon.

Corrosion Protection to Steel Structure Elements

Corrosion protection methods: The methods of corrosion protection are governed by actual environmental conditions as per IS: 9077 and IS: 9172. The main corrosion protection methods are given below:

(*a*) Controlling the Electrode Potential

(*b*) Inhibitors

(*c*) Inorganic/Metal Coatings or Organic/Paint systems.

Taking care of the following points can provide satisfactory corrosion protection to most structural steel elements: The design, fabrication and erection details of exposed structure should be such that good drainage of water is ensured. Standing pool of water, moisture accumulation and rundown of water for extended duration are to be avoided. The details of connections should ensure that:

- All exposed surfaces are easily accessible for inspection and maintenance.
- All surfaces not so easily accessible are completely sealed against-ingress of moisture.
- Avoiding of entrapment and accumulation of moisture and dirt in components and connections by suitable detailing as shown in Figure 4.15.
- Avoiding contact with other materials such as bimetallic connections.
- Detailing the structural steel work to enhance air movement and thereby keeping the surfaces dry as shown in Figure 4.16.

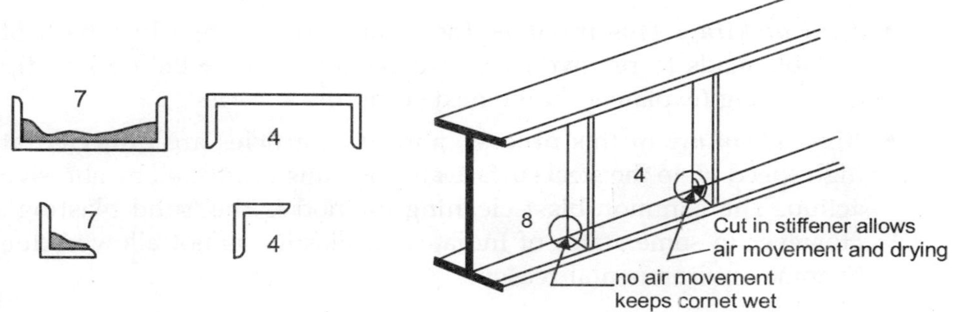

Fig. 4.15 : Simple orientation of members to avoid dirt and water entrapment.

Fig. 4.16 : Detailing to enhance air movement between joints.

- Providing suitable drain holes wherever possible to initiate easy draining of the entrapped water as shown in Figure 4.17.

- Providing suitable access to all the components of steel structures for periodic maintenance, cleaning and carrying out inspection and maintenance at regular intervals.

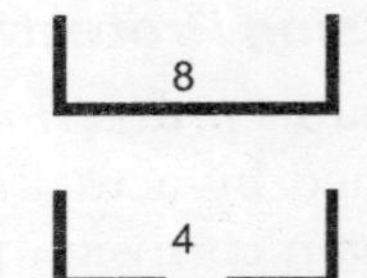

Fig. 4.17 : Provision of drain holes wherever possible.

- Providing coating applications to structural steel elements. Metallic coatings such as hot-dip galvanising, metal spray coatings, etc. are very effective forms of corrosion protection. Cleaning of the surfaces and applying suitable paints is the most commonly used and reliable method of corrosion protection.

Structural steel comes out of the mill with a mill scale on its surface. On weathering, water penetrates into the fissures of the mill scale and rusting of the steel surface occurs. The mill scale loses its adhesion and begins to shed. Mill scale therefore needs to be removed before any protective coatings are applied. The surface of steel may also contain dirt or other impurities during storage, transportation and handling.

The various surface preparation methods are briefly explained below:

- ***Manual preparation:*** This is a very economical surface cleaning method but only 30 per cent of the rust and scale may be removed. This is usually carried out with a wire brush.
- ***Mechanical preparation:*** This is carried out with power driven tools and up to 35 per cent cleaning can be achieved. This method is quite fast and effective.
- ***Flame cleaning:*** In this process an Oxy-gas flame causes differential thermal expansion and removes mill scale more effectively.
- ***Acid pickling:*** This involves the immersion of steel in a bath of suitable acids to remove rust. Usually this is done before hot dip galvanising (explained in the next section).
- ***Blast cleaning:*** In this process, abrasive particles are projected at high speed on to the steel surface and cleaning is effected by abrasive action. The common blast cleaning method is the 'sand blasting'. However in some states of India, sand blasting is not allowed due to some environmental reasons.

Protective Coatings

The principal protective coatings applied to structural steel work are paints, metal coatings or combination of these two. Paints basically consist of a pigment, a binder and solvent. After the paint has been applied as a wet film, the solvent evaporates leaving the binder and the pigment on the surface.

In codes of practices relating to corrosion protection, the thickness of the primer, the type of paints and the thickness of the paint in term of microns are specified depending upon the corrosive environment. The codes of practice also specify the frequency with which the change of paint is required. Metal coatings on structural steel work are almost either zinc or aluminium. Hot dip Zinc coatings known as "galvanising", involves dipping of the steelwork into a bath of molten Zinc at a temperature of about 450°C. The work piece is first degreased and cleaned by pickling to enhance the wetting properties. Sometimes hot dip aluminising is also done. Alternatively, metal coating could also be applied using metal spraying.

Weathering Steels

To protect steel from corrosion, some countries produce steels which by themselves can resist corrosion. These steels are called as "Weathering steels or Corten steels". Weathering steels are high strength alloy weldable structural steels, which possess excellent weathering resistance in many non-polluted atmospheric conditions. They contain up to 3 per cent of alloying elements such as chromium, copper, nickel, phosphorous, etc. On exposure to air, under suitable conditions, they form adherent protective oxide coatings. This acts as a protective film, which with time and appropriate conditions causes the corrosion rate to reduce until it is a low terminal level. Conventional coatings are, therefore, not usually necessary since the steel provides its own protection. Weathering steels are 25 per cent costlier than the mild steel, but in many cases the total cost of the structure can be reduced if advantage is taken of the 30 per cent higher yield strength compared to mild steel.

Uniform Corrosion

Uniform corrosion is normally characterized by a chemical or electrochemical reaction that proceeds uniformly over the entire exposed surface or large fraction of total area. Uniform corrosion is relatively easily measured and predicted making disastrous failures. It is an unexpected or premature failure of protective coating system on structures.

Concentration Cell Corrosion

Concentration cell corrosion is due to electrochemical attack on the metal surface, exposed to an electrolyte of varying concentration or of varying aeration. It may be the result of local differences in metal-ions concentration or temperature differences or inadequate agitation or slow diffusion of metal ions, produced by corrosion.

Soil Corrosion

Soil corrosion is a special case of electrochemical reaction. It depends on many factors like soil composition, its acidity, degree of aeration, electro-chemical activity, moisture, presence of bacteria and micro organisms etc.

Intergranular Corrosion

This type of corrosion is due to the fact that the grain boundaries contain material which shows electrode potential, more anodic than that of the grain centre in the particular corroding medium. This may be due to precipitation of certain compounds at the grain boundaries, thereby leaving the solid metal solution (just adjacent to the grain boundary) impoverished (or depleted) in one constituent.

Water line Corrosion

When water is stored in a steel tank, it is generally found that the maximum amount of corrosion takes along a line just beneath the level of the water meniscus. The area above the waterline (highly-oxygenated) acts as the cathodic. However, if the water is relatively free from acidity, little corrosion takes place.

Corrosion of Plastic and Elastomers

Polymeric materials corrode by processes quite different from those associated with metallic corrosion. Physicochemical processes, rather than electrochemical reactions, are responsible for the degradation, rather than electrochemical reactions, are responsible for the degradation of plastics and elastomers. Polymeric materials are attacked by:

1. Swelling
2. Dissolution
3. Bond rupture due to
   (*i*) Chemical reaction (*e.g.*, oxidation)
   (*ii*) Heat
   (*iii*) Radiation (*e.g.*, sunlight).

These reactions can occur singly or in combination. Swelling and dissolution, with and without chemical-bond breaking, are the chief causes of attack during exposure to liquids.

Erosion Corrosion and Fretting

It is caused by the combined effect of the abrading action of turbulent flow of gases, vapours and liquids: and the mechanical rubbing action of solids over a metal surface. Erosion corrosion is most frequently encountered in piping, agitators, condenser-tubes or such vessels in which streams of liquids or gases emerge from an opening and strike the side-walls with high velocities. The same stagnant or slow flowing fluid will cause a low corrosion rate but rapid movement of corrosive fluid physically erodes and removes the protective corrosion. Fretting is another type of erosion corrosion but in vapor phase it is caused by two surfaces rubbing together at very small amplitude.

Where does Corrosion Matter in Structural Steel Work?

The requirement of durability should always be balanced with the cost of corrosion protection and the cost of the structure itself. Higher cost of protection is justified in structures such as bridges where longer life is desirable and the cost of repair or replacement is higher. The cost of repair and replacement should also take into account the cost due to loss of service over the repair period. With this in mind, the following discussions can be better understood.

The corrosion of steel in a dry interior environment is virtually insignificant. For example, structural steel work in the interiors of offices, shops, schools, hostels, residences, airport terminals, hospitals etc. will not corrode noticeably during the expected 50-year life of the structure. Hence in these situations no protective coating is required and the structural steel work may be left exposed. Only when the structural steel work is exposed to moisture in an interior environment such as kitchens, sports halls etc. a little attention is needed in the detailing of the steel work or in the form of thin protective coatings. Structural steel work will need protective coatings in slightly intensive corrosive environment such as some industrial buildings, dairies, laundries, breweries etc. The above mentioned situations can be termed as 'low to medium' risk categories. Structural steel work exposed to high humidity and atmosphere, chemical plants, foundries, steel bridges, offshore structures would fall into the "high risk" category.

Structural steel work that is categorised into high-risk group requires better surface preparation and sufficient thickness of the anti-corrosive paints. As we review the protective coatings such as the paints available in the market today many of the paints can perform very satisfactorily for 5-7 years. Specially prepared epoxy paints when applied in sufficient thickness after a good surface preparation, can last as high as 20 years! Corrosion of steel is no longer the major problem that it once was and the protective methods no longer pose any major disincentive for using steel in the building industry. For the purpose of selecting a suitable paint system, the corrosion risk groups of structural steel work are classified according to their location and their intended service; however the same classification can also be done depending on the exterior environment of the structural steel work as in Table 4.1.

The general environment, to which steel structure is exposed during its working life, is classified into five levels of exposure conditions namely mild, moderate, severe, very severe and extreme. For example, surfaces which are protected as in interior of buildings are classified as mild while those exposed to saturated salt air in coastal area are classified as severe. The code gives a description of each of these exposure conditions and they can be assumed to correspond to a certain atmospheric condition as shown in Table 4.1. For each atmospheric condition, the coating system to be adopted for a desired number of years is given. For desired life of 18 years in polluted inland environment coating system 4 to be selected and so on. The coating system may consist of a primer, a thickening coat and a wearing coat of paint.

Table 4.1 : Protection Guide for Steel Work Application

(*a*) Desired life in different environments (in years) under various coating systems

Exposure Condition	Atmospheric Condition	Coating System					
		1	2	3	4	5	6
Mild	Normal Inland (Rural and Urban areas)	12	18	20	20	20	>20
Moderate	Polluted Inland (High airborne sulphur dioxide)	10	15	12	18	15-20	>20
Severe	Normal Coastal (As normal inland plus high airborne salts levels)	10	12	20	20	20	>20
Very severe	Polluted Coastal (As polluted Inland plus high airborne salt levels)	8	10	10	15	15-20	>20
Extreme							

Electrochemical Theory of Corrosion

The mechanism of corrosion was not known until eighteenth century, while the problem of corrosion is as old as man's knowledge. Regarding the mechanism of corrosion, the first paper was produced in 1801 by Wallaston. There are various theories namely Acid theory, Direct chemical theory, Colloidal theory to study the mechanism of corrosion by the most acceptable, given by Whlenty in 1903, is electrochemical theory of corrosion. It is one of the best theories for corrosion processes. In corrosion reaction there are two partial reactions, which can be divided in to two-class oxidation and reduction. For every oxidation reaction there must be simultaneously reduction reaction. Some examples of oxidation and reduction are as follows:

Oxidation or anodic reactions are those that result in a surplus of electron and for corrosion these typically correspond to various metal dissolution reaction such as:

$$Fe \rightarrow Fe^{2+} + 2e^-$$

$$Fe^{2+} \rightarrow Fe^{3+} + e^-$$

$$Fe^{2+} + 2OH^- \rightarrow Fe(OH)_2$$

Reduction or cathodic reactions result in the consumption of electrons, and for corrosion these typically correspond to the oxygen reduction or hydrogen evolution reactions:

$$O_2 + 2H_2O + 4e^- \rightarrow 4OH^-$$

$$2H_2O + 2e^- \rightarrow H_2 + 2\,OH^-$$

Oxidation-reduction reactions can be understood by example of corrosion of mild steel in sulphuric acid contaminated by ferric ions:

$$M_{(s)} \rightarrow M^{n+1} + ne^-$$

All the components of mild steel (*e.g.* Fe, Mn etc.) go into the solution. The electrons produced by these anodic reactions will be consumed by the cathodic reaction. In this case reaction can be represented as:

$$Fe^{3+} + e^- \rightarrow Fe^{2+}$$

Removing one of the available cathodic reactions will reduce the corrosion rate. In electrochemical corrosion theory, electrochemical corrosion involves two half-cell reactions these are oxidation reaction at the anode and a reduction at the cathode. For iron corroding in water with a nearly neutral pH, these half-cell reactions can be represented as:

Anodic reaction : $2Fe \longleftrightarrow 2Fe^{2+} + 4e^-$

Cathodic reaction : $O_2 + 2H_2O + 4e^- \longleftrightarrow 4\,OH^-$

There are obviously different anodic and cathodic reactions for diffrent alloys exposed to various environments. This half-cell reactions are thought to occur (at least initially) at microscopic anodes and cathodes covering a corroding surface. Microscopic anodes and cathodes can develop as corrosion damage with progresses with time. From the above theory it should be apparent that there are four fundamental components in an electrochemical corrosion cell. There are an anode, a cathode, a conducting environment for ionic movement (electrolyte) and an electrical connection between the anode and cathode for the flow of electron current.

Electrochemical Equilibrium

Thermodynamic reversible reactions will adopt an equilibrium potential, which is described by the Nernst equation

$$E = E_0 + \frac{RT}{nF} \text{In} \frac{\pi[O]}{\pi[R]}$$

where π [O] = Product of concentrations of oxidized species

π[R] = Products of concentrations of reduce species

Eo = Standard Electrode Potential,

R = Gas constant,

F = Faraday constant,

n = Number of electrons transferred in the reaction.

The potential is related to its free energy [ΔG] given by

$$\Delta G = -nFE.$$

A negative value for the free energy corresponds to spontaneous reaction while positive value of ΔG indicates that reaction has no tendency to occur. It is the redox potential by which one can predict whether a metal will corrode in a given environment or not.

Electrochemical Kinetics

There is a tendency for charged species to be attached to or repelled from the metal-solution interface. This gives rise to a separation of charge and layer of solution with different composition from the bulk solution is known as the electrochemical double layer. There are a number of theoretical descriptions of the structure of this layer, including the Helmholtz model, the Gouy Chapman model and the Gouy Chapman stem model. As a result of the variation of the charge separation with the applied potential, the electrochemical double layer has an apparent capacitance (known as the double layer capacitance).

Kinetics of Electrochemical Reaction

An activation controlled reaction is one for which the rate of reaction is controlled solely by the rate of the electrochemical charge transfer process, which in turn is an activation-controlled process. This gives rise to kinetics and are described by the Butler Volmer Equation:

$$i = io\left[\exp\left(\frac{\alpha AnF}{nRT}\eta\right)-\exp\left(\frac{\alpha CnF}{RT}\eta\right)\right]$$

where i_o = exchange current density

n = number of electrons

αA = anodic transfer coefficient

αC = cathodic transfer coefficient

η = overpotential (= $E - Eo$).

While the Butler-Volmer equation is valid over the full potential range, we can obtain simpler approximate solutions over more restricted ranges of potential.

Linear Polarization Resistance and the Stern-Geary Equation

With this widely used technique in corrosion monitoring, the polarization resistance of a material is defined as the slope of the potential-current density (DE/Di) curve at the free corrosion potential, yielding the polarization resistance R_p that can be related (for reactions under activation control) to the corrosion current by the Stern-Geary equation:

$$R_P = \frac{B}{I_{corr}} = \frac{(\Delta E)}{(\Delta i)} \Delta E \to 0$$

where

R_P is the polarization resistance and I_{corr} is the corrosion current

The proportionality constant (B), for a particular system can be determined empirically (calibrated from separate weight loss measurements) or, as shown by Stern and Geary, can be calculated from b_a and b_c the slopes of the anodic and cathodic Tafel slopes *i.e.*

$$B = \frac{ba.bc}{2.3(ba + bc)}$$

Losses due to Corrosion

The most comprehensive study of annual cost of metallic corrosion in the United State was conducted by the National Bureau of Standards (NBS) and Battelle Memorial institute in response to a congressional directive. Results are published in seven parts of series. Corrosion is recognized as one of the most serious problems in our modern societies and the resulting losses each year are in the hundreds of billions of dollars. Cost of corrosion studies have been undertaken by several countries including, the United States, the United Kingdom, Japan, Australia, Kuwait, Germany, Finland, Sweden, India, and China.

5

Metallic Corrosion

Corrosion may be classified by the forms in which it manifests itself; the basis for cation belongs to the appearance of the corroded metal.

(i) ***Uniform or General corrosion:*** Uniform corrosion is the most common form of all corrosions. It is normally characterized by a chemical or electrochemical reaction, which proceeds uniformly over the entire exposed surface. Owing to this attack the metal becomes thinner and eventually fails.

The example for this type of corrosion is a piece of steel or zinc immersed in dilute sulphuric acid which normally dissolves at a uniform rate over its entire surface. A sheet of iron roof also shows essentially the same degree of rusting over its entire outside surface.

(ii) ***Galvanic corrosion or Bimetallic corrosion:*** When two dissimilar metals are immersed in a corrosive or conductive solution, the potential difference usually exists between them. This potential difference produces electron flow between them. Corrosion of the less resistant metal is usually increased and attack of the more resistant material is decreased, as compared with the behaviour of these metals when they are not in contact. Because of the electric currents and dissimilar metals involved, this form of corrosion is called galvanic or bi-metallic corrosion. The dry cell battery is a good example of this point.

(iii) ***Pitting corrosion:*** Pitting is a form of extremely localized attack that results in holes in the metal. These holes may be small or large in diameter, but in most cases they are relatively small. Pits are sometimes

isolated or so close together that they look like a rough surface. Generally a pit may be described as a cavity or hole with a surface diameter about the same as or less than the depth. Example of this corrosion is that of stainless steel by sulphuric acid containing ferric chloride.

(iv) ***Crevice corrosion:*** Intense localized corrosion frequently occurs within crevices and other shielded areas on metal surfaces exposed to corrosive environment. This type of attack is usually associated with small volume of stagnant solution caused by holes, gasket, surfaces, lap joints, surface deposits and crevices under bolt and rivet heads. The result of this leads to corrosion and this form of corrosion is called crevice corrosion or sometimes deposit or gasket corrosion. The crevice corrosion may result due to the deposits of sand, dirt and other solid corrosion products on the crevices.

(v) ***Intergranular corrosion:*** If a metal corrodes, uniform attack results since grain boundaries are usually only slightly more reactive than the matrix. However under certain conditions grain interfaces are very reactive which leads to intergranular corrosion. Localised corrosion attacks at and adjacent to grain boundaries with relatively little corrosion of the grain is called intergranular corrosion. The metal disintegrates and loses its strength.

Intergranular corrosion can be caused by impurities at the grain boundaries, enrichment of one of the alloying elements, or depletion of one of these elements in the grain-boundary areas. Small amount of iron in aluminium wherein the solubility of iron is low, have been shown to segregate in the grain boundaries and causes intergranular corrosion.

(vi) ***Selective leaching:*** Selective leaching is the removal of the element from a solid alloy by corrosion process. The most common example is the selective removal of zinc in brass alloys (Dezincification). Similar process occurs in other alloy systems in which aluminium, iron, cobalt, chromium and other elements are removed.

(vii) ***Erosion corrosion:*** Erosion corrosion is the acceleration or increase in rate of deterioration or attack on a metal surface because of relative movement between a corrosive fluid and metal surface. Generally this movement is quite rapid and mechanical wear effect or abrasion is involved. Examples are aluminium, lead and stainless steel corrosion.

(viii) ***Stress corrosion cracking:*** Stress corrosion cracking refers to cracking caused by the simultaneous presence of tensile stress and a specific

corrosive medium. Cathodic protection is an effective method of preventing stress corrosion cracking whereas it rapidly accelerates hydrogen embrittlement effect.

The classic examples of stress-corrosion cracking are seasonal cracking of brass and the caustic embrittlement of steel.

(ix) ***Film-forming corrosion:*** It is a special type of rusting which occurs on certain metals under protective films like paints and is characterized by a thread like growth. Film-forming corrosion may be found on tools coated with oil films, refrigerator door, etc.

(x) ***Cavitation corrosion:*** This is a special type of corrosion which is caused due to the formation of vapour bubbles in a corrosive environment near a metal surface and when the bubbles collapse attack arises. It is similar to pitting corrosion but the surface is rougher and has many close spaced pits.

(xi) ***Dealloying or Selective leaching:*** Dealloying is the corrosion process in which one constituent of an alloy is removed preferentially from the alloy leaving an altered residual structure. This process is also known as selective leaching, occurs due to selective corrosion of a phase or an element. Examples of this process are dezincification, graphitization, etc. The primary physical difference between dealloying and other forms of corrosion is that the size and shape of structure undergoing attack are basically unaltered but the density of the residual metal generally is less than that of the original alloy.

(xii) ***Exfoliation:*** Loss of material in the form of layers or leaves from a solid metal or alloy is called exfoliation. This type of corrosion is generally observed in wrought products that exhibit elongated structures. It is observed in Al-Mg, Al-Cu, Al-Zn-Mg and Al-Mg-Si alloys. Certain environmental factors such as presence of chloride or bromide ions in the environment, higher temperatures and acidic conditions make the metals tend towards exfoliation.

(xiii) ***Fretting corrosion:*** Fretting corrosion describes corrosion occurring at constant area between the two surfaces of any material under load subjected to slight relative motion of small amplitude.

Tribocorrosion

Tribocorrosion is a material *degradation* process due to the combined effect of *corrosion* and *wear*. The name tribocorrosion expresses the underlying disciplines of *tribology* and *corrosion*. Tribology is concerned with the study of friction, lubrication and wear (its name comes from the Greek "tribo" meaning to rub) and corrosion is concerned with the chemical and electrochemical interactions between a material, normally a metal, and its environment. As a field of research tribocorrosion is relatively new, but tribocorrosion phenomena have been around ever since machines and installations are being used.

Wear is a mechanical material degradation process occurring on rubbing or impacting surfaces, while corrosion involves *chemical* or *electrochemical reactions* of the material. Corrosion may accelerate wear and wear may accelerate corrosion. One then speaks of corrosion accelerated wear or wear accelerated corrosion. Both these phenomena, as well as fretting corrosion (which results from small amplitude oscillations between contacting surfaces) fall into the broader category of tribocorrosion. Erosion-corrosion is another tribocorrosion phenomenon involving mechanical and chemical effects: impacting particles or fluids erode a solid surface by abrasion, chipping or fatigue while simultaneously the surface corrodes.

Phenomena in Different Engineering Fields

Tribocorrosion occurs in many engineering fields. It reduces the life-time of pipes, valves and pumps, of *waste incinerators,* of mining equipment or of *medical implants,* and it can affect the safety of *nuclear reactors* or of transport systems. On the other hand, tribocorrosion phenomena can also be applied to good use, for example in the chemical-mechanical planarization of wafers in the electronics industry or in metal grinding and cutting in presence of aqueous emulsions. Keeping this in mind, we may define tribocorrosion in a more general way independently of the notion of usefulness or damage or of the particular type of mechanical interaction: Tribocorrosion concerns the irreversible transformation of materials or of their function as a result of simultaneous mechanical and chemical/electrochemical interactions between surfaces in relative motion.

Biotribocorrosion

Biotribocorrosion covers the science of surface transformations resulting from the interactions of mechanical loading and chemical/electrochemical reactions that occur between elements of a triblogical system exposed to biological environments. It has been studied for artificial joint prostheses. It is important to understand material degradation processes for joint implants to achieve longer service life and better safety issues for such devices.

Passive Metals

While tribocorrosion phenomena may affect many materials, they are most critical for metals, especially the normally corrosion resistant so-called *passive metals.* The vast majority of corrosion resistant metals and alloys used in engineering (stainless steels, *titanium, aluminium* etc.) fall into this category. These metals are thermodynamically unstable in the presence of oxygen or water and they derive their corrosion resistance from the presence at the surface of a thin oxide film, called the passive film, which acts as a protective barrier between the metal and its environment. Passive films are usually just a few atomic layers thick. Nevertheless, they can provide excellent corrosion protection because if damaged accidentally they spontaneously self-heal by metal oxidation. However, when a metal surface is subjected to severe rubbing or to a stream of impacting particles the passive film damage becomes; continuous and extensive. The self-healing process may no longer be effective and in addition it requires a high rate of metal oxidation. In other words, the underlying metal will strongly corrode before the otective passive film is reformed, if at all. In such a case, the total material loss due to tribocorrosion vill be much higher than the sum of wear and corrosion one would measure in experiments with the ame metal where only wear or only corrosion takes place. The example illustrates the fact that the rate of tribocorrosion is not simply the addition of the rate of wear and the rate of corrosion but it is strongly laffected by synergistic and antagonistic effects between mechanical and chemical mechanisms. To study such effects in the laboratory, one most often uses mechanical wear testing rigs which are equipped with an electrochemical cell. This permits one to control independently the mechanical and chemical parameters. For example, by imposing a given potential to the rubbing metal one can simulate the oxidation potential of the environment and in addition, under certain conditions, the current flow is a measure of the instantaneous corrosion rate. For a deeper understanding tribocorrosion experiments are supplemented by detailed microscopic and analytical studies of the contacting surfaces.

At high temperatures, the more rapid generation of oxide due to a combination of temperature and tribological action during sliding wear can generate potentially wear resistant oxide layers known as *'glazes'*. Under such circumstances, tribocorrosion can be used potentially in a beneficial way.

Stress Corrosion Cracking

Stress corrosion cracking (SCC) is the unexpected sudden failure of normally ductile metals subjected to a tensile stress in a corrosive environment, especially at elevated temperature in the case of metals. SCC is highly chemically specific in that certain alloys are likely to undergo SCC only when exposed to a small number of chemical environments. The chemical environment that causes SCC for a given alloy is often one which is only mildly corrosive to the metal otherwise. Hence, metal parts with severe SCC can appear bright and shiny, while being filled with microscopic cracks. This factor makes it common for SCC to go undetected prior to failure. SCC often progresses rapidly, and is more common among alloys than pure metals. The specific environment is of crucial importance, and only very small concentrations of certain highly active chemicals are needed to produce catastrophic cracking, often leading to devastating and unexpected failure.

The stresses can be the result of the crevice loads due to stress *concentration*, or can be caused by the type of assembly or residual stresses from fabrication (*e.g.* cold working); the residual stresses can be relieved by *annealing*.

Metals Attacked

Certain *austenitic stainless* steels and *aluminium alloys* crack in the presence of *chlorides*, mild *steel* cracks in the presence of alkali (boiler cracking) and *nitrates*, *copper* alloys crack in ammoniacal solutions (season cracking). This limits the usefulness of austenitic stainless steel for containing water with higher than few ppm content of chlorides at temperatures above 50 °C. Worse still, high-tensile structural steels crack in an unexpectedly brittle manner in a whole variety of aqueous environments, especially containing chlorides. With the possible exception of the latter, which is a special example of *hydrogen cracking*, all the others display the phenomenon of subcritical crack growth, *i.e.* small surface flaws propagate (usually smoothly) under conditions where *fracture mechanics* predicts that failure should not occur. That is, in the presence of a corrodent, cracks develop and propagate well below K_{Ic}. In fact, the subcritical value of the stress intensity, designated as K_{ISCC}, may be less than one per cent of K_{IC}, as the following table shows:

Alloy	K_{IC} MN/m$^{3/2}$	SCC environment	K_{Iscc} MN/m$^{3/2}$
13Cr steel	60	3% NaCl	12
18Cr-8Ni	200	42% $MgCl_2$	10
Cu-30Zn	200	NH_4OH, pH7	1
Al-3Mg-7Zn	25	Aqueous halides	5
Ti-6Al-1V	60	0.6M KCl	20

Polymers Attacked

A similar process occurs in polymers, when products are exposed to aggressive chemicals such as *acids* and *alkalis*. As with metals, attack is confined to specific polymers and particular chemicals. Thus polycarbonate is sensitive to attack by alkalis, but not by acids. On the other hand, *polyesters* are readily degraded by acids, and SCC is a likely failure mechanism. Polymers are also susceptible to *environmental stress cracking* where attacking agents do not necessarily degrade the materials chemically. *Nylon* is sensitive to degradation by acids, a process known as *hydrolysis* and nylon mouldings will crack when attacked by strong acids.

For example, the fracture surface of a fuel connector showed the progressive growth of the crack from cid attack (Ch) to the final cusp (C) of polymer. In this case the failure was caused by hydrolysis of the polymer by contact with *sulphuric acid* leaking from a *car battery*. The degradation reaction is the reverse of the synthesis reaction of the polymer:

$$n\,HO{-}\overset{O}{\overset{\|}{C}}{-}R{-}\overset{O}{\overset{\|}{C}}{-}OH + nH_2N{-}R'{-}NH_2 \longrightarrow \left[{-}\overset{O}{\overset{\|}{C}}{-}R{-}\overset{O}{\overset{\|}{C}}{-}\underset{H}{N}{-}R'{-}\underset{H}{N}{-}\right]_n + 2H_2O$$

$$R{-}\overset{O}{\overset{\|}{C}}{-}\underset{H}{N}{-}R' \longrightarrow R{-}\overset{O}{\overset{\|}{C}}{-}OH + H{-}\underset{H}{N}{-}R'$$

Cracks can be formed in many different *elastomers* by *ozone* attack, another form of SCC in polymers. Tiny traces of the gas in the air will attack double bonds in rubber chains, with *Natural rubber*, Styrene-butadiene rubber and NBR being most sensitive to degradation. Ozone cracks form in products under tension, but the critical strain is very small. The cracks are always oriented at right angles to the strain axis, so will form around the circumference in a rubber tube bent over. Such cracks are very dangerous when they occur in fuel pipes because the cracks will grow from the outside exposed surfaces into the bore of the pipe, so fuel leakage and fire may follow. The problem of ozone cracking can be prevented by adding anti-ozonants to the rubber before vulcanization. Ozone cracks were commonly seen in automobile tire sidewalls, but are now seen rarely thanks to the use of these additives. On the other hand, the problem does recur in unprotected products such as rubber tubing and seals.

Crack Growth

The subcritical nature of propagation may be attributed to the chemical energy released as the crack propagates. That is:

elastic energy released + chemical energy = surface energy + deformation energy

The crack initiates at K_{ISCC} and thereafter propagates at a rate governed by the slowest process, which most of the time is the rate at which corrosive ions can diffuse to the crack tip. As the crack advances so K rises (because crack length appears in the calculation of stress intensity). Finally it reaches K_{IC}, whereupon fast fracture ensues and the component fails. One of the practical difficulties with SCC is its unexpected nature. *Stainless steels,* for example, are employed because under most conditions they are "passive", *i.e.* effectively inert. Very often one finds a single crack has propagated while the rest of the metal surface stays apparently unaffected. The crack propagates perpendicular to the applied stress.

Prevention

SCC is the result of a combination of three factors—a susceptible material, exposure to a corrosive environment, and tensile stresses above a threshold. If you eliminate any one of these factors SCC initiation becomes impossible. The conventional approach to controlling the problem has been to develop new alloys that are more resistant to SCC. This is a costly proposition and can require a massive time investment to achieve only marginal success.

Examples

SCC caused the catastrophic collapse of the *Silver Bridge* in December 1967, when an eyebar suspension bridge across the Ohio river at *Point Pleasant. West Virginia,* suddenly failed. The main chain joint failed and the whole structure fell into the river, killing 46 people in vehicles on the bridge at the time. Rust in the eyebar joint had caused a stress corrosion crack, which went critical as a result of high bridge loading and low temperature. The failure was exacerbated by a high level of *residual stress* in the eyebar. The disaster led to a nationwide reappraisal of bridges.

Suspended ceilings in indoor swimming pools are safety-relevant components. As was demonstrated by the collapses of the ceiling of the *Uster* (*Switzerland*) indoor *swimming pool* (1985) and again at *Steenwijk* (*Netherlands,* 2001), attention must be paid to selecting suitable materials and inspecting the state of such components. The reason for the failures was stress corrosion cracking of metal fastening components made of stainless steel. The active chemical was chlorine added to the water as a disinfectant.

A classic example of SCC is *season cracking* of brass cartridge cases, a problem experienced by the British army in *India* in the early 19th century. It was initiated by *ammonia* from dung and horse manure decomposing at the higher temperatures of the spring and summer. There was substantial residual stress in the cartridge shells as a result of *cold forming*. The problem was solved by annealing the shells to ameliorate the stress.

Bacterial Anaerobic Corrosion

Bacterial anaerobic corrosion is a bacterially-induced oxidation of metals.

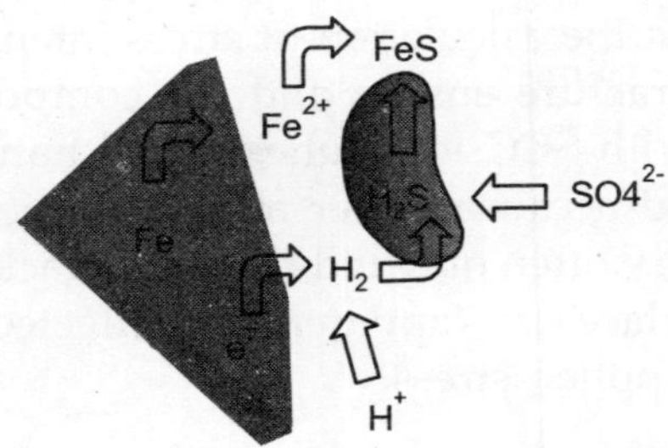

Diagram of bacterially-induced corrosion

In a humid environment and anoxic conditions the corrosion of metals occurs as a result of a redox reaction that generates molecular hydrogen from hydrogen ions, requiring bacteria, unlike anacrobic corrosion that occurs spontaneously.

A base metal, such as iron (Fe) goes into aqueous solution as positively charged cation, Fe^{2+}. As the metal is oxidized under anaerobic condition by the protons of water, H^+ ions are reduced to form molecular H_2. This can be written in the following ways under acidic and neutral conditions respectively:

$$Fe + 2H^+ \rightarrow Fe^{2+} + H_2$$

$$Fe + 2H_2O \rightarrow Fe(OH)_2 + H_2$$

Usually, a thin film of molecular hydrogen forms on the metal. Sulfate-reducing bacteria, oxidize the molecular hydrogen to produce hydrogen sulphide ions (HS^-) and water:

$$4H_2 + SO_4^{2} \rightarrow HS^- + 3H_2O + OH^-$$

The iron ions partly precipitate to from iron (II) sulphide. A reaction with water also occurs, producing *iron hydroxide*.

$$Fe^{2+} + HS^- \rightarrow FeS + H^+$$

$$3Fe^{2+} + 6H_2O \rightarrow 3Fe(OH)_2 + 6H^+$$

The net equation comes to:

$$4Fe + SO_4^{2-} + H^+ + 3H_2O \rightarrow FeS + 3Fe(OH)_2 + OH^-$$

This form of corrosion by sulphate-reducing bacteria can, in this way, be far more harmful than anaerobic corrosion.

Anaerobic Corrosion

Hydrogen corrosion is a form of metal corrosion occurring in the presence of anoxic water. Hydrogen corrosion involves a redox reaction that reduces hydrogen ions, forming molecular hydrogen.

Metals enter aqueous solution and are oxidized.

Oxidation reaction (pH independent):

$$Fe \rightarrow Fe^{2+} + 2e^-$$

Reduction reaction in acid solution:

$$2H^+ + 2e^- \rightarrow H_2$$

In an acidic solution, the water molecules are protonated and the hydronium ions (H_3O^+) are directly reduced into H_2.

Reduction reaction in neutral or slightly alkaline solution:

$$2H_2O + 2e^- \rightarrow H_2 + 2OH^-$$

In a neutral or slightly alkaline solution, the protons of water are reduced into molecular hydrogen giving rise to the production of hydroxide ions responsible of the precipitation of the slightly soluble ferrous hydroxide ($Fe(OH)_2$).

This finally leads to the global reaction of the anaerobic corrosion of iron in water:

$$Fe + 2H_2O \rightarrow Fe(OH)_2 + H_2$$

Transformation of Ferrous Hydroxide into Magnetic

Under anaerobic conditions, the *ferrous hydroxide* ($Fe(OH)_2$) can be oxidized by the protons of water to form magnetite and molecular *hydrogen*. This process is described by the *Schikorr reaction.*

$$3Fe(OH)_2 \rightarrow Fe_3O_4 + H_2 + 2H_2O$$

Ferrous hydroxide → magnetite + hydrogen + water

The well crystallized magnetite (Fe_3O_4) is thermodynamically more stable than the ferrous hydroxide ($Fe(OH)_2$).

This process also occurs during the anaerobic corrosion of *iron* and *steel* in *oxygen-free groundwater* and in reducing soils below the *water table.*

Nominally Anaerobic Corrosion of Carbon Steel in Near-Neutral pH Saline Environments

Gas transmission pipeline corrosion commences when coatings disbond, exposing the steel to groundwater. When this occurs, a number of anaerobic and aerobic corrosion scenarios can be envisaged. The initial nominally anaerobic corrosion period has been investigated by applying a combination of electrochemical methods (*i.e.,* corrosion potential, linear polarization resistance, and electrochemical impedance spectroscopy [EIS] measurements) and surface analytical techniques (scanning electron microscopy, energy-dispersive x-ray spectroscopy, and Raman spectroscopy). An volution in film properties was observed and attributed to the entry of adventitious oxygen into faults within the preformed film. This leads to an increase in overall corrosion and a change in properties of he film as detected by EIS and Raman analysis. This section describes the mechanism involved in this transition, and provides a basis for a more extensive study of the corrosion process encountered on switching between anaerobic and aerobic conditions. The overall goal of this study was to provide a mechanistic basis for the corrosion scenarios possible on gas transmission pipelines.

Iron Bacteria

In the management of water-supply wells, iron bacteria are bacteria that derive the energy they need to live and multiply by oxidizing dissolved ferrous iron (or the less frequently available manganese). The resulting ferric oxide is insoluble, and appears as brown gelatinous slime that will stain plumbing fixtures, and clothing or utensils washed with the water carrying it. They are known to grow and proliferate in waters containing as low as 0.1 mg/1 of iron. However, at least 0.3 ppm of dissolved oxygen is needed to carry out oxidation.

Common effects of excess iron in water are a reddish-brown color and stained laundry. Iron bacteria are a natural part of the environment in most parts of the world. These microorganisms combine dissolved iron or manganese with oxygen and use it to form rust-coloured deposits. In the process, the bacteria produce a brown slime that builds up on well screens, pipes, and plumbing fixtures.

Bacteria known to Feed on Iron are Thiobacillus Ferrooxidans and Leptospirillum Ferrooxidans

Habitat

Iron bacteria colonize the transition zone where de-oxygenated water from an anaerobic environment flows into an aerobic environment. Groundwater containing dissolved organic material may be de-oxygenated by *micro-organisms* feeding on that dissolved organic material. Where concentrations of organic material exceed the concentration of dissolved oxygen required for complete oxidation, microbial populations with specialized *enzymes* can reduce insoluble ferric oxide in aquifer soils to soluble ferrous hydroxide and use the oxygen released by that change to oxidize some of the remaining organic material.

$$H_2O + Fe_2O_3 \rightarrow 2Fe(OH)_2 + O_2$$

$$\text{(water)} + \text{(Iron[III]oxide)} \rightarrow \text{(Iron[II] hydroxide)} + \text{(oxygen)}$$

When the de-oxygenated water reaches a source of oxygen, iron bacteria use that oxygen to convert the soluble ferrous iron back into an insoluble reddish precipitate of ferric iron:

$2Fe(OH)_2$	+	O_2	→	H_2O	+	Fe_2O_3
(Iron[II] hydroxide)	+	(oxygen)	→	(water)	+	(Iron[III] oxide)

Since the latter reaction is the normal equilibrium in our oxygen atmosphere while the first requires biological coupling with a simultaneous oxidation of carbon, organic material dissolved in water is often the underlying cause of an iron bacteria population. Groundwater may be naturally de-oxygenated by decaying vegetation in *swamps*; and useful mineral deposits of *bog iron* ore have formed where that groundwater has historically emerged to be exposed to atmospheric oxygen. *Anthropogenic* sources like *landfill leachate, septic drain fields*, or leakage of light *petroleum* fuels like *gasoline* are other possible sources of organic materials allowing soil *microbes* to de-oxygenate groundwater.

A similar reversible reaction may form black deposits of manganese dioxide from dissolved manganese, but is less common because of the relative abundance of iron (5.4%) in comparison to manganese (0.1%) in average soils. Other conditions associated with iron bacteria result from the anaerobic laqueous environment rather than the iron bacteria visibly colonizing that habitat. Corrosion of pipes is another source of soluble iron for the first reaction above and the sulfurous smell of rot or decay results from enzymatic conversion of soil sulfates to volatile hydrogen sulfide as an alternative source of oxygen in anaerobic environments.

Possible Indicators

Clues which indicate that iron bacteria may be present in well water:

- Iron bacteria often produce unpleasant tastes and odors commonly reported as
  - swampy
  - oily or petroleum
  - cucumber
  - sewage
  - rotten vegetation
  - musty

  The taste or odor may be more noticeable after the water has not been used for some time.
- Iron bacteria will usually cause yellow, orange, red, or brown stains and colored water.

- It is sometimes possible to see a rainbow colored, oil-like sheen on the water.
- Iron bacteria produce a sticky slime which is typically rusty in color, but may be yellow, brown, or grey.
- A feathery or filamentous growth may also be seen, particularly in standing water such as a toilet tank.

The dramatic effects of iron bacteria are seen in surface waters as brown slimy masses on stream bottoms and lakeshores or as an oily sheen upon the water. More serious problems occur when bacteria build up in well systems. Iron bacteria in wells do not cause health problems, but they can reduce well yields by clogging screens and pipes.

Prevention

Iron bacteria can be introduced into a well or water system during drilling, repair, or service. Elimination of iron bacteria once a well is heavily infested can be extremely difficult. Normal treatment techniques may be only partly effective. Good housekeeping practices can prevent iron bacteria from entering a well:

- Water placed in a well for drilling, repair, or priming of pumps should be disinfected, and should never be taken from a lake or pond.
- The well casing should be watertight, properly capped, and extend a foot or more above ground.
- When pumps, well pipes, and well equipment are repaired, they should not be placed on the ground where they could pick up iron bacteria.
- The well, pump, and plumbing should be disinfected when repaired.

Control

Treatment techniques which may be successful in removing or reducing iron bacteria include physical removal, pasteurization, and chemical treatment. Treatment of heavily infected wells may be difficult, expensive, and only partially successful.

Physical removal is typically done as a first step in heavily infected wells. The pumping equipment in the well must be removed and cleaned, which is usually a job for a well contractor or pump installer. The well casing is then scrubbed by use of brushes or other tools. Physical removal is usually followed by chemical treatment. Pasteurization has been successfully used to control iron bacteria. Pasteurization involves a process of injecting steam or hot water into the well and maintaining a water temperature in the well of 60°C (140 °F) for 30 minutes. Pasteurization can be effective, however, the process may be expensive.

Chemical treatment is the most commonly used iron bacteria treatment technique. The three groups of chemicals typically used include: surfactants; acids (and bases); and disinfectants, biocides, and oxidizing agents.

Surfactants are detergent-like chemicals such as phosphates. Surfactants are generally used in conjunction with other chemical treatment. It is important to use chlorine or another disinfectant if phosphates are used, since bacteria may use phosphates as a food source.

Acids have been used to treat iron bacteria because of their ability to dissolve iron deposits, destroy bacteria, and loosen bacterial slime. Acids are typically part of a series of treatments inolving chlorine, and at times, bases. Extreme caution is required to use and properly dispose of these chemicals. Acid and chlorine should never be mixed together. Acid treatment should only be done by trained professionals.

Disinfectants are the most commonly used chemicals for treatment of iron bacteria, and the most common disinfectant is household laundry bleach, which contains chlorine. Chlorine is relatively inexpensive and easy to use, but may have limited effectiveness and may require repeated treatments. Effective treatment requires sufficient chlorine strength and time in contact with the bacteria, and is often improved with agitation. Continuous chlorine injection into the well has been used, but is not normally recommended because of concerns that the chlorine will conceal other bacterial contamination and cause corrosion and maintenance problems.

Shock Chlorination

"Shock" chlorination is the process of introducing a strong chlorine solution into the well, usually at a concentration of 1000 parts per million or more. Ideally, the well should be pumped until clear, or physically cleaned before introducing chlorine. Approximately two gallons of chlorine bleach can be mixed with at least 10 gallons of water, and poured into the well. If possible, the chlorinated water should be circulated through the well and household plumbing by running the water back into the well through a clean hose, washing down the sides of the well casing. The chlorinated water should be drawn into the household plumbing and remain overnight, and if possible for 24 hours. Heavy infestations of iron bacteria may require repeated disinfections. Shock chlorination may only control, not eliminate, iron bacteria.

Before attempting to chlorinate, or doing any maintenance on a well, it is important to disconnect the electricity and understand how the well and water system works. It is usually advisable to hire a licensed pump installer or well contractor.

High concentrations of chlorine may affect water conditioning equipment, applicances such dishwashers, and septic systems. You may want to check with the manufacturer of the appliances before chlorinating. The equipment can be bypassed, however, iron bacteria or other organisms may remain in the units and spread through the water system. It may be possible to disinfect the well with higher chlorine concentrations; and if the water storage and treatment units are not heavily infected, disinfect the treatment unit and piping with lower concentrations circulated through the water system.

After the chlorine has been in the well and plumbing overnight or for 24 hours, the water should be pumped out. If possible, water with high chlorine concentrations should not be disposed of in the septic system. It may be possible to discharge the water to a gravel area, run the water into a tank or barrel until the chlorine dissipates, or contract with a hauler to properly dispose of the water. Water from the well should not be consumed until the chlorine has been removed.

Copper Band Corrosion

Copper

Copper (s) is a *chemical element* with the symbol Cu (from Latin: *cuprum*) and atomic number 29. It is a ductile, semi-precious metal with very high thermal and electrical conductivity. Pure copper is soft and malleable; an exposed surface has a reddish-orange tarnish. It is used as a conductor of heat and electricity, a building material, and a constituent of various metal alloys.

The metal and *its alloys* have been used for thousands of years. In the Roman era, copper was principally mined on *Cyprus*, hence the origin of the name of the metal as cypriurn (metal of Cyprus), later shortened to cuprum. Its compounds are commonly encountered as copper(II) salts, which often impart blue or green colors to minerals such as *turquoise* and have been widely used historically as pigments. Architectural structures built with copper corrode to give green *verdigris* (or patina). *Decorative art* prominently features copper, both by itself and as part of pigments.

Copper(II) ions are water-soluble, where they function at low concentration as bacteriostatic substances, fungicides, and wood preservatives. In sufficient amounts, they are poisonous to higher organisms; at lower concentrations it is an essential trace nutrient to all higher plant and animal life. The main areas where copper is found in animals are tissues, liver, muscle and bone.

Characteristics

Physical

Copper, silver and gold are in *group 11* of the periodic table, and they share certain attributes: they have one s-orbital electron on top of a filled *d-electron shell* and are characterized by high ductility and electrical conductivity. The filled d-shells in these elements do not contribute much to the interatomic interactions, which are dominated by the s-electrons through metallic bonds. Contrary to metals with incomplete d-shells, metallic bonds in copper are lacking a *covalent* character and are relatively weak. This explains the low hardness and high *ductility* of single crystals of copper. At the macroscopic scale, introduction of extended defects to the crystal lattice, such as grain boundaries, hinders flow of the material under applied stress thereby increasing its hardness. For this reason, copper is usually supplied in a fine-grained *polycrystalline* form, which has greater strength than *monocrystalline* forms.

The low hardness of copper partly explains its high electrical (59.6×10^6 S/m) and thus also high thermal conductivity, which are the second highest among pure metals at room temperature. This is because the resistivity to electron transport in metals at room temperature mostly originates from scattering of electrons on thermal vibrations of the lattice, which are relatively weak for a soft metal. The maximum permissible current density of copper in open air is approximately 3.1×10^6 A/m^2 of cross-sectional area, above which it begins to heat excessively. As with other metals, if copper is placed against another metal, galvanic corrosion will occur.

Together with *osmium* (bluish), and *gold* (yellow), copper is one of only three elemental metals with a natural color other than gray or silver. Pure copper is orange-red and acquires a reddish *tarnish* when exposed to air. The characteristic color of copper results from the electronic transitions between the filled 3d and half-empty 4s atomic shells—the energy difference between these shells is such that it corresponds to orange light. The same mechanism accounts for the yellow color of gold.

Chemical

Copper forms a rich variety of compounds with *oxidation states* +1 and +2, which are often called cuprous and cupric, respectively. It does not react with water, but it slowly reacts with atmospheric [oxygen forming a layer of brown-black copper oxide. In contrast to the oxidation of iron by wet air, this oxide layer stops the further, bulk corrosion. A green layer of verdigris (copper carbonate) can often be seen on old copper constructions, such as the *Statue of Liberty*, the largest copper statue in the world build using *repousse and chasing*. *Hydrogen sulphides* and *sulphides* react with copper to form various copper sulphides on the surface. In the latter case, the copper corrodes, as is seen when copper is exposed to air containing sulphur compounds. Oxygen-containing ammonia solutions give water-soluble complexes with copper, as do oxygen and hydrochloric acid to form copper chlorides and acidified *hydrogen peroxide* to form copper(II) salts. Copper(II) chloride and copper comproportionate to form copper(I) chloride.

Isotopes

There are 29 isotopes of copper. ^{63}Cu and ^{65}Cu are stable, with ^{63}Cu comprising approximately 69 per cent of naturally occurring copper; they both have a spin of 3/2. The other isotopes are radioactive, with the most stable being ^{67}Cu with a half-life of 61.83 hours. Seven metastable isotopes have been characterized, with ^{68m}Cu the longest-lived with a half-life of 3.8 minutes. Isotopes with a *mass number* above 64 decay by β^-, whereas those with a mass number below 64 decay by β^+. ^{64}Cu, which has a half-life of 12.7 hours, decays both ways.

^{62}Cu and ^{64}Cu have significant applications. ^{64}Cu is a *radiocontrast* for X-ray imaging, and complexed with a *chelate* can be used for *treating* cancer. ^{62}Cu is used in ^{62}Cu-PTSM that is a *radioactive tracer* for positron emission tomography.

Occurrence

Copper can be found as either native copper or as part of minerals. Native copper is a polycrystal, with the largest single crystals found to date measuring 4.4 × 3.2 × 3.2 cm. The largest mass of elemental copper weighed 420 tonnes and was found in 1857 on the Keweenaw Peninsula in Michigan, US. There are many examples of copper-containing minerals: chalcopyrite and chalcocite are copper sulphides, azurite and malchite are copper carbonates and cuprite is a copper oxide. Copper is present in the Earth's crust at a concentration of about 50 parts per million (ppm) and is also synthesised in massive stars.

Production

Most copper is mined or extracted as copper sulphides from large open pit mines in porphyry copper deposits that contain 0.4 1.0 per cent copper. Examples include Chuquicamata in Chile, Bingham Canyon Mine in Utah, United States and El Chino Mine in New Mexico, United States. According to the British Geological Survey, in 2005, Chile was the top mine producer of copper with at least one-third world share followed by the United States, Indonesia and Peru. The amount of copper in use is increasing and the quantity available is barely sufficient to allow all countries to reach developed world levels of usage.

Reserves

Copper has been in use at least 10,000 years, but more than 95 per cent of all copper ever mined and smelted has been extracted since 1900. As with many natural resources, the total amount of copper on Earth is vast (around 10^{14} tons just in the top kilometer of Earth's crust, or about 5 million years worth at the current rate of extraction). However, only a tiny fraction of these reserves is economically viable, given present-day prices and technologies. Various estimates of existing copper reserves available for mining vary from 25 years to 60 years, depending on core assumptions such as the growth rate. Recycling is a major source of copper in the modern world. Because of these and other factors, the future of copper production and supply is the subject of much debate, including the concept of *Peak copper*, analogue to *Peak Oil*.

The price of copper has historically been unstable, and it quintupled from the 60-year low of US$0.60/lb (US$1.32/kg) in June 1999 to US$3.75 per pound (US$8.27/kg) in May 2006. It dropped to US$2.40/lb (US$5.29/kg) in February 2007, then rebounded to US$3.50/lb (US$7.7I/kg) in April 2007. In February 2009, weakening global demand and a steep fall in commodity prices since the previous year's highs left copper prices at US$1.51/lb.

Methods

The concentration of copper in ores averages only 0.6 per cent, and most commercial ores are sulphides, especially chalcopyrite ($CuFeS_2$) and to a lesser extent chalcocite (Cu_2S). These minerals are concentrated from crushed ores to the level of 10-15 per cent copper by *froth flotation* or *bioleaching*. Heating this material with silica in flash smelting removes much of the iron as slag. The process exploits the greater ease of converting iron sulphides into its oxides, which in turn react with the silica to form the silicate slag, which floats on top of the heated mass. The resulting copper matte consisting of Cu_2S is then roasted to convert all sulphides into oxides:

$$2\,Cu_2S + 3\,O_2 \rightarrow 2\,Cu_2O + 2\,SO_2$$

The cuprous oxide is converted to blister copper upon heating:

$$2\,Cu_2O \rightarrow 4\,Cu + O_2$$

This step exploits the relatively easy reduction of copper oxides to copper metal. Natural gas is blown across the blister to remove most of the remaining oxygen and *electrorefining* is performed on the resulting material to produce pure copper:

$$Cu^{2+} + 2\,e^- \rightarrow Cu$$

Recycling

Copper, like aluminium, is 100 per cent recyclable without any loss of quality whether in a raw state or contained in a manufactured product. In volume, copper is the third most recycled metal after iron and aluminium. It is estimated that 80 per cent of the copper ever mined is still in use today. According to the *International Resource Panel's Metal Stocks in Society report*, the global per capita stock of Copper in use in society is 35-55 kg. Much of this is in more-developed countries (140-300 kg per capita) rather than less-developed countries (30-40 kg per capita).

The process of recycling copper follows roughly the same steps as is used to extract copper, but requires fewer steps. High purity scrap copper is melted in a furnace and then *reduced* and cast into *billets* and *ingots;* lower purity scrap is refined by electroplating in a bath of sulphuric acid.

Binary Compounds

As for other elements, the simplest compounds of copper are binary compounds, *i.e.* those containing only two elements. The principal ones are the oxides, sulphides and *halides*. Both *cuprous* and *cupric oxides* are known. Among the numerous *copper sulfides* important examples include *copper(II) sulphide* and *copper(II) sulphide.*

The cuprous halides with *chlorine, bromine* and *iodine* are known, as are the cupric halides with *fluorine, chlorine* and *bromine.* Attempts to prepare copper(II) iodide give cuprous iodide and iodine.

$$2Cu^{2+} + 4\ I^- \rightarrow 2CuI + I_2$$

[edit] Coordination chemistry

Copper (II) gives a deep blue coloration in the presence of ammonia ligands. The one used here is tetramminecopper(II) sulphate.

Copper, like all metals, forms coordination complexes with *ligands.* In aqueous solution, copper(II) exists as $[Cu(H_2O)_6]^{2+}$. This complex exhibits the fastest water exchange rate (speed of water ligands attaching and detaching) for any transition *metal aquo complex*. Adding an aqueous *sodium hydroxide* causes the precipitation of light blue solid *copper(II) hydroxide.* A simplified equation is:

$$Cu^{2+} + 2OH^- \rightarrow Cu(OH)_2$$

An *aqueous ammonia* causes the same precipitate to form. Upon adding excess ammonia, the precipitate dissolves, forming *tetraamminecopper(II):*

$$Cu(H_2O)_4(OH)_2 + 4NH_3 \rightarrow [Cu(H_2O)_2(NH_3)_4]^{2+} + 2H_2O + 2OH^-$$

Many other oxyanions form complexes; these include copper(II) acetate, copper(II) nitrate, and copper(II) carbonate. Copper(II) sulphate forms a blue crystalline pentahydrate, which is the most familiar copper compound in the laboratory. It is used in a *fungicide* called the *Bordeaux mixture.*

Ball-and-stick model of the complex $[Cu(NH_3)_4(H_2O)_2]^{2+}$, illustrating the *octahedral coordination geometry* common for copper (II).

Polyols, compounds containing more than one alcohol *functional group,* generally interact with cupric salts. For example, copper salts are used to test for reducing sugars. Specifically, using *Benedict's reagent* and *Fehling's solution* the presence of the sugar is signaled by a color change from blue Cu(II) to reddish copper(I) oxide. Schweizer's reagent and related complexes with ethylenediamine and other amines dissolve cellulose. Amino acids form very stable chelate complexes with copper(II). Many wet-chemical tests for copper ions exist, one involving potassium ferrocyanide, which gives a brown precipitate with copper(II) salts.

Organocopper Chemistry

Compounds that contain a carbon-copper bond are known as organocopper compounds. They are very reactive towards oxygen to form copper(I) oxide and have many uses in chemistry. They are synthesised by treating copper(I) compounds with *Grignard reagents*, terminal alkynes or *organolithium* reagents; in particular, the last reaction described produces a *Gilman reagent*. These can undergo substitution with alkyl halides to form coupling products: as such, they are important in the field of organic synthesis. *Copper(I) acetylide* is highly shock-sensitive but is an intermediate in reactions such as the *Cadiot-Chodkiewicz coupling* and the *Sonogashira coupling*. Conjugate addition to enones and carbocupration of alkynes can also be achieved with Organocopper compounds. Copper(I) forms a variety of weak complexes with alkenes and carbon monoxide, especially in the presence of amine ligands.

Copper(III) and Copper(IV)

Complexes of copper(III) are frequent intermediate in reactions of organocopper compounds. Dicopper oxo complexes also feature copper(III). Fluoride ligands, being highly basic, stabilize metal ions in high oxidation states; indeed, representative copper(III) and copper(IV) complex are fluorides. These include K_3CuF_6 and Cs_2CuF_6. With di-and tripeptides, purple-colored complexes of copper(III) have been observed, this high oxidation state being stabilized by the deprotonated amide ligands.

Erosion Corrosion of Copper Water Tubes

Erosion corrosion, also known as impingement damage, is the combined effect of corrosion and erosion caused by rapid flowing turbulent water. It is probably the second most common cause of copper tube failures behind Type 1 pitting which is also known as *Cold Water Pitting of Copper Tube*.

Copper Water Tubes

Copper tubes have been used to distribute drinking water within buildings for many years, and hundreds of miles are installed throughout Europe every year. The long life of copper when exposed to natural waters is a result of its thermodynamic stability, its high resistance to reacting with the environment, and the formation of insoluble corrosion products that insulate the metal from the environment. The corrosion rate of copper in most drinkable waters is less than 2.5 μm/year, at this rate a 15 mm tube with a wall thickness of 0.7 mm would last for about 280 years. In some soft waters the general corrosion rate may increase to 12.5 μm/year, but even at this rate it would take over 50 years to perforate the same tube.

Occurrence

If the general water speed or the degree of local turbulence in an installation is high, the protective film that would normally be formed on a copper tube as a result of slight initial corrosion, may be torn off the surface locally, permitting further corrosion to take place at that point. If this process continues it can produce deep localised attack of the type known as erosion-corrosion or impingement damage. The actual attack on the metal is by the corrosive action of the water to which it is exposed while the erosive factor is the mechanical removal of the corrosion product from the surface.

Impingement attack produces highly characteristic water-swept pits, which are often horseshoe shaped, or it can produce broader areas of attack. The leading edge of the pit is frequently undercut by the swirling action of the water. Usually, the surface of the metal within the pits or areas of attack is smooth and carries no substantial corrosion product. Erosion-corrosion is known to occur in pumped-circulation hot water distribution systems, and even in cold water distribution systems, if the water velocities are too high. The factors influencing the attack include the chemical character of the water passing through the system, the temperature, the average water velocity in the system and the presence of any local features likely to induce turbulence in the water stream.

It is unusual for the general water velocity in a system to be so high that impingement attack occurs throughout the whole of the copper pipework. More commonly, the velocity is just sufficiently low for satisfactory protective films to be formed and to remain in position on most of the system, with impingement damage more likely to occur where there is an abrupt change in the direction of water flow giving rise to a high degree of turbulence, such as at tee pieces and elbow fittings. It is not generally realised how great an effect small obstructions can have on the flow pattern of water in a pipe-work system and the extent to which they can induce turbulence and cause corrosion-erosion. For example, it is most important, as far as possible, to ensure that copper tubes cut with a tube cutter are deburred before making the joint. Also a gap between the tube end and the stop in the fitting, due to the tube not having been cut to the correct length and fully inserted into the socket of the fitting, can also induce turbulence in the water stream.

Zinc Pest

Zinc pest, (from German Zinkpest), is a destructive, intercrystalline corrosion process of zinc alloys containing lead impurities. It was first discovered to be a problem in 1923.

Zinc pest affects primarily die-cast zinc articles that were manufactured during the 1930s, 1940s, and early 1950s. In Germany, articles made from *Zamak* during *World War II* and several years thereafter may be affected. Purer alloys were not available to the manufacturers as they were used for the war effort, or were just not on the market after the war. While impurities of the alloy seem to be the cause of the problem, environmental conditions such as high humidity (greater than 65%) may accelerate the process. Also, significant temperature changes can be damaging.

Affected objects may show surface irregularities such as blisters or pitting. They expand, buckle, tear, and in the end, crumble. The irreversible process will eventually destroy the object. Due to the expansion process, attached normal material may be damaged secondarily. Zinc pest is different from a superficial white oxidation process (*"Weissrost")* that may affect some zinc articles.

Zinc pest is dreaded by collectors of old *model trains*, toys, or radios where the zinc *die-cast process* was used. Valuable items are rendered worthless but for their residual parts. Also parts of engines of older vehicles or airplanes and military medals may be affected.

Articles made after 1960 are generally considered free of the risk of zinc pest. Use of purer materials and more controlled manufacturing conditions make it unlikely that modern zinc articles will encounter degradation by zinc pest. However, some model aircraft produced between 2001-2003 by certain brands have fallen victim to zinc pest.[citation needed]

Zinc pest is not related to tin pest.

Environmental Stress Fracture

In materials science, environmental stress fracture or environment assisted fracture is the generic name given to premature failure under the influence of tensile stresses and harmful environments of materials such as metals and alloys, composites, plastics and ceramics.

Metals and alloys exhibit phenomena such as *stress corrosion cracking, hydrogen embrittlement, liquid metal embrittlement* and *corrosion fatigue* all coming under this category. Environments such as moist air, sea water and corrosive liquids and gases cause environmental stress fracture. *Metal matrix composites* are also susceptible to many of these processes.

Plastics and plastic-based composites may suffer swelling, debonding and loss of strength when exposed to organic fluids and other corrosive environments, such as acids and alkalies. Under the influence of stress and environment, many structural materials, particularly the high-specific strength ones become brittle and lose their resistance to fracture. While their *fracture toughness* remains unaltered, their threshold stress intensity factor for crack propagation may be considerably lowered. Consequently, they become prone to premature fracture because of *sub-critical crack growth*. This article aims to give a brief overview of the various degradation processes mentioned above.

Stress Corrosion Cracking

Stress corrosion cracking is a phenomenon where a synergistic action of corrosion and tensile stress leads to brittle fracture of normally ductile materials at generally lower stress levels. During stress corrosion cracking, the material is relatively unattacked by the corrosive agent, but fine cracks form within it. This process has serious implications on the utility of the material because the applicable safe stress levels are drastically reduced in the corrosive medium. Season cracking and caustic embrittlement are two stress corrosion cracking processes which affected the serviceability of brass cartridge cases and riveted steel boilers respectively.

Hydrogen Embrittlement

Small quantities of hydrogen present inside certain metallic materials make the latter brittle and susceptible to sub-critical crack growth under stress. Sôme materials may exhibit a marked decrease in their load carrying capacity and fail in a brittle fashion when stressed in an atmosphere containing hydrogen. Both of these processes may be called hydrogen embrittlement. Hydrogen embrittlement may occur as a side effect of electroplating processes.

Delayed failure, the fracture of a component under stress after an elapsed time, is a characteristic feature of hydrogen embrittlement. Hydrogen entry into the material may be effected during melting, casting, welding, and service life. Corrosion during service in moist environments generates hydrogen, part of which may enter the metal and cause embrittlement. Presence of a tensile stress, either inherent or externally applied, is necessary for metals to be damaged. As in the case of stress corrosion cracking, hydrogen embrittlement may also lead to a decrease in the threshold stress intensity factor for crack propagation or an increase in the sub critical crack growth velocity of the material. The most visible effect of hydrogen in materials is a drastic reduction in ductility during tensile tests. It may increase, decrease or leave unaffected the *yield strength* of the material. Hydrogen may cause serrated yielding in certain metals such as *Niobium, Nickel* and some *steels*.

Over the years several theories have been proposed to explain hydrogen embrittlement. Pressure theory and surface adsorption theory are among the earliest of these. Later, decohesion theory and slip softening theory were introduced to resolve defects in the earlier theories. The hydride embrittlement theory explains the behaviour of hydride forming metals such as *Titanium, Zirconium, Vanadium* and *Niobium*.

Case Studies

One of the worst disasters caused by stress corrosion cracking was the fall of the *Silver Bridge*, WV in 1967, when a single brittle crack formed by rusting grew to criticality. The crack was on one of the tie bar links of one of the suspension chains, and the whole joint failed quickly by overload. The event escalated and the whole bridge disappeared in less than a minute, killing 46 drivers or passengers on the bridge at the time.

Fracture

A fracture is the (local) separation of an object or material into two, or more, pieces under the action of *stress*.

The word fracture is often applied to *bones* of living creatures (that is a *bone fracture*), or to *crystals* or crystalline materials, such as *gemstones* or *metal*. Sometimes, in crystalline materials, individual crystals fracture without the body actually separating into two or more pieces. Depending on the substance which is fractured, a fracture reduces *strength* (most substances) or inhibits *transmission* of *light* (*optical* crystals).

Environmental Stress Cracking

Environmental Stress Cracking (ESC) is one of the most common causes of unexpected *brittle* failure of *thermoplastic* (especially amorphous) *polymers* known at present. Environmental stress cracking may account for around 15-30 per cent of all plastic component failures in service.

ESC and polymer resistance to ESC (ESCR) have been studied for several decades. Research shows that the exposure of polymers to liquid chemicals tends to accelerate the *crazing* process, initiating crazes at stresses that are much lower than the stress causing crazing in air. The action of either a tensile stress or a corrosive liquid alone would not be enough to cause failure, but in ESC the initiation and growth of a crack is caused by the combined action of the stress and a corrosive environmental liquid.

It is somewhat different from *polymer degradation* in that stress cracking does not break polymer bonds. Instead, it breaks the secondary linkages between polymers. These are broken when the mechanical stresses cause minute cracks in the polymer and they propagate rapidly under the harsh environmental conditions. It has also been seen that catastrophic failure under stress can occur due to the attack of a *reagent* that would not attack the polymer in an unstressed state.

Metallurgists typically use the term *Stress corrosion cracking* or *Environmental stress fracture* to describe this type of failure in metals.

Stress Fractures

One of the most common injuries in sports is a stress fracture. Overcoming an injury like a stress fracture can be difficult, but it can be done.

What is a Stress Fracture?

A stress fracture is a common overuse injury most often seen in athletes. Usually, a fracture, *or broken bone,* is caused by an acute event, such as a car crash or a fall. When this is the case, the bone experiences a very high force that causes the stress fracture.

Causes

A stress fracture occurs when the forces are much lower, but happen repetitively for a long period of time; these injuries are also known as "fatigue fractures." Stress fractures are commonly seen in athletes who run and jump on hard surfaces, such as distance runners, basketball players, and ballet dancers.

A stress fracture can occur in any bone, but is commonly seen in the foot and shin bones. They rarely occur in the upper extremity because the weight of your body is not supported by your arms as it is in your legs.

How is a Stress Fracture Diagnosed?

Physical examination and history are important in diagnosing stress fractures. Because these overuse injuries have a typical course and common physical findings, the history and examination can be critical in the diagnostic evaluation. X-Rays usually do not show a stress fracture, but they may show evidence of bone attempting to heal around the stress fracture. Further studies, including an MRI or bone scan may be necessary if the diagnosis is unclear or if the problem does not resolve with treatment.

Why Did I get a Stress Fracture?

Bone is constantly undergoing changes to adapt to its environment. When astronauts go into space, they are known to develop a thinning of the bone similar to osteoporosis. The reason is that their skeleton is not under the constant demands of gravity, and the bone adapts to that environment. Stress fractures are usually seen in athletes who increase their level of activity over a short period of time. The increased demand placed on the bones causes the bone to remodel and become stronger in the areas of higher stress. However, if the response of the bone cannot maintain the pace of the repetitive demands, a stress fracture may result.

Another factor that can contribute to the development of a stress fracture are dietary abnormalities and menstrual irregularities. Because both factors contribute to bone health, any problems with diet (*e.g.* poor nutrition, anorexia, bulimia) or menstruation (amenorrhea) may place an individual at higher risk for these injuries. This is one reason that adolescent female athletes are at particularly high risk for development of a stress fracture.

What is the Treatment for a Stress Fracture?

The best treatment is almost always resting the injured leg. If there is no evidence that the stress fracture may displace, then avoiding the overuse activity may be sufficient treatment. However, if there is a concern of displacement of the stress fracture, then, weight-bearing should be avoided (*i.e.* use crutches), and a cast may be placed. One rule of thumb (but not an absolute rule) is: if there is pain, don't do it. This means if jogging causes pain where you have a stress fracture, don't jog. If walking causes pain in that location, use crutches.

Concrete

Concrete is a *composite* construction material, composed of cement (commonly *Portland cement)* and other cementitious materials such as *fly ash* and *slag cement, aggregate* (generally a coarse aggregate made of gravel or crushed rocks such as *limestone,* or *granite,* plus a fine aggregate such as sand), *water* and *chemical* admixtures.

The word concrete comes from the Latin word "concretus" (meaning compact or condensed), the perfect passive participle of "concrescere", from "con" (together) and "crescere" (to grow).

Concrete solidifies and hardens after mixing with water and placement due to a *chemical process* known as *hydration*. The water reacts with the cement, which bonds the other components together, eventually creating a robust stone-like material. Concrete is used to make *pavements,* pipe, *architectural structures, foundations,* motorways/roads, bridges/overpasses, *parking* structures, brick/block walls, *footings* for gates, *fences* and poles and even *boats.*

Concrete is used more than any other man-made material in the world. As of 2006, about 7.5 billion cubic metres of concrete are made each year—more than one cubic metre for every person on Earth.

Concrete powers a US$35 billion industry, employing more than two million workers in the United States alone.[citation needed] More than 55,000 miles (89,000 km) of highways in the United States are paved with this material. *Reinforced concrete, prestressed concrete* and *precast concrete* are the most widely used types of concrete functional extensions in modern days.

Electrical Resistivity Measurement of Concrete

The 4 point electrical resistivity measurement device (wenner array probe) is used to measure the electrical resistivity of concrete for analyzing the corrosion potential and offers an indication of its permeability.

Method

Corrosion is an electro-chemical process. The rate of flow of the *ions* between the *anode* and *cathode* areas, and therefore the rate at which corrosion can occur, is affected by the *resistivity* of the concrete. To measure the electrical resistivity of the concrete a current is applied to the two outer probes and the potential difference is measured between the two inner probes. Empirical tests have arrived at the following threshold values which can be used to determine the likelihood of corrosion.

- When $\rho \geq 120\ \Omega$-m corrosion is unlikely
- When $\rho = 80$ to $120\ \Omega$-m corrosion is possible
- When $\rho \leq 80\ \Omega$-m corrosion is fairly certain

The electrical resistivity of the concrete cover layer decreases due to:

- Increasing concrete water content
- Increasing concrete porosity
- Increasing temperature
- Increasing chloride content
- Decreasing carbonation depth.

When the electrical resistivity of the concrete is low, the rate of corrosion increases. When the electrical resistivity is high, *e.g.* in case of dry and carbonated concrete, the rate of corrosion decreases.

Transformer Method

In this method a transformer is used to measure resistivity without any direct contact with the specimen. The transformer consists of a primary coil which energises the circuit with an AC voltage and a secondary which is formed by a toroid of the concrete sample. The current in the sample is detected by a current coil wound around a section of the toroid (a *current transformer*). This method is good for measuring the setting properties of concrete, its hydration and strength. Wet concrete has a resistivity of around 1 Ω-m which progressively increases as the cement sets.

Standards

- ASTM Standard C1202-94: Standard Test Method for Electrical Indication of Chloride's Ability to Resist Chloride Ion Penetration.

Application

The presence of rebars disturbs electrical resistivity measurement as they conduct current much better than the surrounding concrete. This is particularly the case when the cover depth is less than 30 mm. In order to minimize the effect, none of the electrodes should be placed above a rebar when measuring, or if this is unavoidable, then perpendicular to the rebar.

6

Corrosion in Non-metals

Most ceramic materials are almost entirely immune to corrosion. The strong ionic and/or covalent bonds that hold them together leave very little free chemical energy in the structure; they can be thought of as already corroded. When corrosion does occur, it is almost always a simple dissolution of the material or chemical reaction, rather than an electrochemical process. A common example of corrosion protection in ceramics is the lime added to soda-lime glass to reduce its solubility in water; though it is not nearly as soluble as pure sodium silicate, normal glass does form sub-microscopic flaws when exposed to moisture. Due to its brittleness, such flaws cause a dramatic reduction in the strength of a glass object during its first few hours at room temperature.

Polymer degradation is due to a wide array of complex and often poorly-understood physiochemical processes. These are strikingly different from the other processes discussed here, and so the term "corrosion" is only applied to them in a loose sense of the word. Because of their large molecular weight, very little entropy can be gained by mixing a given mass of polymer with another substance, making them generally quite difficult to dissolve. While dissolution is a problem in some polymer applications, it is relatively simple to design against. A more common and related problem is *swelling*, where small molecules infiltrate the structure, reducing strength and stiffness and causing a volume change. Conversely, many polymers (notably flexible vinyl) are intentionally swelled with plasticizers, which can be leached out of the structure, causing brittleness or other undesirable changes. The most common form of degradation, however, is a decrease in polymer chain length. Mechanisms which break polymer chains are familiar to biologists because of their effect on DNA: ionizing radiation (most commonly ultraviolet light), free radicals, and oxidizers such as oxygen, ozone, and chlorine. Additives can slow these process very effectively, and can be as simple as a UV-absorbing pigment (*i.e.*, titanium dioxide or carbon black). Plastic shopping bags often do not include these additives so that they break down more easily as litter.

Corrosion of Glasses

Glass disease is the corrosion of silicate glasses in aqueous solutions. It is governed by two mechanisms: diffusion-controlled leaching (ion exchange) and glass network hydrolytic dissolution. Both corrosion mechanisms strongly depend on the pH of contacting solution: the rate of ion exchange decreases with pH as $10^{-0.5\,pH}$ whereas the rate of hydrolytic dissolution increases with pH as $10^{0.5\,pH}$.

Mathematically, corrosion rates of glasses are characterised by normalised corrosion rates of elements NR_i (g/cm² d) which are determined as the ratio of total amount of released species into the water M_i (g) to the water-contacting surface area S (cm²), time of contact t (days) and weight fraction content of the element in the glass f_i:

$$NR_i = \frac{M_i}{Sf_i t}$$

The overall corrosion rate is a sum of contributions from both mechanisms (leaching + dissolution) $NR_i = Nrx_i + NRh$. Diffusion controlled leaching (ion exchange) is characteristic of the initial phase of corrosion and involves replacement of alkali ions in the glass by a hydronium (H_3O^+) ion from the solution. It causes an ion-selective depletion of near surface layers of glasses and gives an inverse square root dependence of corrosion rate with exposure time. The diffusion controlled normalised leaching rate of cations from glasses (g/cm²d) is given by:

$$NRx_i = 2\rho\sqrt{\frac{D_i}{\pi t}}$$

where t is time, D_i is the ith cation effective diffusion coefficient (cm²/d), which depends on pH of contacting water as $D_i = D_{i0} \cdot 10^{-pH}$, and ρ is the density of the glass (g/cm³).

Glass corrosion

Glass network dissolution is characteristic of the later phases of corrosion and causes a congruent release of ions into the water solution at a time-independent rate in dilute solutions (g/cm²d):

$$NRh = \rho r_{h'}$$

where r_h is the stationary hydrolysis (dissolution) rate of the glass (cm/d). In closed systems the consumption of protons from the aqueous phase increases the pH and causes a fast transition to hydrolysis. However, further silica saturation of solution impedes hydrolysis and causes the glass to return to an ion-exchange, *e.g.* diffusion-controlled regime of corrosion.

In typical natural conditions normalised corrosion rates of silicate glasses are very low and are of the order of $10^{-7} - 10^{-5}$ g/cm²d. The very high durability of silicate glasses in water makes them suitable for hazardous and nuclear waste immobilisation.

Glass Corrosion Tests

There exist numerous standardized procedures for measuring the corrosion (also called chemical durability) of glasses in neutral, basic, and acidic environments, under simulated environmental conditions, in simulated body fluid, at high temperature and pressure and under other conditions.

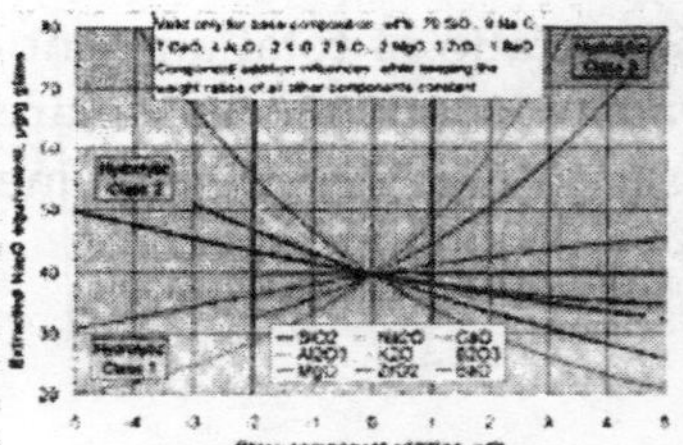

Influences of selected glass component additions on the chemical durability against water corrosion of a specific base glass (corrosion test ISO 719).

In the standard procedure ISO 719 a test of the extraction of water soluble basic compounds under neutral conditions is described: 2 g glass, particle size 300-500 µm, is kept for 60 min in 50 ml de-ionized water of grade 2 at 98° C. 25 ml of the obtained solutions is titrated against 0.01 mol/1 HCl solution. The volume of HCl needed for neutralization is recorded and classified following the values in the table below:

0.01M HCl needed to neutralize extracted basic oxides, ml	Extracted Na_2O equivalent, µg	Hydrolytic class
to 0.1	to 31	1
above 0.1 to 0.2	above 31 to 62	2
above 0.2 to 0.85	above 62 to 264	3
above 0.85 to 2.0	above 264 to 620	4
above 2.0 to 3.5	above 620 to 1085	5
above 3.5	above 1085	>5

Corrosion is the distintegration of an engineered material into its constituent atoms due to chemical reactions with its surroundings. In the most common use of the word, this means electrochemical oxidation of metals in reaction with an oxidant such as oxygen. Formation of an oxide of iron due to oxidation of the iron atoms in solid solution is a well-known example of electrochemical corrosion, commonly known as rusting. This type of damage typically produces oxide(s) and/or salt(s) of the original metal. Corrosion can also refer to other materials than metals, such as ceramics or polymers, although in this context, the term degradation is more common.

Materials failure modes
Buckling
Corrosion
Creep
Fatigue
Fouling
Fracture
Impact
Mechanical overload
Thermal shock
Wear
Yielding

In other words, corrosion is the wearing away of metals due to a chemical reaction.

Rust, the most familiar example of corrosion.

Many structural alloys corrode merely from exposure to moisture in the air, but the process can be strongly affected by exposure to certain substances. Corrosion can be concentrated locally to form a pit or crack, or it can extend across a wide are more or less uniformly corroding the surface. Because corrosion is a diffusion controlled process, it occurs on exposed surfaces. As a result, methods to reduce the activity of the exposed surface, such as passivation and chromate-conversion, can increase a materials's corrosion resistance. However, some corrosion mechanisms are less visible and less predictable.

Volcanic gases have sped the corrosion of this abandoned mining machinery.

Galvanic Corrosion

Galvanic corrosion occurs when two different metals electrically contact each other and are immersed in an electrolyte. In order for galvanic corrosion to occur, an electrically conductive path and an ionically conductive path are necessary. This effects a galvanic couple where the more active metal corrodes at an accelerated rate and the more noble metal corrodes at a retarded rate. When

Corrosion on exposed metal.

immersed, neither metal would normally corrode as quickly without the electrically conductive connection (usually via a wire or direct contact). Galvanic corrosion is often utilized in sacrificial anodes. What type of metal(s) to use is readily determined by following the galvanic series. For example, zinc is often used as a sacrificial anode for steel structures, such as pipelines or docked naval ships. Galvanic corrosion is of major interest to the marine industry and also anywhere water can contact pipes or metal structures.

Factors such as relative size of anode (smaller is generally less desirable), types of metal, and operating conditions (temperature, humidity, salinity, etc.) will affect galvanic corrosion. The surface area ratio of the anode and cathode will directly affect the corrosion rates of the materials.

Galvanic Series

In a given sea environment (one standard medium is aerated, room-temperature seawater), one metal will be either more *noble* or more *active* than the next, based on how strongly its ions are bound to the surface. Two metals in electrical contact share the same electrons, so that the tug-of-war at each surface is translated into a competition for free electrons between the two materials. The noble metal will tend to take electrons from the active one, while the electrolyte hosts a flow of ions in the same direction. The resulting mass flow or electrical current can be measured to establish a hierarchy of materials in the medium of interest. This hierarchy is called a *galvanic series*, and can be a very useful in predicting and understanding corrosion.

Corrosion Removal

Often it is possible to chemically remove the products of corrosion to give a clean surface, but one that may exhibit artifacts of corrosion such as pitting. For example phosphoric acid in the form of naval jelly is often applied to ferrous tools or surfaces to remove rust.

Corrosion removal should not be confused with Electropolishing which removes some layers of the underlying metal to make a smooth surface. For example phoshporic acid (again) may be used to electropolish copper but it does this by removing copper, not the products of copper corrosion.

Resistance to Corrosion

Some metals are more intrinscially resistant to corrosion than others, either due to the fundamental nature of the electrochemical processes involved or due to the details of how reaction products form. For some examples, see galvanic series. If a more susceptible material is used, many techniques can be applied during an item's manufacture and use to protect its materials from damage.

Intrinsic Chemistry

The materials most resistant to corrosion are those for which corrosion is thermodynamically unfavourable. Any corrosion products of gold or platinum tend to decompose spontaneously into pure metal, which is why these elements can be found in metallic form on Earth, and is a large part of their intrinsic value. More common "base" metals can only be protected by more temporary means.

Some metals have naturally slow reaction kinetics, even though their corrosion is thermodynamically favourable. These include such metals as zinc, magnesium, and cadmium. While corrosion of these metals is continuous and ongoing, it happens at an acceptably slow rate. An extreme example is graphite, which releases large amounts of energy upon oxidation, but has such slow kinetics that it is effectively immune to electrochemical corrosion under normal conditions.

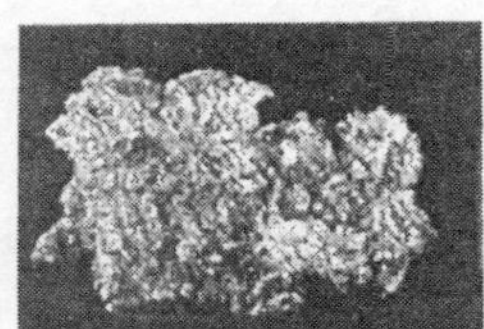

Gold nuggets do not naturally corrode, even on a geological time scale.

Passivation

Given the right conditions, a thin film of corrosion products can form on a metal's surface spontaneously, acting as a barrier to further oxidation. When this layer stops growing at less than a micrometre thick under the conditions that a material will be used in, the phenomenon is known as passivation (rust, for example, usually grows to be much thicker, and so is not considered passivation, because this mixed oxidized layer is not protective). While this effect is in some sense a property of the material, it serves as an indirect kinetic barrier: the reaction is often quite rapid unless and until an impermeable layer forms. Passivation in air and water at moderate pH is seen in such materials as aluminium, stainless steel, titanium, and silicon.

These conditions required for passivation are specific to the material. The effect of pH is recorded using Pourbaix diagrams, but many other factors are influential. Some conditions that inhibit passivation include: high pH for aluminium, low pH or the presence of chloride ions for stainless steel, high temperature for titanium (in which case the oxide dissolves into the metal, rather than the electrolyte) and fluoride ions for silicon. On the other hand, sometimes unusual conditions can bring on passivation in materials that are normally unprotected, as the alkaline environment of concrete does for steel rebar. Exposure to a liquid metal such as mercury or hot solder can often circumvent passivation mechanisms.

Corrosion in Passivated Materials

Passivation is extremely useful in alleviating corrosion damage, but care must be taken not to trust it too thoroughly. Even a high-quality alloy will corrode if its ability to form a passivating film is hindered. Because the resulting modes of corrosion are more exotic and their immediate results are less visible than rust and other bulk corrosion, they often escape notice and cause problems among those who are not familiar with them.

Pitting Corrosion

The scheme of pitting corrosion

Certain conditions, such as low concentrations of oxygen or high concentrations of species such as chloride which compete as anions, can interfere with a given alloy's ability to re-form a passivating film. In the worst case, almost all of the surface will remain protected, but tiny local fluctuations will degrade the oxide film in a few critical points. Corrosion at these points will be greatly amplified, and can cause *corrosion pits* of several types, depending upon conditions. While the corrosion pits only nucleate under fairly extreme circumstances, they can continue to grow even when conditions return to normal, since the interior of a pit is naturally deprived of oxygen and locally the pH decreases to very low values and the corrosion rate increases due to an auto-catalytic process. In extreme cases, the sharp tips of extremely long and narrow corrosion pits can cause stress concentration to the point that otherwise tough alloys can shatter; a thin film pierced by an invisibly small hole can hide a thumb sized pit from view. These problems are especially dangerous because they are difficult to detect before a part or structure fails. Pitting remains among the most common and damaging forms of corrosion in passivated alloys[citation needed] , but it can be prevented by control of the alloy's environment.

Weld Decay and Knifeline Attack

Stainless steel can pose special corrosion challenges, since its passivating behaviour relies on the presence of a minor alloying component (Chromium, typically only 18%). Due to the elevated temperatures of welding or during improper heat treatment, chromium carbides can form in the grain boundaries of stainless alloys. This chemical reaction robs the material of chromium in the zone near the grain boundary, making those areas much less resistant to corrosion. This creates a galvanic couple with the well-protected alloy nearby, which leads to *weld decay* (corrosion of the grain boundaries near welds) in highly corrosive environments. Special alloys, either with low carbon content or with added carbon "getters" such as titanium and niobium (in types 321 and 347, respectively), can prevent this effect, but the latter require special heat treatment after welding to prevent the similar phenomenon of *knifeline attack.* As its name applies, this is limited to a small zone, often only a few micrometres across, which causes it to proceed more rapidly. This zone is very near the weld, making it even less noticeable.

Crevice Corrosion

Crevice corrosion is a localized form of corrosion occurring in spaces to which the access of the working fluid from the environment is limited and a concentration cell, areas with different oxygen concentration, will take place with consequent high corrosion rate. These spaces are generally called crevices. Examples of crevices are gaps and contact areas between parts, under gaskets or seals, inside cracks and seams, spaces filled with deposits and under sludge piles.

Microbial Corrosion

Microbial corrosion, or bacterial corrosion, is a corrosion caused or promoted by microorganisms, usually chemautorophs. It can apply to both metals and non-metallic materials, in both the presence and lack of oxygen. Sulphate-reducing bacteria are common in lack of oxygen; they produce hydrogen sulphide, causing sulphide stress cracking. In presence of oxygen, some bacteria directly oxidize iron to iron oxides and hydroxides, other bacteria oxidize sulphur and produce sulphuric acid causing biogenic sulphide corrosion. Concentration cells can form in the deposits of corrosion products, causing and enhancing galvanic corrosion.

Accelerated Low Water Corrosion (ALWC) is a particularly aggressive form of MIC that affects steel piles in seawater near the low water tide mark. It is characterised by an orange sludge, which smells of Hydrogen Sulphide when treated with acid. Corrosion rates can be very high and design corrosion allowances can soon be exceeded leading to premature failure of the steel pile. Piles that have been coating and have cathodic protection installed at the time of construction are not susceptible to ALWC. For unprotected piles, sacrificial anodes can be installed local to the affected areas to inhibit the corrosion or a complete retrofitted sacrificial anode system can be installed. Affected areas can also be treated electrochemically by using an electrode to first produce chlorine to kill the bacteria, and then to produced a calcareous deposit, which will help shield the metal from further attack.

High Temperature Corrosion

High temperature corrosion is chemical deterioration of a material (typically a metal) under very high temperature conditions. This non-galvanic form of corrosion can occur when a metal is subject to a high temperature atmosphere containing oxygen, sulphur or other compounds capable of oxidising (or assisting the oxidation of) the material concerned. For example, materials used in aerospace, power generation and even in car engines have to resist sustained periods at high temperature in which they may be exposed to an atmosphere containing potentially highly corrosive products of combustion.

The products of high temperature corrosion can potentially be turned to the advantage of the engineer. The formation of oxides on stainless steels, for example, can provide a protective layer preventing further atmospheric attack, allowing for a material to be used for sustained periods at both room and high temperature in hostile conditions. Such high temperature corrosion products in the form of compacted oxide layer glazes have also been shown to prevent or reduce wear during high temperature sliding contact of metallic (or metallic and ceramic) surfaces.

METHODS OF PROTECTION FROM CORROSION

Surface Treatments

Applied Coatings

Plating, painting, and the application of enamel are the most common anti-corrosion treatments. They work by providing a barrier of corrosion-resistant material between the damaging environment and the (often cheaper, tougher, and/or easier-to-process) structural material. Aside from cosmetic and manufacturing issues, there are tradeoffs in mechanical flexibility versus resistance to abrasion and high temperature. Platings usually fail only in small sections, and if the plating is more noble than the substrate (for example, chromium on steel), a galvanic couple will cause any exposed area to corrode much more rapidly than an unplated surface would. For this reason, it is often wise to plate with a more active metal such as zinc or cadmium. Painting either by roller or brush is more desirable for tight spaces; spray would be better for larger coating areas such as steel decks and waterfront applications.

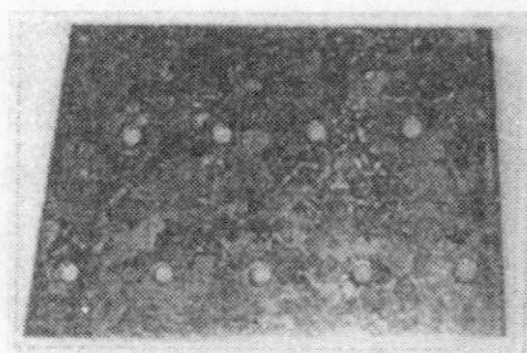
Galvanized surface

Flexible polyurethane coatings, like Durabak-M26 for example, can provide an anti-corrosive seal with a highly durable slip resistant membrane. Painted coatings are relatively easy to apply and have fast drying times although temperature and humidity may cause dry times to vary.

Reactive Coatings

If the environment is controlled (especially in recirculating systems), corrosion inhibitors can often be added to it. These form an electrically insulating and/or chemically impermeable coating on exposed metal surfaces, to suppress electrochemical reactions. Such methods obviously make the system less sensitive to scratches or defects in the coating, since extra inhibitors can be made available wherever metal becomes exposed. Chemicals that inhibit corrosion include some of the salts in hard water (Roman water systems are famous for their mineral deposits), chromates, phosphates, polyaniline, other conducting polymers and a wide range of specially-designed chemicals that resemble surfactants (*i.e.* long-chain organic molecules with ionic end groups).

Anodization

Aluminium alloys often undergo a surface treatment. Electrochemical conditions in the bath are carefully adjusted so that uniform pores several nanometers wide appear in the metal's oxide film. These pores allow the oxide to grow much thicker than passivating conditions would allow. At the end of the treatment, the pores are allowed to seal, forming a harder-than-usual surface layer. If this coating is scratched, normal passivation processes take over to protect the damaged area. Anodizing is very resilient to weathering and corrosion, so it is commonly used for building facades and other areas that the surface will come into regular contact with the elements. Whilst being resilient, it must be cleaned frequently. If left without cleaning Panel Edge Staining will naturally occur.

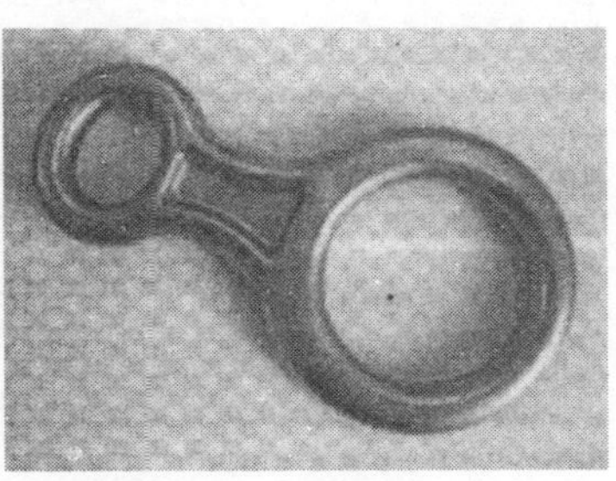

The descender is anodized with a yellow finish. Climbing equipment is available in a wide range of anodized colors.

Biofilm Coatings

A new form of protection has been developed by applying certain species of bacterial films to the surface of metals in highly corrosive environments. This process increases the corrosion resistance substantially. Alternatively, antimicrobial-producing biofilms can be used to inhibit mild steel corrosion from sulphate-reducing bacteria.

Controlled Permeability Formwork

Controlled permeability formwork (CPF) is a method of preventing the corrosion of reinforcement by naturally enhancing the durability of the cover during concrete placement,. CPF has been used in environments to combat the effects of carbonation, chlorides, frost and abrasion.

Cathodic Protection

Cathodic protection (CP) is a technique to control the corrosion of a metal surface by making that surface the cathode of an electrochemical cell. Cathodic protection systems are most commonly used to protect steel, water, and fuel pipelines and tanks; steel pier piles, ships, and offshore oil platforms.

Sacrificial Protection

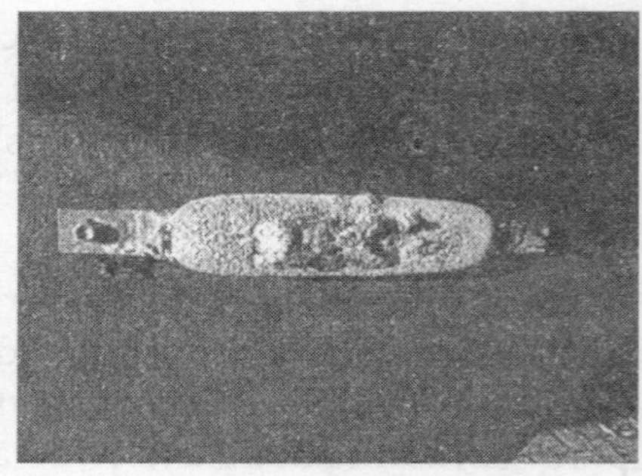
Sacrificial anode in the hull of a ship.

For effective CP, the potential of the steel surface is polarized (pushed) more negative until the metal surface has a uniform potential. With a uniform potential, the driving force for the corrosion reaction is halted. For galvanic CP systems, the anode material corrodes under the influence of the steel, and eventually it must be replaced. The polarization is caused by the current flow from the anode to the cathode, driven by the difference in electrochemical potential between the anode and the cathode.

Impressed Current Cathodic Protection

For larger structures, galvanic anodes cannot economically deliver enough current to provide complete protection. Impressed Current Cathodic Protection (ICCP) systems use anodes connected to a DC power source (such as a cathodic protection rectifier). Anodes for ICCP systems are tubular and solid rod shapes of various specialized materials. These include high silicon cast iron, graphite, mixed metal oxide or platinum coated titanium or niobium coated rod and wires.

Anodic Protection

Anodic protection impresses anodic current on the structure to be protected (opposite to the cathodic protection). It is appropriate for metals that exhibit passivity (*e.g.*, stainless steel) and suitably small passive current over a wide range of potentials. It is used in aggressive environments, *e.g.*, solutions of sulphuric acid.

Economic Impact

The US Federal Highways Administration released a study, entitled *Corrosion Costs and Preventive Strategies in the United States*, in 2002 on the direct costs associated with metallic corrosion in nearly every U.S. industry sector. The study showed that for 1998 the total annual estimated direct cost of corrosion in the U.S. was approximately $276 billion (approximately 3.2% of the US gross domestic product).

The collapsed Silver Bridge, as seen from the Ohio side

Rust is one of the most common causes of bridge accidents. As rust has a much higher volume than the originating mass of iron, its build-up can also cause failure by forcing apart adjacent parts. It was the cause of the collapse of the Mainus river bridge in 1983, when the bearings rusted internally and pushed one corner of the road slab off its support. Three drivers on the roadway at the time died as the slab fell into the river below. The following NTSB investigation showed that a drain.

REFERENCES

Calculation of the Chemical Durability (Hydrolytic Class) of Glasses (http://glassproperties.com/chemical_durability/).

Corrosion of Glass, Ceramics and Ceramic Superconductors. Edited by: D.E. Clark, B.K. Zoitos, William Andrew Publishing/Noyes, 672 pp. (1992).

FHWA Report Number: FHWA-RD-01-156. (http://www.corrosioncost.com/summary.htm).

International Organization for Standardization, Procedure 719 (1985) (http://www.iso.org/iso/iso_catalogue/catalogue_tc/catalogue_detail.htm?csnumber-4948)

Jones, Denny (1996). *Principles and Prevention of Corrosion* (2nd edition ed). Upper Saddle River, New Jersey: Prentice Hall. ISBN 0-13-359993-0.

Management of Accelerated Low Water Corrosion in Steel Maritime Structures, JE Breakell, M Siegwart, K Foster, D Marshall, M Hodgson, R Cottis, S Lyon. ISBN 0-86017-634-7.

Ojovan, M.I., W.E. Lee. *New Developments in Glassy Nuclear Wasteforms.* Nova Science Publishers, New York, 136 pp. (2007).

Vapor Hydration Testing (VHT) (http://www.vscht.cz/sil/english/chemtech_ag/vht.htm)

Varshneya, A.K., *Fundamentals of Inorganic Glasses.* Society of Glass Technology, Sheffield, 682 pp. (2006).

Working Safely with Corrosive Chemicals (http://www.llnl.gov/es_and_h/hsm/doc_14-08/doc14-08 html).

Zuo, R., D. Ornek, B.C. Syrett, R.M. Green, C.-H. Hsu, F.B. Mansfeld and T.K. Wood, Inhibiting mild steel corrosion from sulphate-reducing bacteria using antimicrobial-producing biofilms in Three-Mile-Island process water Appl. Microbiol. Biotechnol. (2004) 64:275-283 http://dx.doi.org/10.1007/s00253-003-1403-7.

7

Theories of Corrosion

Heterogeneous Theory

Heterogeneous theory points out that the presence of impurity on metals causes corrosion and thus a local cell is set up between the anodic and cathodic parts of the corroding surface. The metal becomes unstable and corrosion occurs as a consequence of the electrochemical reactions occurring at the interface of the metal and ionically conducting moisture films or actual solution.

Thus it is evident that a corroding metal consists of:

(*i*) an electron sink area at which a de-electronation reaction occurs (metal dissolution), and an electron source area where electronation reaction occurs;

(*ii*) an electronic conductor to carry the electrons to the electron source area; and

(*iii*) an ionic conductor to keep the ion current flowing and to function as a medium for the electrodic reaction.

This model is often termed as 'Local cell theory of corrosion' or 'Heterogeneous theory of corrosion'.

Homogeneous Theory

According to Wagner and Traud, impurities or other heterogeneities are not essential on the surface for corrosion to occur. Homogenous theory states that the metals become unstable because of different electrodic charge transfer reactions occurring simultaneously and in opposite direction at the surface. Thus Wagner-Traud mechanism emphasizes that the necessary condition for corrosion is that the metal dissolution reaction and some electronation reaction proceed simultaneously at the metal/environment interface. For this it is necessary that the potential difference across the interface should be more positive than the equilibrium potential of metal dissolution reaction and/or more negative than the equilibrium potential of the electronation reaction.

Expressions for Corrosion Rate

In literature corrosion rates are expressed in a number of ways [7]. The following are some of the major systems of corrosion units.

(*i*) ipy ..... Inches per year

(*ii*) mpy ..... Mils per year (1 mil = 0.001 inch = 0.0245 mm)

(*iii*) ipmo ..... Inches per month

(*iv*) mdd ..... Milligrams per square decimeter per day

(*v*) mmpy ..... Millimeter per year

Usually corrosion rates are expressed in basic units mpy, mmpy and mdd.

From the following expressions, the corrosion rates in mpy and mdd scales can be directly calculated

$$mpy = \frac{82.75\,W}{A \times t \times D} \quad ...(7.1)$$

$$mmpy = \frac{87.6\,W}{A \times t \times D} \quad ...(7.2)$$

where

W-Weight loss in mg

A-Area in square centimeter

t-Time in hour

and D-Density of the specimen.

Using the conversion table, the other expressions of corrosion rates can be calculated using these two basic units.

$$\text{mpy} = 1000 \text{ X ipy}$$
$$= 12100 \text{ X ipmo}$$

It can be mentioned here that in general a corrosion rate of less than 5 mpy indicates satisfactory service behaviour, 5-50 mpy indicates moderate to fair corrosion resistance and corrosion rate above 50 mpy would be unsatisfactory for service.

Corrosion Monitoring Techniques

The following are the techniques used for non-electrochemical methods and monitoring the corrosion electrochemical methods.

Non-Electrochemical Methods

The technique like weight loss measurement and gasometric methods are generally termed as non-electrochemical methods. The main disadvantage of these methods is that they require relatively long exposure times of the corroding systems. The chemical methods are also in general restricted to systems which do not form adherent layers of corrosion products.

(*i*) ***Weight loss measurement:*** This method is considered to be the most reliable method. In this technique the specimen is immersed generally in the corrosive medium for a fixed time and the loss in weight of the specimen is determined. The weight loss is generally expressed in mils per year, millimeter per year or milligrams per square decimeter per day. This method is used to evaluate the inhibitors.

(*ii*) ***Gasometric method:*** In this method the volume of hydrogen gas (in acid corrosion) evolved during a corrosion reaction is measured at a constant temperature. From the corresponding metal loss can be calculated. This method yields reliable and accurate results with a high degree of reproducibility. This technique has been used for the inhibitor studies by Nathan and also by Hackerman. Mathur *et al.* have designed a gasometric unit with which corrosion rates could be monitored under controlled condition. This technique has also been successfully applied for the determination of corrosion kinetic parameters by them.

However, this technique has certain limitations and it cannot be applied to strong oxidizing medium like nitric acid and to systems where the inhibitor used undergoes reduction with the hydrogen gas evolved.

Electrochemical Methods

Different electrochemical techniques have been employed for the determination of corrosion rates. Since most of the corrosion processes in aqueous solution are electrochemical in nature, the electrochemical methods are more advantageous than the non-electrochemical techniques. Some of them are:

(*i*) the relatively short measuring time

(*ii*) high accuracy and

(*iii*) the possibility of continuous corrosion monitoring.

The main disadvantage of all electrochemical methods is the necessity for perturbation of the corroding system by an externally imposed polarisation which leads to inevitable changes of the system-specific properties.

These methods use direct or alternating current (or voltage) and the resultant voltage (or current) is followed. Accordingly they are known as D.C. methods and A.C. methods.

The corrosion rate can be calculated using the formula

Rate in mpy = $0.1288 I_{corr} (W/\rho)$ ...(7.3)

where

ρ = density of the metal used

W = equivalent weight of the metal.

While D.C. methods have been widely used for the measurement of corrosion rate, A.C. (impedance) techniques have been applied only more recently for these purpose Mansfeld and Lorenz have shown that electrochemical D.C. and A.C. techniques can be successfully applied for the determination of metal corrosion rates for many systems.

The results obtained from linear polarisation D.C. method have been shown to be in good agreement with weight loss data by Driver and Meakins.

D.C. Methods

Some of the important D.C. methods used for the determination of corrosion rate:

(*i*) Tafel extrapolation method;

(*ii*) Linear polarisation method;

(*iii*) Coulostatic method;

(*iv*) Small amplitude cyclic voltammetry method.

(i) Tafel Extrapolation Method: This method is based on electrochemical theory of corrosion. It involves the measurement of potential (E) of the electrode (against S.C.E.) for various applied current densities (I). The plot of E Vs log I gives a Figure known as polarisation diagram. At low current density the plot is non-linear and at high current densities the plot is linear in accordance with Tafel equation.

$$E = a + b \log I \quad ...(7.4)$$

where

E-potential of the speciman

I-current density

a and *b*-constants.

Usually both cathodic and anodic polarisation curves are obtained. The two lines in the linear regions are extrapolated to intersect at a point which corresponds to "Corrosion Current" (I_{corr}).

The polarisation curves can be obtained by galvanostatic, potentiostatic or potentiodynamic method. The main disadvantages in this method are

(*i*) A lot of values are required for each curve.

(*ii*) For systems with more than one cathodic reaction the linear or Tafel region is distorted.

(*iii*) Surface conditions of the systems are altered as a result of polarisation.

(*iv*) This method is applicable for reactions controlled by activation reactions and requires a conducting medium.

(*v*) The evaluation of Tafel constant through extrapolation is only approximate.

(ii) Linear Polarisation Method: The polarisation resistance R_p is defined as the tangent of a polarisation curve at E_{corr}

$$R_p = \left(\frac{dE}{di}\right) \qquad ...(7.5)$$

Stern-Greary observed that within ± 10 mV (or 20 mV) from corrosion potential, the applied current density is a linear function of the electrode potential. The slope of the curve, *i.e.*, R_p is related to corrosion current (i_{corr}) by the expression

$$\frac{dE}{di} = R_p = \frac{b_a b_c}{2.303 i_{corr}(b_a + b_c)} \qquad ...(7.6)$$

or

$$i_{corr} = \frac{(b_a b_c)}{2.303(b_a + b_c)} \times \frac{1}{R_p} \qquad ...(7.7)$$

where

b_a and b_c are anodic and cathodic Tafel slopes. If the cathodic process is diffusion controlled then eqn. (7.7) becomes

$$i_{corr} = \frac{b_a}{2.303} \frac{1}{R_p} \qquad ...(7.8)$$

Assuming b_a and b_c values to be 0.12 volt, the eqn. (7.8) reduces to

$$i_{corr} = \frac{0.026}{R_p} \qquad ...(7.9)$$

This equation may be used to calculate the corrosion rate of a system without the knowledge of its electrode-kinetic parameters.

Mansfeld and Kending have given the suitable sweep rates to be employed. Mansfeld used a computer programme (CORFIT) for curve fitting of experimental data to evaluate Tafel slopes from polarisation resistance.

A modified expression for certain corrosion system in which the electrode surface does not remain 'clean' has been proposed by the researchers.

He introduced a correlation factor which has been expressed as

$$Q_c = K \frac{E_{mv}}{\text{In t}} \qquad ...(7.10)$$

where K is the function for the process hindering the normal dissolution of test electrode.

(E_{mv}/In t) is the slope for the potential difference (E_{mv}) Vs the natural logarithm of time (In t) plot for the freely corroding surface $K = 1$.

It has been shown that R_p values are affected by I.R. drop. Williams and Taylor have used a current interrupt method for obtaining polarisation curves free of I.R. drop.

Methods like Coulostatic and Small Amplitude Cyclic Voltammetry (SACV) are some other important corrosion monitoring D.C. techniques.

A.C. Methods

(i) Impedance method: In recent years the impedance technique has become a popular tool for the measurement of corrosion rate. There are many advantages in this method. Some of them are

(*i*) Solution resistance is completely eliminated

(*ii*) Applicable to low conductivity systems

(*iii*) Provides mechanistic information.

The electrical equivalent circuit for the corroding system is given as

R_s - Solution resistance

R_t - Charge transfer resistance

W - Warburg impedance

C_{dl} - Double layer capacity.

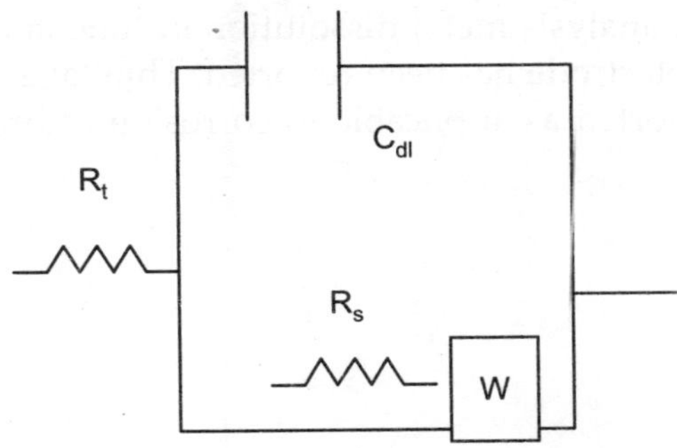

The cell impedance consists of real (Z′) and imaginary (Z″) parts. A sinusoidal current (or potential) perturbation of very small amplitude is applied as a function of frequency (usually 10 KHz to 10 MHz) for the determination of R_z. The impedance of corroding system for various frequencies can be measured using Lock-in amplifier or by using more sophisticated modern digital techniques.

A plot of Z′ Vs Z″ for various frequencies gives a semicircle which cuts the real axis at higher and at lower frequencies. At high frequency, Z corresponds to R_s and to low frequency Z corresponds to $(R_s + R_t)$. The difference between the two values gives R_t.

From the corresponding R_t value the corrosion current can be calculated using Stern-Geary equation.

$$I_{corr} = \frac{b_a b_c}{2.303(b_a + b_c)} x \frac{1}{R_t} \quad ...(7.11)$$

The double layer capacitance can be determined from the frequency at which Z″ is maximum

$$f_{(z''\max)} = \frac{1}{2\pi C_{dl} R_t} \quad ...(7.12)$$

Only R_t can be determined directly and the Tafel parameters have to be obtained by other methods.

The impedance diagrams are rather complex and exhibit several inductive and capacitive loops. For most corrosion systems, in the presence and the absence of the inhibitor, the impedance diagrams are rather complex and exhibit several inductive and capacitive loops. This makes interpretation of impedance diagram very difficult. More pracical A.C impedance measurements are described by Ohno and co-workers.

Others methods: Faradaic rectification method and Faradaic distortion method are some other important corrosion monitoring A.C. techniques [36-39]. Transient analysis metal dissolution in time and frequency domains by channel flow electrode has been reported. Thin layer activation technique has also been reported as applicable to corrosion of bronze.

8

Theory of Atmospheric Corrosion

A fundamental requirement for electrochemical corrosion processes is the presences of an electrolyte.Thin-film "invisible" electrolyte tend to form on metallic surfaces under atmospheric exposure conditions after a certain critical humidity level is reached. It has been shown that for iron, the critical humidity is 60 per cent in an atmosphere free of sulphur dioxide. The critical humidity level is not constant and depends on the corroding material, the tendency of corrosion products, surface deposits to absorb moisture and the presence of atmospheric pollutants. In the presence of thin-film electrolytes, atmospheric corrosion proceeds by balancing anodic and cathodic reactions. The anodic oxidation reaction involves the dissolution of the metal, while the cathodic reaction is often assumed to be the oxygen reduction reaction. It should be noted that corrosive contaminant concentrations can reach relatively high values in the thin electrolyte films, especially under conditions of alternate wetting and drying. Oxygen from the atmosphere is also readily supplied to the electrolyte under thin-film corrosion conditions. The cathodic process: If it is assumed that the surface electronic in extremely thin layers is neutral or even slightly acidic, then the hydrogen production reaction (Eq. 8.1) can be ignored for atmospheric corrosion of most metals and alloys.

$$2H^+ + 2e^- \rightarrow H_2 \qquad \text{(Eq. 8.1)}$$

Exceptions to this assumption would include corrosive attack under coatings, when the production of hydrogen can cause blistering of the coating, and other crevice corrosion conditions. The reduction of atmospheric oxygen is one of the most important reactions in which electrons are consumed. In the presence of gaseous air pollutants, other reduction reactions involving ozone and sulphur and nitrogen species have to be considered. For atmospheric corrosion in near-neutral electrolyte solution, the oxygen reduction reaction is applicable (Eq.)

$$O_2 + 2H_2O + 4e^- \rightarrow 4O\,H- \quad \text{(Eq. 8.2)}$$

Two reaction steps may actually be involved, with hydrogen peroxide as an intermediate, in accordance with

$$O_2 + 2H_2O + 2e^- \rightarrow 2H_2O_2 + 2e^- \quad \text{(Eq. 8.3)}$$

If oxygen from the atmosphere diffuses through the electrolyte film to the metal surface, a diffusion limited current density should apply. It has been shown that a diffusion transport mechanism for oxygen is applicable only to an electrolytelayer thickness of approximately 30 μm and under strictly isothermal conditions. The predicted theoretical limiting current density of oxygen reduction in an electrolyte-layer thickness of 30 μm significantly exceeds practical observations of atmospheric corrosion rates. It can be argued, therefore, that the over-all rates of atmospheric corrosion are likely to be controlled not by the cathodic oxygen reduction process, but rather by the anodic reactions. The anodic process: Equation represents the generalized anodic reaction that corresponds to the rate-determining step of atmospheric corrosion.

$$M \rightarrow Mn^+ + ne^- \quad \text{(Eq. 8.4)}$$

The formation of corrosion products, the solubility of corrosion products in the surface electrolyte, and the formation of passive films affect the overall rate of the anodic metal dissolution process and cause deviations from sample rate equations. Passive films distinguish themselves from corrosion products, in the sense that these films tend to be more tightly adherent, are of lower thickness, and provide a higher degree of protection from corrosive attack. Atmospheric corrosive attack on a surface protected by a passive film tends to be of a localized nature. Surface pitting and stress corrosion cracking in aluminum and stainless alloys are examples of such attack. Relatively complex reaction sequences have been proposed for the corrosion product formation and breakdown processes to explain observed atmospheric corrosion rates for different classes of metals. Fundamentally, kinetic modeling rather than equilibrium assessments appears to be appropriate for the dynamic conditions of alternate wetting and drying of surfaces corroding in the atmosphere. A framework for treating atmospheric corrosion phenomena on a theoretical basis, based on six different regimes, has been presented by Graedel. The regimes in this so-called GILDES-type model are the gaseous region (G), the gas-to-liquid interface (I), the surface liquid (L), the deposition layer (D), the electrodic layer (E), and the corroding solid (S). For the gaseous-layer effects, such as entrainment and detrainment of species across the liquid interface, chemical transformations in the gas phase, the effects of solar radiation on photosensitive atmospheric reactions, and temperature effects on the gas phase, reaction kinetics are important. In the interface regime, the transfer of molecules into the liquid layer prior to their chemical interaction in the liquid layer is studied. Not only does the liquid regime "receive" species from the gas phase, but species from the liquid are also volatilized into the gas phase. Important variables in the liquid regime include the aqueous film thickness and its effect on the concentration of species, chemical transformations in the liquid, and reactions involving metal ions originating from the electrochemical corrosion reactions. In the deposition zone, corrosion products will accumulate, following their nucleation on the substrate. The corrosion products formed under thin film atmospheric conditions are closely related to the formation of naturally occurring minerals. Over long periods of time, the most thermodynamically stable species will tend to dominate. The natures of corrosion products found on different metals exposed to the atmosphere are shown in Table 8.1. The solution known as the "inner electrolyte" can be trapped inside or under the corrosion products formed. The deposited corrosion product layers can thus be viewed as membranes, with varying degrees of resistance to ionic transport. Passivating films tend to represent strong barriers to ionic transport.

Table 8.1 : Nature of Corrosion Products formed on Four Metals

Common species	Rarer species
Al	$Al(OH)_3$, Al_2O_3, $Al_2\,O_3$, $3H_2\,OAlOOH$, Alx (OH)Y (SO_4)Z, $AlC(OH)_2$, $4H_2O$
Fe	Fe_2O_3, FeOOH, $FeSO_4$, $4H_2\,O$ Fex (OH)Y Clz, $FeCO_3$
Cu	$Cu_2\,O$, $Cu_4\,SO_4\,(OH)_6$, $Cu_4SO_4(OH)_6$, $2H_2\,O$, $Cu_3\,SO_4$ (OH)
	$_4Cu_2\,Cl(OH)_3$, $Cu_2\,CO_3\,(OH)_2$, $Cu_2\,NO_3\,(OH)_3$
Zn	ZnO, $Zn_5(OH)_6\,(CO_3)2$, $ZnCO_3\,Zn(OH)_2$, $ZnSO_4$, $Zn_5\,Cl_2$ $(OH)_8$, H_2O

Any corroding surface has a complex charge distribution, producing in the adjacent electrolyte a microscopic layer with chemical and physical properties that differ from those of the nominal electrolyte. This electrodic regime influences the overall reaction kinetics in atmospheric corrosion processes. In the solid regime, the detailed mechanistic steps (sequences) in the dissolution of the solid and their kinetic characteristics are relevant.

Experimental Procedure

Inhibitors (VCI)

2-Dec-9-enyl-2-imidazoline was synthesized according to the literature and the salt were prepared by dissolving equimolar fatty acids in ethanol. The reaction was stirred for 60 minute at 40°C. The precipitated compounds were filtered and crystallized from ethanol. All compounds were purified by crystallization and their purity was conformed using thin layer chromatography. Name, structural formula of the compounds is shown in Table 8.2.

Table 8.2 : Structural Formula of Compound *s* used as VPIs

Molecular structure of the compounds used

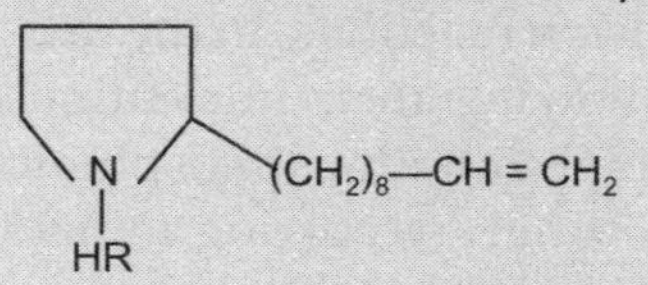

N — $(CH_2)_8$—CH = CH_2

HR

(2-Dec-9-enyl-2-imidazoline nitrobenzoate)

(DIN)

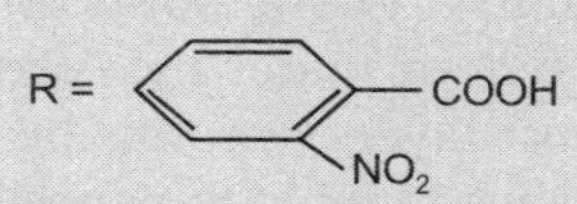

R = — COOH, NO_2

(2-Dec-9-enyl-2-imidazoline phthalate)

(DIP)

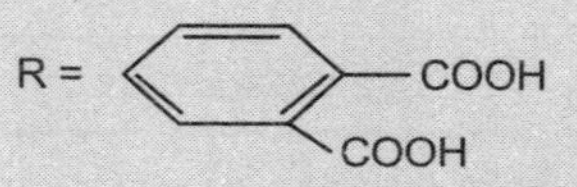

R = — COOH, COOH

(2-Dec-9-enyl-2-imidazoline cinnamate

(DIC)

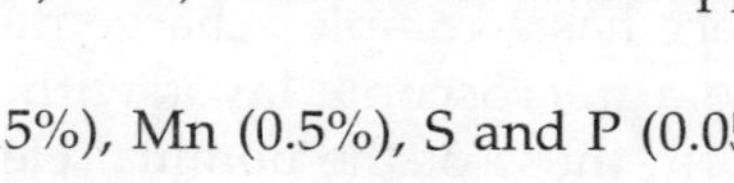

R = — CH=CH.COOH

Samples and their Composition

Test plates of mild steel, zinc, aluminium and copper have the following chemical composition:

(*a*) Mild steel C-(0.15%), Mn (0.5%), S and P (0.05%) and balance Fe.

(*b*) Zinc 98% purity.

(*c*) Aluminium, commercially available.

(*d*) Copper, commercially available.

The determination of corrosion rate of specimen a special frame will be designed and it is insulated with insulating material, in this arrangement the frame is fixed upon 20-30 ft height on ground level and fixing sample on horizontal of ground making an angle approximately 90°.

Corrosion Rate Expressions

Mostly the rates of corrosion of metals are expressed as mpy or mmpy.

The relative scale for corrosion of metal is given as:

Safe: Less than 5 mpy or 0.125 mmpy.

Moderate: 5 mpy to 50 mpy or 0.125 mmpy to 1.25 mmpy.

Severe: Greater than 50 mpy or 1.25 mmpy.

The rate of corrosion of metal is usually measured either by gravimetric method or by electrochemical methods. The conversion factors for the two methods are.

Gravimetric Method

$$\text{Corrosion rate (mmpy)} = \frac{87.6 \times \text{weight loss (mg)}}{\text{Area (cm}^2) \times \text{time (hrs)} \times \text{Density}}$$

Weight Loss Studies

All samples were hanging with the support of designed frame with nylon threads. Three types of time duration *viz.* monthly, seasonal and yearly were considered for the determination of corrosion rate. All tests were carried out in triplicate and their mean values were taken as final values were taken. After exposure period test plates were warped in a plastic bag and coded to laboratory for cleaning weighted and corrosion rate is calculated using corrosion rate expressions.

Table 8.3 : Weight Loss Parameters Obtained for 500 ppm Concentration of VCIs at (40 ± 1) °C and 90% Humidity for 30 days for various Metals

System	Weight loss (mg)	Inhibition Efficiency %	CR (mmpy × 10^{-2})
Mild Steel	34.5	—	8.00
DIN	1.7	95.12	0.39
DIP	1.5	95.75	0.35
DIC	1.0	97.12	0.23
Copper	5.7	—	1.16
DIN	0.8	86.20	0.16
DIP	0.6	89.65	0.12
DIC	0.5	91.37	0.10

The same composition samples were used for the weight loss measurement in laboratory carried out in the presence and absence of inhibitors at a fixed concentration of 500 ppm, using tight fitting rubber cork 250 ml conical flasks containing 25 ml of water-glycerin mixture to produce 90 per cent relative humidity. The metal specimen were suspended in these flask by nylon tags and just below these specimens weighed VCIs samples were kept in a glass container as not to be contact with the liquid kept inside the conical flask. The temperature of flask were maintained (40±1°C) and relative humidity 90% during the day and were removed at night to allow condensation of moisture on metal specimen. The experiment was conducted for 30 days. The weight loss parameter such as weight loss, percentage inhibition efficiency and corrosion rate using corrosion rate expression are listed in Table 8.3.

Results and Discussion

Meteorological and Pollution Data

Temperature data with minimum and maximum of year 2005 and 2006 is shown in Figure 8.1. It was found that April, May, June and July are the hot months of the year whereas December, January and February are considered to be cold months. The data of rain fall of the year 2005 and year 2006 is mentioned in Figure 8.2. Generally the rain starts in last June or July and continues upto October. Total annual rain fall was measured as 706 mm in 2005 and 698 mm in 2006. The prominent direction of wind is south west during the summer and monsoon season. Under these conditions, polluted gases from industries would travel to north east direction. The mean relative humidity data of the year 2005 and year 2006 is mentioned in Figure 8.3.

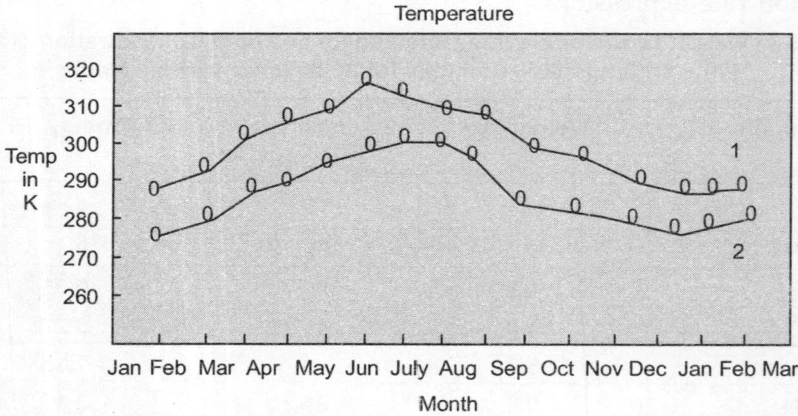

Fig. 8.1 : Maximum and minimum Temperature at Delhi in 2005-2006 (1 max) and (2 min).

Mild Steel (MS)

Monthly mass loss of mild steel was found in the range of 258 to 1265 mg/sq.dm/month whereas yearly mass loss was found in the range of 12000 to 13205 mg/sq.dm is presented in Figure 8.4. Monthly mass loss of mild steel indicates a satisfactory correlation with rain fall as well as with mean relative

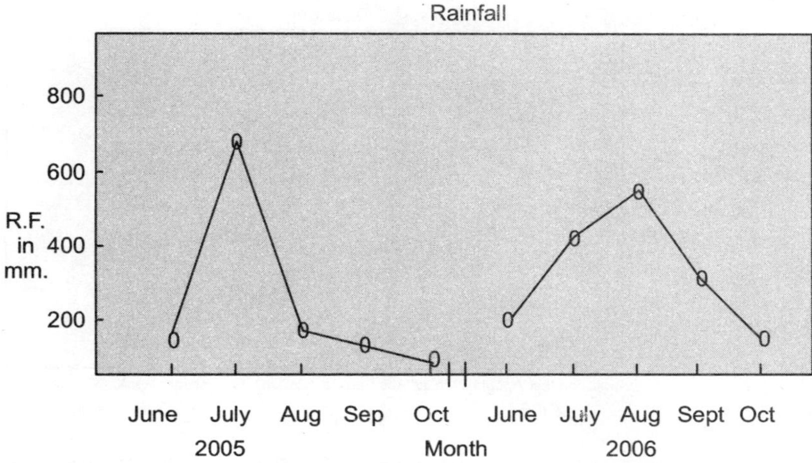

Fig. 8.2 : Rainfall (in mm) at Delhi in 2005-2006.

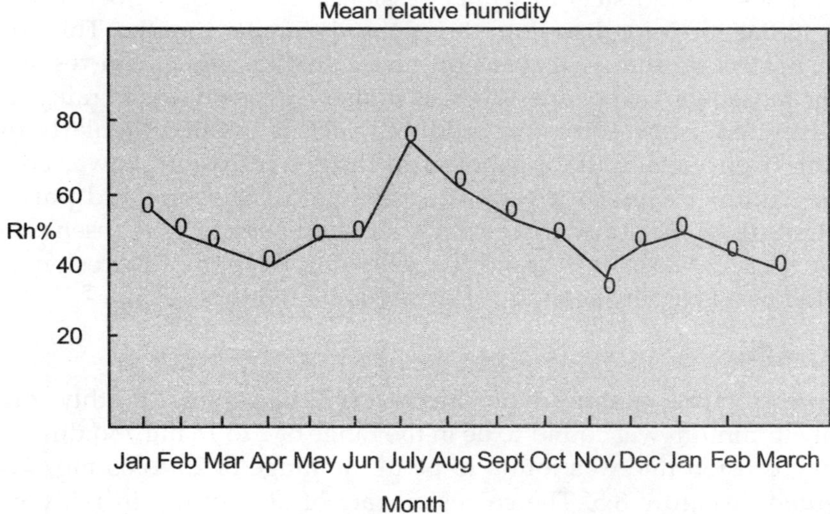

Fig. 8.3 : Mean relative Humidity (% Rh) at Delhi in year 2005-2006.

humidity. No correlation appeared to exist between temperature and mass loss of mild steel. Corrosion rate of mild steel in rainy month is higher than that of hot month and winter months because the humidity is high in rainy month. It is found that the rate of corrosion is approximately doubled in rainy month's compaired to hot as well as winter session. Samples of mild steel exposed to rainy months initially developed tiny (1 to 2 mm in diameter) yellow spots within a weak which turn reddish yellow then orange brown and finally black in colour after three months exposure period.

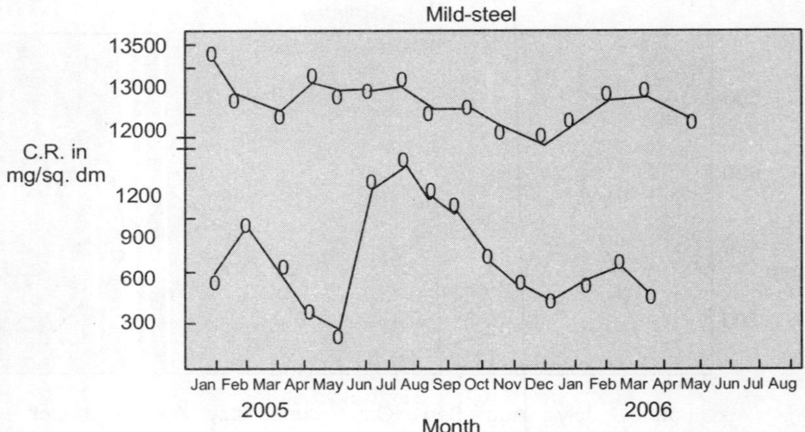

Fig. 8.4 : Monthly and Yearly Corrosion Rate of Mild Steel under Outdoor Exposure during Different Months in 2005-2006 (1 Yearly) and (2-Monthly).

Samples of mild steel in winter session indicate (December to January) lower initial corrosion loss than the exposed to rainy months. This suggests that a protective film is formed on metal surface which can resist attack during subsequent exposure. Whereas higher corrosion rate in rainy months are attributed to the corrosion product which is washed regularly by rain keeping fresh metal surface exposed to further corrosion. Lower corrosion rate in summer months are due to removal of gaseous and particulate pollutants from the atmosphere by higher wind velocity and absence of rain. On the seasonal basis it is found the following relation of corrosion of mild steel follows as: Rainy session > Hot session > Winter session.

Aluminium

The corrosion rate of aluminium shows very little values. Monthly corrosion rate of aluminium was found to be in the range of 2 to 18 mg./sq.dm whereas yearly corrosion rate was found to be in the range of 25 to 65 mg/sq.dm is presented in Figure 8.5. The corrosion rate of aluminium in rainy months (12.5 mg/sq.dm) was higher than the rate of summer months (6.5 mg/sq.dm) and winter months (3.8 mg/sq.dm). No correlation appeared to exist between corrosion rate of aluminium and temperature. Low corrosion rate of aluminium in outdoor exposure is attributed to the formation of a protective oxide layer on the metal surface which might have offered protection to the metal from reacting with the surrounding environment. The results agree well with a previous report that aluminium is highly resistant to normal out door exposure condition and the rate of attack greatly decreases with increase in the time of exposure due to a self stopping action.

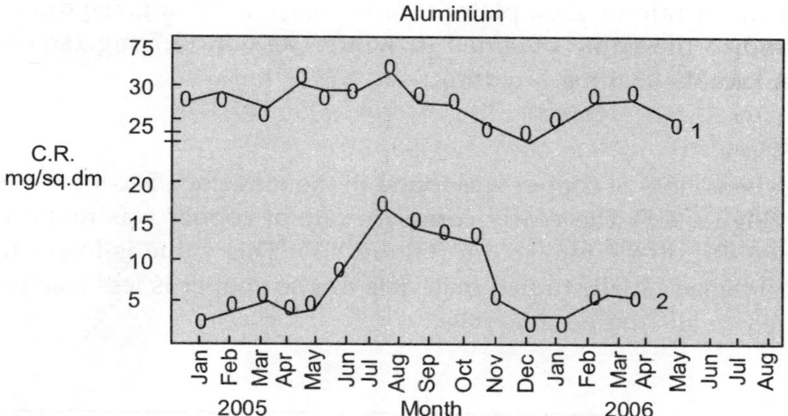

Fig. 8.5 : Monthly and Yearly Corrosion Rate of Aluminium under Outdoor exposure during Different Months in 2005-2006 (1-Yearly) and (2-Monthly).

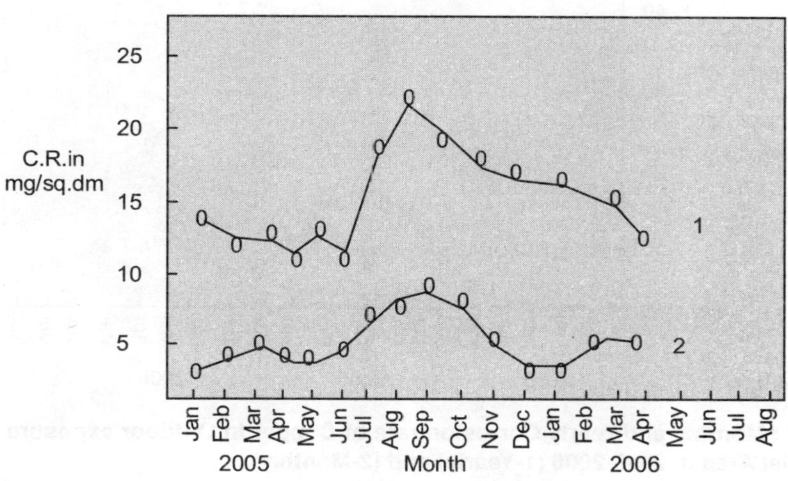

Fig. 8.6 : Monthly and Yearly Corrosion Rate of Zinc under Outdoor exposure during Different Months in 2005-2006 (1-Yearly) and (2-Monthly).

Zinc

Monthly mass loss of Zinc at Delhi was found in the range of 2.5 to 9.6 mg/sq.dm/month, is presented in Figure 8.6 whereas the monthly corrosion rate was found in the range of 67 to 167 mg/sq.dm at Ankleshwar, 3.2 to 10.8 mg/sq.dm at Kanpur [14], 12 to 40 mg/sq.dm at Mumbai, and 10.7 to 42.5 mg/sq.dm at Baroda. The yearly corrosion rate of Zinc was found to be in the range of 12 to 23.5 mg/sq.dm (Figure 8.6). This value is lower than the values obtained at Kanpur (27 mg/sq.dm) and Mumbai (111 to 545 mg/sq.dm)

Corrosion rate of Zinc plate in rainy season (9.6 mg./sq.dm.) is high compared to the value obtained in winter session (2.7 mg./sq.dm.) and summer months (3.8 mg./sq.dm.).

Copper

Monthly mass loss of copper was found in the range of 1.5 to 4.6 mg/sq./dm month (Figure 8.7) The yearly corrosion rate of copper was found to be in the range of 2 to 8.5 mg/sq.dm (Figure 8.7). This value is lower than the values obtained on all studied materials this so copper is less reactive metal compared to all studied materials.

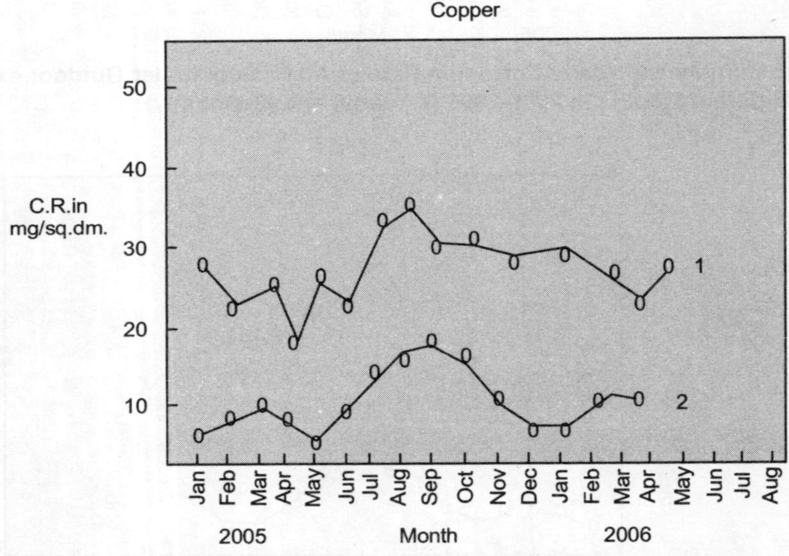

Fig. 8.7 : Monthly and Yearly Corrosion rate of Copper in Outdoor exposure at Delhi Industrial Area in 2005-2006 (1-Yearly) and (2-Monthly).

Corrosion rate of copper plate in rainy season (5.2 mg/sq.dm) is high compared to the value obtained in winter session (2.4 mg/sq.dm) and summer months (3.5 mg/sq.dm).

Weight Loss Measurements

The values of percentage inhibition efficiency (% I.E) and corrosion rate (CR) obtained by weight loss methods at 500 ppm concentration of VCIs for mild steel and copper at 40 ± 1 °C are summarized in Table 8.3. The weight per cent I.E. was calculated using the following equation:

$$\%I.E. = [(CR'' - CR)/CR''] \times 100$$

Where CR″ and CR are the corrosion rate in the absence and presence of inhibitors, respectively. The corrosion rate was calculated using corrosion rate expression.

All studied VCIs have shown good inhibition efficiency, which may be attributed to the formation of a physical barrier between metal and corrosive environment by the interaction of metal and inhibitor molecules. The corrosion inhibiting action of the volatile corrosion inhibitors is attributed to the presence of lone pair of electrons present on the N atom of the inhibitor molecules, which facilitate adsorption of these inhibitors onto the metal surface. In the present investigation, all studied cinnamate salt exhibited highest inhibition efficiency for all the metals. It gave 95-97 percent for mild steel and 86-91 per cent for copper respectively. The high inhibition efficiency of this VPIs is due to the presence of an additional π-bond between C = C which further facilitate greater adsorption on the metal surface.

Conclusion

All the examined samples were corroded in outdoor exposure of environment; mild steel corroded rapidly compared to all studied metallic alloys. The corrosion rate of rainy session is higher than the all other session. All the tested organic inhibitors showed good inhibition efficiency (IE) for mild steel and copper at (40±1°C) on relative humidity 90 per cent. These are suggested for the use of the protections of mild steel and copper for outdoor exposure condition because Delhi industrial area temps vary from (2-48°C).

REFERENCES

ASTM Standards, *Method for Chimerical Cleaning after Testing*, 41-72 (1978) 681.

Barton, K., 1976. *Protection against Atmospheric Corrosion*, John Wiley and Sons, London.

Black, H.L. and Lherbier L.W., 1968. *Metal Corrosion in the Atmosphere*, ASTM STP, 435:3.

Briggs, C.W., 1968. *Metal Corrosion in the Atmosphere*. ASTM STP; 435:271.

Brown, P.W. and Masters L.W.,1982. *Atmospheric Corrosion*, Wiley, New York.

Brown, P.W. and Masters L.W.,1982. *Atmospheric Corrosion*, Wiley, New York.

Chawla, S.K. and Payer J.H., 1990. *Corros*. 46:860.

Evans, U.R. and Hoar T.P., 1932. *Proc. Roy. Soc.* (A), 137-343.

Fontana, M.G. 1987. *Corrosion Engineering*, 3rd Ed. McGraw-Hill Book Company Inc., New York.

Graedel, T.E., 1996. *Corros. Sci.*, 38:2153.

Grossman, P.R., 1987. *Atmospheric Factors Affecting Engineering Metals*, ASTM ST, 646.

Lipfert, F.W. 1987. *Mater. Perf.*, 26:12.

Money, K.L., 1987. *Metals Handbook Corrosion*, Metals Park, Ohio, ASM International, 204.

Naeemi, A.H. and Albrecht P., 1984. *Int. Cong. Metallic Corros.*, Toronto, Canada, 418.

Naixin, X, Zhao L, Ding C, Zhang C, Li R and Zhong Q, *Corros. Sci.*, (2002) 44-163.

Oesch, S and Faller M, 1997. *Corros. Sci.*, 39:1505.

Pourbaix, M and Pourbaix A., 1989. *Corros.* 45: 71.

Quraishi, M.A. and D. Jamal. *Indian Journal of Chemical Tech.* 11 (2004) 459-464.

Sanyal, B. and G.K. Singhania, Atmospheric Corrosion of Metals, Part-I, *Journal of Sci Industrial Research*, 15-B (1956) 448.

Sanyal, B., A.N. Nandi, A. Natrajan and D. Bhadwar, Atmospheric Corrosion of Metals, Pt II Corrosion of Metals in Bombay. *Journal of Mandapam Camp*, India, Corrosion, 15 (1958) 25.

Scully, J.C., 1990. *The Fundamentals of Corrosion* 3rd Edn., Pergamon Press, New York.

Speller, F.N., 1951. *Corrosion (Causes and Prevention)* McGraw-Hill Book Company Inc., New York.

Spller, F.N., Corrosion courses and Prevention, McGraw-Hill, New York (1961) 163.

Stiles, D.C. and Edney E.O. 1989. *Corros.* 45: 896.

Talati, J.D. and B.M. Patel, *Atmospheric Corrosion of Metals in Patan* (NG), Vidya, X-2 (1967) 182-186.

Thomas, H.E. and Alderson H.N., 1968. *Metal Corrosion in the Atmosphere*, ASTM STP; 435:83.

Trimgham, T.C.E., 1958. *Causes and Prevention of Corrosion in AIR Craft*, SIR ISAAC, Pitman & Sons, Ltd.

Uhlig, H.H., *Corrosion Hand Book*, John Wiley and Sons, Inc, New York (1961) 51.

Uhling, H.H., *Corrosion*, 29 (1950) 6.

Vashi, R.T. and R.N. Patel, Atmospheric Corrosion Study of Barodra Industrial Area. Bulletin of Electrochemistry, 13(8-9). (1997) 343-347.

Vashi, R.T. and R.N. Patel, Atmospheric Corrosion Study of Surat Industrial Area. *Bulletin of Electrochemistry* 12(7-8) (1996) 477-481.

Vashi, R.T., G.M. Malek, V.A. Champaneri and R.N. Patel., Atmopsheric Corrosion Study at Ankleshwar Industrial Area, *Bulletin of Electrochemistry*, 18(2) (2002), 91-96.

Vassie P.R., 1987. Br. Corros. J., 22:37.

Vernon, W.H.J., *Metallic Corrosica and Conservation. The Conservation of National Resources*, Institution of Civil Engineers, London (1957) 105 to 133.

Vilche, J.R., Varela F.E., Acuna G., Codaro E.N., Rosales B.M., 1995. Fernandez A and Moriena G., *Corros. Sci.*, 37:941.

Walters, G.W., 1991. *Corros. Sci.*, 32: 1331.

Walters, G.W., 1991. *Corros. Sci.*, 32:1353.

9

Methods of Corrosion Control

In this field of combating corrosion both economic and scientific considerations are involved. The greater knowledge of the electrochemical aspects of corrosion science has paved the way for the development of newer techniques for combating corrosion.

The methods of corrosion prevention are many and varied. The general classification may be given below:

Corrosion Control Methods

Modification of metal		Modification of environment		Change of metal environment potential
↓		↓		↓
By alloying (or surface modification		By the use of inhibitors		Cathodic and anodic protection

As the present work relates to the use of inhibitors for acid corrosion of mild steel, it is being separately dealt with in the next chapter. However, the other methods are briefly mentioned in this chapter.

Modification of Metal

By bulk alloying or surface coating, the metal is modified to get protected from corrosion. Surface coating is far more economic than bulk alloying. Surface coatings may pose problems related to adhesion, thermal expansion compatibility, etc. Surface processing of metals has been improved by ion implantation technique and Laser treatment which result in a homogenous often single phase surface layer.

Electron beam surface area glazing has been found to increase the wear life of ironbase tool materials.

Cathodic Protection

Cathodic protection is an important method to reduce the corrosion rate. An external D.C. power source and an auxiliary power source are used to pass a net cathodic current, thereby corrosion rate is reduced. By applying a suitable cathodic current it is possible to bring down the corrosion rate to the desired level. This method becomes expensive for large structures like pipelines, ships, etc. In such cases "sacrificial anodes" are used to protect the metal cathodically, *e.g.*, in the protection of the hulls of ships and boats from corrosion an active metal, generally zinc, is used as a sacrificial anode in contact with corrodible metal. The two metals in contact form a cell and the terminals of them have been shorted. Zinc slowly dissolves while the other metal is cathodically protected.

Impressed current anodes are also used for cathodic protection. In this system the anodes are not used as the source of electrical energy. Instead, an external source of direct current is connected within the structure to be protected. The positive terminal of the power source is always connected to the anode and the negative terminal is connected to the structure to be protected.

Examples of impressed current anodes are graphite, scrap iron and platinum and lead-silver alloys. Rectifiers are used as power sources in this system.

The main advantage of impressed current system over galvanic system, which has a definite maximum current input, is that the protecting current can be increased, if necessary by increasing the applied voltage.

The impressed current system is a more versatile method. But the main difficulty anode leads must be insulated well and water proofed and continuous electrical must be available. Online monitoring of cathodic protection and the performance of embeddable reference electrodes has been reported.

Anodic Protection

Here the potential is set in the positive region and the structure to be protected is made as the anode. The nature of auxiliary electrode is of little importance in this case since it is the cathode and is cathodically protected. The current density in the passive region is extremely small and so the electric power needed for anodic protection is much smaller than that required for cathodic protection.

In the presence of Cl^- ions the passivation does not occur on iron and ferrous alloys. This is the limitation of this method. Anodic protection is applied to steel containers for storage of sulphuric and phosphoric acid. A detailed analysis of the nature and quality of passive films by electrochemical techniques for stainless steel has been reported.

Corrosion Inhibitors

The corrosion inhibitor may be described as a chemical species or combination of species that when present in the appropriate concentration reduce but not necessarily eliminate the corrosion. These species can range from chemical species that chemically adsorb into a surface to those that react with the surface to change its structure to a more inert state.

In industries acid solutions are widely used for most important purposes such as acid pickling, industrial acid cleaning, acid descaling, etc. Among the commercially acids the most frequently used for pickling are hydrochloric acid and sulphuric acid. Other acids such as nitric, phosphoric, oxalic, tartaric, citric and acetic acids are also widely used only for special applications.

The most formed in the metal is usually removed by pickling. It is a process carried out to remove the oxide scales (mills scale or rust) from a metal by immersing in a suitable acid solution called pickling bath. The acid after dissolving the scale, attacks the metal. Certain substances are added to acid solution in small concentration to reduce the metal corrosion and they are called inhibitors. Schmitt has carried out detailed study of prominent inhibitors which protect ferrous metals from the above mentioned acids during acid pickling. Inhibition is the most extensively studied topic in the field of corrosion.

Researchers have done a detailed review study on corrosion inhibitors. Various papers on corrosion inhibitors have been published. Generally, organic compounds such as amines, aldehydes, thiophenols, mercaptans, sulphides and phosphonium compounds are used as acid pickling inhibitors.

Classification of Inhibitors

Inhibitors are classified in different ways. Depending on the environment they are called acid, neutral, alkaline and vapour phase inhibitors. They are also classified as cathodic, anodic and mixed inhibitors, based on the inhibition nature of the inhibitors.

The following observations have been concluded for inhibitors:

- Type A forms a protective film on the metal surface.
- Type B reduces the aggressiveness of corrosion media.
- Type AB forms a protective film and also reduces the aggressiveness of the corrosive agent.

(i) Acid Inhibitors: These may be further classified into (*a*) Organic and (*b*) Inorganic inhibitors.

(a) Organic inhibitors: A large number of organic compounds have been studied widely as inhibitors. These compounds include alcohols, amines, aldehydes, mercaptans, alkaloids, sulphur compounds such as thiourea and its derivatives and quaternary ammonium and quaternary phosphonium compounds.

Those compounds which have active hetero atoms such as N, S, O or P are found to have good inhibition capacity.

The effectiveness of a large number of organic inhibitors has been correlated to different factors like compound structure, molecular weight, carbon chain length, basicity (pK_a), dipole moment, magnetic susceptibility, NMR shift, etc.

An organic corrosion inhibitor can be anodic, cathodic or mixed type depending on its reaction at the metal surface and how the potential of the metal is affected. Generally the cathodic inhibitors enhance cathodic polarisation and shift the corrosion potential to more negative values while the anodic inhibitors increase anodic polarisation and shift the corrosion potential to more positive values.

The effectiveness of an organic inhibitor depends mainly on the following factors:

(*i*) molecular size;

(*ii*) carbon chain length;

(*iii*) bonding strength to metal surface;

(*iv*) aromaticity and/or conjugated bonding;

(*v*) nature and number of bonding atoms; and

(*vi*) atoms with lone pair of electrons.

The influences of N-heterocyclics and heterocyclic anils on the corrosion inhibition and hydrogen permeation through mild steel in acidic environment have been reported by Venkatakrishna Iyer *et al.*

(b) Inorganic inhibitors: Many inorganic compounds have been studied as inhibitors. The oxides like As_2O_3, Sb_2O_3 have been reported as pickling inhibitors in acid media. In strong acid solutions, Br^-, Cl^- have been found to be effective inhibitors. Recently it has been reported that addition of heavy metal ions like Pb^{2+}, Mn^{2+}, Cd^{2+} is found to inhibit corrosion of iron in acids. The effect is explained as due to under potential deposition of metal ions leading to complete coverage on the iron surface. The inhibition effects of some inorganic multivalent cations for iron corrosion in aerated sodium sulphate solution have also been reported.

(ii) Alkaline and Neutral Inhibitors: These inhibitors include cathodic inhibitors, anodic inhibitors (passivating inhibitors) and mixed or general inhibitors.

Anodic inhibitors form an oxide or some other insoluble film. Insufficient concentration of anodic inhibitors will lead to poor pitting.

Sodium chromate is one of the most widely used inhibitors in alkaline and neutral media. Sodium silicate is generally used in hot water systems. The other compounds other compounds used in neutral and alkaline media are borates, molybdates and salts of organic acids, like benzoates and salicylates.

(iii) Vapour Phase Inhibitors: These inhibitors are mainly used to reduce the volatile corrosion. Hence these are also called volatile corrosion inhibitors. They are transported to the site of corrosion in a closed system by volatalisation from a source. They are used in boilers, to prevent corrosion, in condenser tubes by neutralizing the acidic CO_2. Compounds of this type inhibit corrosion by making the environment alkaline.

Protection of mild steel corrosion by some amine based vapour phase inhibitors and vapour phase inhibitor coated paper have been reported. Volatile solids such as nitrite and benzoate salts of dicyclohexylamine and cyclohexylamine and its derivatives are used in closed vapour phase like shipping containers.

The vapour inhibitor condenses on contacting a metal surface and is hydrolysed by moisture present to liberate nitrate and benzoate ions which in the presence of available oxygen passivates the steel surface as they do in aqueous solution.

Adsorption and its Influence on Inhibition of Corrosion

The ions and molecules of the inhibitor adsorb on the metal surface. This adsorption of ions and molecules at an electrified interface is of fundamental importance in all aspects of aqueous corrosion.

Rose and Jones used the radio-active technique by using labelled thiourea (S^{35}) that the adsoption of the inhibitor on iron was found to be uniform and about 90 per cent adsorption occurs in 5-10 minutes.

Since the corrosion reaction is heterogeneous, the reaction sequence involves at least one surface step. Organic inhibitors which presumably are not capable of oxidizing or precipitating the metal ion, but have the ability to adsorb and also alter either cathodic, lie or both the reactions.

Most of the organic inhibitors such as the heterocyclic nitrogenous compounds believed to be cathodic inhibitors, *i.e.*, they get adsorbed on cathodic sites and prevent the cathodic reaction. But it has been shown by Hoar that in some cases (beta naphthaquinoline) anodic inhibition has also been observed.

The mode of adsorption depends on:

(*i*) the nature of the metal surface,

(*ii*) the structure of the molecule.

The following are the principal types of adsorption associated with organic inhibitors:

(*i*) Electrostatic adsorption or Electrosorption

(*ii*) Chemisorption and π-orbital adsorption

(*iii*) Physical or Van der Waal's type of adsorption.

Electrostatic Adsorption

As most of the corrosion reactions in aqueous solutions are electrochemical in nature, organic molecules adsorb at metal-solution interface and it is termed as electrostatic adsorption or electrosorption. Electrosorption is different from chemisorption. In electrosorption the coulombic electrical forces which stretch out from the metal to affect the solution are much longer in range than the chemical forces which affect the molecules in chemisorption.

(*i*) **Coulombic adsorption (Similar to physical adsorption):** A layer of water molecules at the surface of the electrode divides the electrode metal from the solution. In this case there are no ions in direct contact with the metal.

(*ii*) **Contact adsorption:** It is analogous to chemisorption. Ions actually come into contact with the electrode in this kind of adsorption. But there need not necessarily be a chemical bond between the adsorbed species and the metal. The ions simply contact the electrode and remain attached.

(*iii*) **Zero charge potential (Z.C.P.) and Electrostatic adsorption:** The potential at which there is zero charge on a metal is called, zero charge potential. The Zero Charge Potential values are of fundamental importance in electrochemistry, since it provides information on adsorption of ions and molecules. It is significant that the tendency of the metal to have excess negative and an excess positive charge are equally balanced resulting no charge on it.

Electrostatic adsorption depends on Z.C.P. of a metal surface and the position of corrosion potential with respect to Z.C.P. The adsorption of organic inhibitor depends on the sign and magnitude of 'rational' corrosion potential $\theta(\theta = E_{corr} - E_{q=0})$ and on the sign of the charge on the inhibitor. The Z.C.P. values of various metal electrolyte systems can be used to determine the rational corrosion potential. Thus for the adsorption of cationic species θ potential must be positive. It has been shown that the inhibitor efficiency of organic nitrogen containing compounds for ion in acid is higher when the θ potential is more negative.

Chemisorption and π-Orbital Adsorption

A chemical bond which is established through an atom containing an unshared pair of electrons is known as the chemisorption of organic molecules. Besides the electrosorption and chemisorption, the adsorption may result from π-orbital interaction with the metal. Organic compounds with double and triple bonds, and those containing aromatic nucleus interact with metal by their π-bond orbitals.

Physical or Van der Wall's Type of Adsorption

Here the adsorbed molecules are held by weak Van der Wall's forces. Since there is no chemical bond formation, the heat of adsorption is very small (ranging from 0 to 20 kJ mol^{-1} of the adsorbate) compared to heat of chemisorption (80 to 400 kJ mol^{-1}). Physically adsorbed molecules on solids often from multilayer. As the forces operating are Van der Wall's type, the adsorbed molecules may easily be removed or desorbed from the surface by lowering the bulk concentration of the adsorbate.

Correlation Between Adsorption and Inhibition of Corrosion

The inhibition of corrosion both in acidic and neutral medium is initiated by adsorption. The adsorption of organic inhibitor on the metal surface forms an indispensable condition for the inhibiting action. The magnitude of sign and charge on the metal is important in adsorption.

The adsorption of dimemylsulphoxide on mercury is found to be less by Subramanyan which clearly agrees with the poor inhibition of corrosion of mild steel in acid by the organic compound.

A correlation between the electro capillary behaviour and corrosion inhibitive nature of few organic sulphur compounds like dimethyl sulphides, dibutyl sulphides, diphenylsulphide and thiophene using H_2SO_4 as the electrolyte has been done by Subramanyan. Except for thiophenes a quantitative correlation was observed between the electro capillary behaviour and corrosion inhibition. Methyl group enhances the activity of sulphur to cause greater adsorption of dimethyl sulphide on mercury and improved corrosion prevention, whereas the phenyl group in diphenyl sulphide has the opposite effect.

All these studies clearly prove a correlation between adsorption and the corrosion inhibition.

Adsorption Isotherms

An adsorption isotherm is the mathematical expression that relates the bulk concentration of an adsorbent to the surface concentration at constant temperature. It gives the relationship between the coverage of an interface with the adsorbate (*i.e.*, the amount adsorbed) and concentration of the species in solution.

Plots of the variation in corrosion rate with various concentrations of inhibitors have the appearance of being mirror images of adsorption isotherms for most of the organic inhibitors. This strongly suggests that adsorption of the inhibitor on the metal surface (partly) accounts for the inhibition mechanism.

Various adsorption isotherms have been formulated. Various isotherms and the corresponding equations are given in the Table 9.1. The adsorption process is related to the chemical structure and the electrochemical process that occur on the metal surface.

Table 9.1

Sl.No.	Isotherm	Equation
1.	Langmuir	$b_c = \frac{\theta}{1-\theta}$
2.	*Freundlich*	$b_c n = \theta$
3.	Frumkin	$b_c = \frac{\theta}{1-\theta} \exp^{(-2a\theta)}$
4.	Temkin	$b_c = \frac{\exp^{a\theta} - 1}{1 - \exp^{(-a(1-\theta)}}$
5.	Parsons	$b_c = \frac{\theta}{1-\theta} \exp \frac{(2-\theta)}{(1-\theta)^2} \exp^{(-2a\theta)}$
6.	Bockris-Devanathan and Muller (B.D.M)	$\log C + \log \frac{\theta}{1-\theta} = C + b\theta^{3/2}$

where

$$b = e^{-\Delta G}_{ads} / RT$$

$$a = \text{Interaction parameter}$$

$$a > 0 = \text{Attraction}$$

$$a < 0 = \text{Repulsion.}$$

Most of the organic inhibitors obey Langmuir or Temkin adsorption isotherm. The inhibitor is found to obey Langmuir, if a plot of log $\theta/(1-\theta)$ Vs log C is linear. Similarly for Temkin a plot of θ Vs log C, for B.D.M. a plot of (log C – log $\theta/(1-\theta)$) Vs $\theta^{3/2}$ and for Frumkin a plot of log $\theta(1-\theta)$C Vs θ will be linear.

Methods of Evaluation of Inhibitors

Non-Electrochemical Methods

The effectiveness of an inhibition is assessed in terms of its inhibition efficiency (I.E.) which is given by the formula

$$\text{I.E\%} = \frac{W_0 - W_1}{W_0} \times 100 \qquad (9.1)$$

where W_0 is the weight loss of specimen in the given medium in the absence of inhibitor, W_1 is the weight loss in the presence of inhibitor. The weight losses are found by keeping exactly identical specimens in the medium in the presence and the absence of inhibitor for the same time at a constant temperature.

Similarly the volumes of hydrogen gas liberated in the presence and the absence of inhibitor can be measured using gasometric technique and the inhibitor efficiency is calculated with the following equation

$$\text{I.E\%} = \frac{V_0 - V_1}{V_0} \times 100 \qquad (9.2)$$

where V_0 is the volume of hydrogen liberated in the absence of inhibitor and V_1 is the volume of hydrogen liberated in the presence of inhibitor. This method is unsuitable when

(*i*) the inhibitors react with hydrogen and

(*ii*) there is considerable hydrogen penetration.

Electrochemical Methods

The following electrochemical methods are most widely used for the study of inhibitors:

Polarisation Method

Corrosion is regarded as an electrochemical phenomenon consisting of anodic (metal dissolution) and cathodic (hydrogen evolution) processes. Hence the behaviour of the inhibitor can be understood by carrying out separately cathodic and anodic polarisation in the presence and absence of inhibitor. The corrosion current can be measured by extrapolating the anodic and cathodic polarisation curve to the value of corrosion potential. The percentage inhibition is calculated from the formula

$$\%\text{I.E.} = \frac{\text{Uninhibited corrosion rate - inhibited corrosion rate}}{\text{Uninhibted corrosion rate}} \times 100$$

Polarisation resistance or linear polarisation method and A.C. impedance method are also used to calculate the corrosion current and to evaluate the inhibitor.

$$\text{i}_{\text{corr}} = \frac{b_a b_c}{2.303(b_a + b_c)} \times \frac{1}{R_p} \tag{9.3}$$

where

$1/R_p$ is polarisation resistance = dI/dN

Impedance Method

The charge transfer resistance (R_t) double layer capacity (C_{dl}) and the surface coverage (θ) of the medium containing the organic compounds are calculated from the impedance studies.

The double layer capacity is calculated from the following equation

$$C_{dl} = \frac{1}{2\pi f_{\text{max}} R_t} \tag{9.4}$$

The degree of surface coverage (θ) is calculated from the relationship

$$\theta = \frac{C_0 - C_i}{C_0} \tag{9.5}$$

where C_0 is the capacity of double layer in the pure electrolyte and C_i is that of solution with inhibitor.

Other Methods

Other methods such as radio tracer technique, spectral methods such as UV, IR NMR, MS and Mossbaur spectroscopic methods, XRD and ellipsometric techniques have also been employed for the study of corrosion inhibition.

Mechanism of Inhibition

The inhibitive action of organic substances in acid solutions has been explained by various theories. Molecular orbital theoretical studies of some organic corrosion inhibitors have been proposed. Organic compounds are adsorbed at the metal-solution interface and the corrosion is inhibited. The adsorbed inhibitor may influence the corrosion of metal by the following ways:

(i) ***Formation of a physical barrier:*** According to this mechanism the inhibiting action is explained as due to the formation of a layer of a complex product obtained by the reaction among the metal, the inhibitor and the ions of corrosive medium. This layer acts as a physical barrier which restricts the diffusion of ions or molecules to or from the metal surface. The metal surface is completely covered by a least a monolayer of inhibitor.

(ii) ***Reduction in metal reactivity due to selective adsorption:*** In this type of mechanism the inhibitor may be selectively adsorbed on the cathodic or anodic sites on the surface of the metal. This results in the decrease of cathodic or anodic reaction rate and thus corrosion is retarded. The adsorption on cathodic sites increases cathodic polarisation and on anodic sites increases anodic polarisation.

(iii) ***Change in the electric double layer structure:*** According to this mechanism, the adsorbed organic molecules physically block the sites on the surface resulting in the change of electrical double layer structure at the metal solution interface.

Though the action of inhibitors has been explained by various considerations, it is now generally accepted that organic compounds inhibit corrosion by adsorbing at the metal-solution interface. But film formation may or may not take place.

REFERENCES

Ailer, W.H., Hand book of Corrosion Testing and Evaluation, John Wiley (1971).

Akiyama, A. and K. Nobe, *J. Electrochem. Soc.*, 117, 999 (1970).

Altsybeeva, S.Z., S.Z. Levin and Dorokhov, 3rd Eur. Symp. on Corr. Inh. Ferrara, Italy, 501 (1970).

Applegate, L.N., Cathodic Protection, Mc Graw Hill Book Co., Inc., New York, (1960).

Aramaki, K., *Corrosion*, 55, 157 (1999).

Arghode, R., S. Venkatakrishna Iyer and D. Mukherjee, *Corr. Bul.*, 3, 235 (1983).

Aromaki, K., *Boshoku Gijutsu*, 26(6), 297 (1977).

Ayers, J.D., *Corrosion*, 37(1), 55 (1981).

Bereket, G. and A. Yurt, *Anti-Corrosion Methods and Materials*, 49(3), 210 (2002).

Bockris, J.O'M and D.A.J. Swinkels, *J. Electrochem. Soc.*, 111, 776 (1964).

Bockris, J.O'M, N. Bonciocat and F. Gutmann, Introduction to Electrochemical Science, London (1973).

Brasher, D.M. and C.P. Dey, *Nature*, 180, 802 (1957).

Breiter, M.W. and S. Gilman, *J. Electrochem. Soc.,* 109, 622 (1962).

Caprani, A., Epelboin, Ph. Morel and Takenouchi, Proc. 4th Eur. Symp. Corrosion Inhibitors, Italy, 517 (1975).

Cavallaro, L., L. Felloni and G. Trabenelli, Symp. N.S. Ses. V, Suppl. 3, 11 (1961).

Cox, P.F., R.L. Ever and O.L. Riggs (Jr), *Corrosion,* 20, 299 (1964).

Damaskin, F.B., O.A. Petri and V.V. Batrakov, 'Adsorption of Organic Compounds on Electrodes', Plenum Press, New York, 86 (1971).

Deans, S.Q. (JR), Richard Derby and G.T. Von Dem Burche, *Materials Performance,* 20, 1247 (1981).

Devay, J. and L. Measros, *Acta Chimica,* 100, 1, (1979).

Doss, K.S.G. and H.P. Agarwal, *Proc. Indian Acad. Sci.,* 34A, 263 (1951).

Driver, R. and R.J. Meakins, *Br. Corros. J.,* 9(4), 227 (1974).

Epelboin, I., M. Keddam and H. Takenouchi, *J. Appl. Electrochem.,* 2, 71 (1972).

Epelboin, I., M. Keddam and H. Takenouti, *J. Appl. Electrochem.,* 2, 71 (1972).

Epoelboin, I., P. Morel and H. Takenouti, *J. Electrochem. Sec.,* 118, 1282 (1971).

Evans, U.R., *'Metallic Corrosion, Passivity and Protection',* Edward Arnold and Co., London, 535 (1948).

Evans, V.R., The Corrosion and Oxidation of Metals, Second Suppl. Edward Arnold Publ., London, 104 (1968).

Fischer, H., *Werkst. Korros.,* 23, 445 (1972).

Fontana, M.G., *Corrosion Engineering,* 3rd edition, 72 (1986).

Foroulis, Z.A., Extended Abstract, *J. Electrochem. Soc.,* 10, 212 (1965).

Foroulis, Z.A., *Proc. Symp. Coupling of Basic and Applied Corrosion Research,* NACE, Houston, Texas (1969).

Franklin, T.C. and R.D. Southern, *J. Phy. Chem.,* 58, 951 (1954).

Frignani, A. and M. Tassinari, Proceedings of the 7th European Symposium on 'Corrosion Inhibitors', Ses, N.S., Supp.9. Ann. Univ. Ferrara, Italy, 895 (1990).

Girijashankar, P.N., J. Balachandra and K.I. Vasu, *J. Electrochem. Soc. India,* 29, 195 (1980).

Grahame, D.C., *J. Am. Chem. Soc.,* 68, 301 (1946).

Haruyama, S., T. Tsuru and M. Anan, *Boshoku Gijutsu,* 27, 449 (1978).

Heckerman, N., *J. Electrochem Soc.,* 115, 1006 (1968).

Hefter, G.T., N.A. North and S.H. Tan, *Corrosion,* 53, 657 (1997)

Hladky, K., L.M. Callow and J.L. Dawson, *Br. Corros. J.,* 15, 21 (1980).

Hluchan, V., B.L. Wheeler and N. Hackerman, *Werkst. Korros.,* 39, 512 (1998).

Hoar, T.P., Pittsburg International Conference on Surface Reactions, 127 (1948).

Ikawa, M. and T. Mukibo, *J. Electrochem. Soc., Japan, 20,* 568 (1962).

Itagaki, M. and K. Watanabe, Electrochem. Soc. Meeting Abstracts, Spring Meeting—Montreal, Quebec, Canada, 4, 138 (1997).

Iyer, S. Venkatakrishna and S. Muralidharan, *Anti-Corrosion Methods and Materials,* 44, 100 (1997).

Iyer, S. Venkatakrishna, M.A.W. Khan, M. Ajmal and S. Muralidharan, *Corrosion,* 53, 475 (1997).

Juttner, K., *Workst. Korros.,* 31, 358 (1980).

Kanno, K., M. Suzuki and Y. Sato, *J. Electrochem. Soc.,* 125, 1389 (1978).
Khurana, S.C. and K.B. Pai, Ninth Nat. Convention of Electrochemists [NCE-IX], Souvenir and Abstrs., Surat, 4, 26 (1999).
Kim, Y.W. and P.R. Strutt, *Mat. Trans.,* 10A, 881 (1979).
Kirtivasan, N., T. Tusru and S. Haruyama, *Boshoku Gijustu,* 29, 275 (1980).
Lacombe, P., 2nd Symp. Eur. Sur. Les. Inhibiteurs de Corrosion, Annali Univ., N.S. Ferrara, Ses. V., Suppl. No. 4, 517 (1966).
Laguzzi, G., L. Tommesani, L. Luvidi, R. Bucci and G. Brunoro, *Corros. Sci.,* 41, 197 (1999).
Lorenz, W.J. and H. Fischer, *Ber. Bunsenges. Phys. Chem.,* 69, 689 (1965).
Macdonald, D.D., B.C. Syrett and S.S. Wing, *Corrosion,* 34, 289 (1978).
Macdonald, D.D., *J. Electrochem. Soc.,* 125, 1443, 1977 (1978).
Macdonald, D.D., *Transient Techniques in Electrochemistry*, Plenum Press, New York (1977).
Mansfeld, F. and M.W. Kendig, *Corrosion,* 38, 478 (1982).
Mansfeld, F. and W.J. Lorenz, *Corros. Sci.,* 21(9), 647 (1981).
Mansfeld, F., *Corrosion,* 29, 397 (1973).
Mansfeld, F., *Corrosion,* 37, 301 (1981) and 38, 570 (1982).
Mathur, P.B. and T. Vasudevan, *Corrosion,* 38(3), 171 (1982).
Mazza, F. and N.D. Greena, 2nd Symp. Eur. Sur. Les. Inh. De Corr. Ferrara, Italy, 13, Ses 5, Suppl. 4(1), 401 (1965).
Murray, P.J., *Br. Corros. J.,* 12, 142 (1977).
NACE, *Glossary of Corrosion Terms, Mat. Prot.,* 4, 79 (1965).
Nathan, C.C., *Corrosion,* 9, 199 (1959).
Ohno, J., T. Tsuru and S. Haruyama, *Proc. Interfinish,* 152, 80 (1990).
Pandiammal, M., S. Vincent, K. Kumar, V.S. Muralidharan and Y.M. Iyer, Ninth Nat. Cong. Corros. Control Souvenir, Goa, 37, 16 (1999).
Potter, E.C., *Electrochemistry, Principles and Applications*, Clever Hume Press Ltd., London (1956).
Powers, R. and M. Hackeman, *J. Electrochem. Soc.,* 100, 314 (1953).
Putilova, I.N., S.A. Balezin and V.P. Barannik, *Metallic Corrosion Inhibitors*, Pergamon Press, 2 (1960).
Quarishi, M.A., J. Rawat and D. Jamal, Ninth Nat. Convention of Electrochemists [NCE-IX], Souvenir and Abstrs., Surat (1999).
Ravidheva, S.N., B.V. Aleksiev and E.I. Sokolova, *Corros. Sci.,* 34, 343 (1993).
Riggs, O.L. (Jr.), *Corrosion,* 26, 2453 (1970).
Ross, T.K. and D.H. Jones, 1st *Symp. Eur. Sur. Les.* Inh. De Corr., Ferrara, (Italy) 163.
Ross, T.K. and D.H. Jones. *J. Appl. Chem.,* 12, 314 (1962).
Rozenfeld, I.L., *Corrosion Inhibitors*, McGraw-Hill Publications, New York (1981).
Sanyal, B., *Progress in Organic Coatings*, 9(2), 165 (1981).
Sathyanarayana, S., *J. Electroanal. Chem.,* 50, 411 (1974).
Sato, Y., K. Kanno and M. Suzuki, Proc. 7th Inter Cong. Met. Corr., Riode Jeneiro, Brazil, 1945 (1978).
Schmitt, G., *Br. Corros. J.,* 19, 4 (1984).
Schwabe, K. and W. Leonhardt, *Chemie-Ingeneur Technik.* 38(1), 59 (1966).

Singer, I.L., C.A. Carosella and J.R. Reed, *Nucl. Instrum.* Methods, McGraw-Hill Publications, New York (1981).

Srinivasan, S. and S. Sathyanarayana, *Br. Corros. J.,* 12, 217 (1977).

Stern, M. and A.L. Greary, *J. Electrochem. Soc.,* 104, 56 (1957).

Stern, M., *Corrosion,* 13, 775 (1957).

Subramanian, A., M. Natesan, K. Balakrishnan, N.S. Rengaswamy and T. Vasudevan, Ninth Nat. Congr. Corros. Conotrol Souvenir, Goa (1999).

Subramanyan, N., *Electrochem. Acta,* 20(8), 539 (1975).

Subramanyan, N., Proc. 13th Seminar on Electrochem., 195 (1972) (CECRI, Karaikudi).

Suetaka, W., *Bull. J. Chem. Soc., Japan.* 38, 148 (1965).

Syrett, B.C. and D.D. Macdonald, *Corrosion,* 35, 505 (1979).

Szklarska, G. Mrowcezynki and Swialowska, *J. Appl. Electrochem.,* 9, 201 (1979).

Taib, F. Heakal and S. Haruyama, *Corros. Sci.,* 20, 887 (1980).

Trabanelli, G. and F. Zucchi, *Reviews on Coatings and Corrosion,* 1(2), 97 (1973).

Trabanelli, G. and V. Carassity, *Advances in Corrosion Science and Technology*, Vol. 1, Plenum Press, New York, 147(1970).

Uhlig, H.H., *Corrosion and Corrosion Control*, John Wiley and Sons, 2nd edition, 40 (1964).

Uhlig, H.H., *Corrosion and Corrosion Control*, John Wiley and Sons, 2nd edition, New York, 68 (1964).

Uhlig, H.N. and A. Geary, *J. Electrochem. Soc.,* 10, 215 (1954).

Wagner, C. and Traud, *Wi Zeit Electrochem.,* 44, 391 (1938).

Williams, L.F.G. and J. Taylor, *J. Electroanal. Chem.,* 108, 305 (1980).

Yu, Y.F. and J. Yao, *Phy. Chem.,* 68, 101 (1964).

Zhong, C.K., *Electrochem. Soc. Meeting Abstracts*, Spring Meeting-Montreal, Quebec, Canada (1997).

10

Inhibitors

The retardation of the rate of any chemical, electrochemical or physical process by influence of any material may be defined as corrosion inhibition and additive used is known as inhibitor. The inhibitor is a preventive measure against corrosive attack on metallic material. It consist of use of chemical compound (organic or inorganic) which when added in small concentration to an aggressive environment are able to decrease corrosion of an exposed metal. By considering the electrochemical nature of corrosion processes contributed by at least two-electrochemical partial reaction, inhibition may also be defined on an electrochemical basis. Inhibitor will reduce the rates of either or both of anodic and cathodic reaction. Corrosion may be prevented by addition of inhibitors either in gaseous or in liquid phase, although corrosion, in some situation would appear as due to presence of solid phase, which can also be inhibited. From 19th century onwards-vegetable wastes, plant extraction and animal proteins were used as inhibitor. Putilova *et. al.*, has reviewed *i.e.* metallic corrosion inhibitors. Several books have been published on this subject. Much work is being carried out at present all over the world on the development and study of corrosion inhibitors. Besides the University of Ferrora, Italy conduct symposium on corrosion inhibition once in five years. Scientific and technical journals are publishing more and more, which deals with problems associated with molecular mechanism of this action. All the international seminars on corrosion discuss the development and application of corrosion inhibitors various books on corrosion review the subject in the manner.

Classification of Inhibitors

Many methods are carried out to classify the inhibitors but none of quit satisfactory and there are no general agreement on allocation of inhibitors. The inhibitors may be classified as passivators, precipitators, vapour phase inhibitors, anodic inhibitors, cathodic inhibitors, neutralizer and adsorbents. Different types of organic compounds are used as corrosion inhibitors and partial account of them can be obtained in review monograph by Putilova and others. A veriety of organic compounds containing heteroatom such as nitrogen, sulpher, oxygen and unsaturated hydrocarbons (double or triple bond) in their ring, which can donate electron pairs are used effective inhibitors on mild steel, brass, aluminium in various aggressive electrolytes. Many authors reported many papers in these aspects *i.e.* thiourea and their derivatives, indole and their derivatives azoles and their derivatives, various types of pyridine and bipyridine have been used as good inhibitors for iron and steel. A number of verifications have been carried out to inhibit the metal corrosion, using heterocyclic compounds containing delocalized pie electrons and heteroatoms in the ring system. An accurate analysis of different modes of inhibiting electrode reaction including corrosion reaction was carried out by Fischer. He distinguished among various mechanisms of action such as:

(*i*) Interface inhibition

(*ii*) Electrolyte layer inhibition

(*iii*) Membrane inhibition

(*iv*) Passivation.

Subsequently, Lorenz and Mansfeld proposed a clear distinguished between interface and interface inhibition representing two different types of retardation mechanism of electrode reaction including corrosion interface inhibition presumes a string interaction between the inhibitor and the corroding surface of metal, in this case the inhibitor adsorbs as a potential dependent two-dimension layer. This layer can affect the basic corrosion reaction in different ways.

By a geometrical blocking effect of electrode surfaces due to adsorption of stable inhibitor at a relatively high degree of coverage of metal surfaces. A blocking effect of active surface sites is due to adsorption of stable inhibitor at a relatively law degree of coverage and by a reactive coverage of metal surface. In this case the adsorption process is followed by electro chemical or chemical reaction of inhibitor at the interface.

The interface inhibition occurs in corroding system exhibiting a bare metal surface in contact with the corrosion medium. Interface inhibition presumes a three dimensional layer between the corroding substrate and the electrolyte. Such layer generally consist of weakly soluble corrosion product and inhibitors. Interface inhibition is mainly observed in natural media.with the formation of porous or non-porous layers. The passivating inhibitors cause a large anodic shift of the corrosion potential forcing the metallic surface into passivation range. There are two type of passivating inhibitors, oxidizing anions *e.g.* chromate, nitrite and nitrate that can passivate steel in the absence of oxygen. Other is a non-oxidising ion such as phosphate, tungstate and molybdate require the presence of oxygen to passivate steel. These inhibitors are the most effective and consequently the most widely used. Passivating inhibitors are also known as danger's inhibitors because uncertain condition increases corrosion. On the basis of mechanism of inhibitors can be classified as Cathodic, Anodic and mixed type. A typical good corrosion inhibitor will give 95 per cent inhibition efficiency at concentration of 80 ppm and 90 per cent at 40 ppm. Some of the mechanisms of its effect are formation of a passivation layer (a thin film on the surface of the material that stops access of the corrosive substances to the metal).

Anodic Inhibitor

Those substances, which reduce the anode area by acting on anodic sites and polarize the anodic reactions, are called anodic inhibitors. They displace the corrosion potential (Ecorr) in positive direction and reduce the corrosion current (Icorr) there by retard anodic reaction and suppress the corrosion rate. Anodic inhibitors are primary inhibitors of oxidizing action. As oxidants, they have a two-fold nature via, (1) They act as depolarizers and therefore, accelerate the cathodic process and (2) They lead to formation of protective film on the anode. In other words, they work as either cathodic simulators or anodic inhibitor. There resulting action can therefore be different depending upon condition. Oxygen often stimulates corrosion, acting as inhibitors or passivators only at rather high concentration and in the absence of string deep passivators such as Cl^-, Br^-, I^-. Such oxidants as chromates, on the contrary are difficult to reduce at the cathode except in sufficiently acid media and are therefore, poor cathodic depolarizers. An example of an anodic inhibitor is chromate which forms a passivation layer on aluminium and steel surfaces which prevents the oxidation of the metal. Sadly chromate is carcinogenic in humans; the toxicity of chromates was featured *e.g.* Like hydrazine, the use of chromate to products. Nitrite is another anodic inhibitor, if anodic inhibitors are used at too low concentration, they can actually aggravate pitting corrosion, as they form a non uniform layer with local anodes.

Cathodic Inhibitor

Those substances, which reduce the cathode area by acting on cathodic sites and polarize the cathodic reaction, are called cathodic inhibitors. They displace the corrosion potential in the negative direction and reduce corrosion current, there by retarding cathodic reaction and suppress the corrosion rate. The cathodic inhibitors with a few exceptions don't lead to intensified or localized attack, since cathode areas are not attacked during corrosion. If corrosion were control by cathodic reaction, the added cathodic inhibitor would decrease cathodic area and hence overall corrosion rate. On the other hand, corrosion is controlled by anodic reaction; decreases in cathodic area would increase cathodic current density but will have no effect on the nature of corrosion. The increase in cathodic current density may cause the reduction of substance present, which is not otherwise being reduced. Mann *et. al.*, and other investigator working on numerous organic inhibitor exist in onium structure and get absorbed on cathodic area of the surface by force of physical adsorption and chemisorption. In contrast, Bockris and Conway that the action cathodic inhibitor is due to an increase of hydrogen over voltage rather than by an adsorbed inhibitor film on the metal surface. The cathodic inhibition due to general adsorption of the inhibitor on the metal surface remains however the most accepted theory. Like anodic inhibitors, cathodic inhibitors are not dangerous but safe, when present in the solution in insufficient quantities, and involved no additional risk of pitting attack. The cathodic inhibitor may be three categories—(1) Those that absorb oxygen *i.e.* oxygen scavengers; (2) Those that reduce the area of cathode precipitate; (3) Those that increase the hydrogen potential of cathodic procedure *i.e.* hydrogen evolution poison. An example of a cathodic inhibitor is zinc oxide, which retards the corrosion by inhibiting the reduction of water to hydrogen gas. As every oxidation requires a reduction to occur at the same time it slows the oxidation of the metal. As an alternative to the reduction of water to form hydrogen, oxygen or nitrate can be reduced. If oxidants such as oxygen are excluded, the rate of the corrosion can be controlled by the rate of water reduction; this is the case in a closed recirculating domestic central heating system, where the water in the radiators soon becomes anaerobic. One very good example of a cathodic inhibitor is a volatile amine present in steam; these are used in the boilers used to drive turbines to protect the pipe work in which the condensed water passes. Here the amine is moved by the steam in a steam distillation to the remote pipe work. The amine increases the pH thereby making proton reduction less favourable. It is also possible that with correct choice, the amine can form a protective film on the steel surface and at same time, act as an anodic inhibitor.

Oxygen Scavengers: The most common scavengers used are sodium sulphite, sodium sulphide and hydragin, which remove dissolve oxygen from aqueous solution according to the reaction:

$$2\,Na_2SO_3 + O_2 \rightarrow Na_2SO_4$$

$$Na_2S + 2O_2 \rightarrow Na_2SO_4$$

$$NH_2\text{–}NH_2 + O_2 \rightarrow N_2 + 2H_2O$$

It is the apparent that such inhibitors will function very efficiently in closed systems where oxygen depolarization in the controlling cathodic reaction, but will not be effective in strong acid solutions.

$$O_2 + 2H_2O + 4e^- \rightarrow 4\,OH^-$$

$$2H^+ + 2e^- \rightarrow H_{2(g)}$$

These inhibitors can be stimulators if the metal is in passive state before introduction of the inhibitor in as much as the loss of oxygen is capable of activating stain less steel in certain corrosive solutions by addition of sulphite.

Mixed Inhibitor

An inhibitor that acts both in an anodic and cathodic manner is termed as a mixed inhibitor. In general, these are organic compounds, which adsorb on the metal surface and suppress metal dissolution and reduction reaction.

Enzyme Inhibitor

Enzyme inhibitors are those molecules that bind to enzymes and decrease their activity. Since blocking an enzyme's activity can kill a pathogen or correct a metabolic imbalance, many drugs molecules are enzyme inhibitors, so their discovery and improvement is an active area of research in biochemistry and pharmacology. A medicinal enzyme inhibitor is often judged by its specificity and its potency. A high specificity and potency ensure that a drug will have few side effects and thus low toxicity. Enzyme inhibitors also occur naturally and are involved in the regulation of metabolism. For example, enzyme in a metabolic path way can be inhibited by downstream products. This type of negative feedback shows flux through a pathway when the products begin to build up and are an important way to maintain homeostasis in a cell. Other cellular enzyme inhibitors are proteins that specifically bind to and inhibit an enzyme target. This can help control enzymes that may be damaging to a cell. Other cellular enzyme inhibitors are proteins that specifically bind to and inhibit an enzyme target.

Inhibitor in Acid Solution

Corrosion of metal in acidic solution environment has been slightly high on metallic alloys depending on many factors like temperature, concentration, metallic structure and metallic composition. This kind of attack can be prevented by using the large number of organic inhibitor. These compounds contain a double or triple bonded hydrocarbons, a heteroatom, like nitrogen, oxygen or sulphur, an aromatic ring and many other families of simple organic compounds or of condensation product formed by the reaction between the two different species such as aldehyde and amines. Generally it is assumed that the first stage in the action mechanism of inhibitor in aggressive acid media is adsorption of the inhibitor, are influenced by the nature and the surface change of the metal, chemical structure of organic inhibitor and by the type of aggressive electrolyte. Physical adsorption and chemisorptions are principal type of interactions between an organic inhibitor and a metal surface.

Interaction between Organic Inhibitor and Metal Surface

Two main types of interaction on adsorption of the organic compounds on the electrode surface: physical adsorption and chemisorptions. Both types of adsorption are influenced by the nature of charge (potential of zero charge Eq =(0) of the metal, the chemical structure of the inhibitor as well as the type of corrosive electrolyte.

Physical Adsorption Mode

This method for the immobilization of an enzyme is based on the physical adsorption of enzyme protein on the surface of water-insoluble carriers. Hence, the method causes little or no conformational change of the enzyme or destruction of its active center. If a suitable carrier is found, this method can be both simple and cheap. However, it has the disadvantage that the adsorbed enzyme may leak from the carrier during use due to a weak binding force between the enzyme and the carrier. The earliest example of enzyme immobilization using this method is the adsorption of beta-D-fructofuranosidase into aluminum hydroxide. The processes available for physical adsorption of enzymes are:

- Static Procedure
- Electro-deposition
- Reactor Loading Process
- Mixing or Shaking Bath Loading

Of the four techniques, the most frequently used in the lab is Mixing-Bath Loading. For commercial purposes the preferred method is Reactor Loading.

A major advantage of adsorption as a general method of immobilizing enzymes is that usually no reagents and only a minimum of activation steps are required. Adsorption tends to be less disruptive to the enzymatic protein than chemical means of attachment because the binding is mainly by hydrogen bonds, multiple salt linkages, and Van der Waal's forces. In this respect, the method bears the createst similarity to the situation found in natural biological membranes and has been used to model such systems.

Because of the weak bonds involved, desorption of the protein resulting from changes in temperature, pH, ionic strength or even the mere presence of substrate, is often observed. Another disadvantage is non-specific, further adsorption of other proteins or other substances as the immobilized enzyme is used. This may alter the properties of the immobilized enzyme or, if the substance adsorbed is a substrate for the enzyme, the rate will probably decrease depending on the surface mobility of enzyme and substrate.

Physical adsorption is a result of electrostatic attractive forces between inhibiting organic ions on dipoles and the electrically charged surface of metal. The surface charge of the metal is due to the electric field at the outer Helmholtz plane of electrical double layer existing at the metal/solution interface. The surface charge can be defined by the potential of the metal (Ecorr) vs. its zero charge potential (ZCP). When the difference E_{corr}-(Eq = 0)= φ is negative, cation adsorption is favoured. Adsorption of anion is favored when it becomes positive. This behaviour is related not only to compounds with formal positive or negative charge but also to dipoles whose orientation is determined by the value of potential. According to Antropob at equal value of different metals, similar behaviours of a given inhibiting species should be expected in the same environment. This has been verified for adsorption of organic charged species on mercury and iron electrodes, at the same potential for the both metals.

In studying the adsorption of the ions at the metal/solution interface, it was first assumed that ions maintained their total charge during the adsorption, giving rise in this way to a pure electrostatic bond. Loreng suggested that a partial charge is present in the adsorption of the ions; in this case a certain amount of covalent bond in the adsorption process must be considered. The partial charge concept was studied by Vetter and Schulze. Who defined as electrosorption valence coefficient for the potential dependency and the charge flow of electrosorption processes. The term electro adsorption valence was chosen because it analogy with the electrode reaction valence which enters into Faraday's Law as well as Nernest equation. Considering the concept discussed above in relation to corrosion inhibition, when an uninhibited solution contains absorbable anions, such as halide ions, these get adsorbed on metal surface by creating oriented dipoles and consequently increase the adsorption of organic cations on the dipoles. In these cases a positive synergistic effect arises; thus the degree of inhibition in the presence of both adsorbable anions and inhibitor cations is higher than the sum of individual effects. This could explain the higher inhibition efficiency of various organic inhibitors in hydrochloric acid solution compared to sulphuric acid solution. A very detailed discussion of electrostatic adsorption has been given by Foroulos who also considered the importance of structural parameters such as hydrocarbon chain length and the nature and position of substituent in aromatic rings influence the electrical charge of organic ion, since this factor could change the degree of inhibition. The inhibiting species whose action is to be attributed to electrostatic adsorption interact rapidly with the electrode surface, but they are also easily removed from the surface. The electrostatic adsorption has low activation energy, and it proves to be relatively independent of temperature. On the other hand electrostatic adsorption appears to depend on:

- The electrical characteristics of organic inhibitors.
- The position of corrosion potential with respect to the zero charge potential.
- The type of adsorbable anion present in the aggressive solution.

Chemisorptions

This process involves charge sharing or charge transfer from the inhibitor molecules to the metal surface in order to form a co-ordinate bonding. It takes place more slowly than electrostatic adsorption and with higher activation energy. It depends on the temperature; higher degree of inhibition should be expected at higher temperature. In other words Chemisorption (or chemical adsorption) is adsorption in which the forces involved are valence forces of the same kind as those operating in the formation of chemical compounds. Some features which are useful in recognizing chemisorptions include:

(*a*) The phenomenon is characterized by chemical specificity;

(*b*) Change in the electronic state may be detectable by suitable physical means (*e.g.* u.v., infrared or microwave spectroscopy, electrical conductivity, magnetic susceptibility);

(*c*) The chemical nature of the adsorptive(s) may be altered by surface dissociation or reaction in such a way that on desorption the original species cannot be recovered; in this sense chemisorption may not be reversible;

(*d*) The energy of chemisorption is of the same order of magnitude as the energy change in a chemical reaction between a solid and a fluid thus chemisorption, like chemical reactions in general, may be exothermic or endothermic and the magnitudes of the energy changes may range from very small to very large;

(*e*) The elementary step in chemisorptions often involves activation energy;

(*f*) Where the activation energy for adsorption is large (activated adsorption), true equilibrium may be achieved slowly or in practice not at all. For example in the adsorption of gases by solids the observed extent of adsorption, at a constant gas pressure after a fixed time, may in certain ranges of temperature increase with rise in temperature. In addition, where the activation energy for desorption is large, removal of the chemisorbed species from the surface may be possible only under extreme conditions of temperature or high vacuum, or by some suitable chemical treatment of the surface.

Effect of Adsorption Inhibitors on Cathodic and Anodic Partial Processes

In the corrosion of metal, the metal electrode under goes a number of simultaneous processes, which are broadly taken as anodic and cathodic process. In anodic process the metal electrode destroyed in the form of their oxide and in cathodic process.

Thermodynamic and Corrosion Kinetics in the Presence of Inhibitors

The increase in temperature leads to different effects according to types of inhibitor. The rate of corrosion of metal can be accelerated by increasing temperature generally in media in which evolution of hydrogen accompanies corrosion. If oxygen takes part in cathodic reaction during corrosion, the relationship between corrosion rate and temperature becomes more complicated owing to the lower solubility of oxygen at elevates temperatures. Speller discovered that in closed system the corrosion rate rises linearly with increasing temperature, while in open system the linear relation was limited upto certain temperature above which corrosion rates fall with rise of temperature owing to lower concentration of dissolved oxygen in solution.

Adsorption Isotherms

An adsorption isotherm is the mathematical expression that relates the bulk concentration of an adsorbent to the surface concentration at constant temperature. It gives the relationship between the coverage of an interface with the adsorbate (*i.e.*, the amount adsorbed) and concentration of the species in solution.

Plots of the variation in corrosion rate with various concentrations of inhibitors have the appearance of being mirror images of adsorption isotherms for most of the organic inhibitors. This strongly suggests that adsorption of the inhibitor on the metal surface (partly) accounts for the inhibition mechanism.

Various adsorption isotherms have been formulated. Various isotherms and the corresponding equations are given in the Table 10.1. The adsorption process is related to the chemical structure and the electrochemical process that occur on the metal surface (83-85).

Table 10.1

Sl.No.	Isotherm	Equation
1.	Langmuir	$b_c = \frac{\theta}{1-\theta}$
2.	Freundlich	$b_c n = \theta$
3.	Frumkin	$b_c = \frac{\theta}{1-\theta} \exp^{(-2a\theta)}$
4.	Temkin	$b_c = \frac{\exp^{a\theta} - 1}{1 - \exp^{(-a(1-\theta)}}$
5.	Parsons	$b_c = \frac{\theta}{1-\theta} \exp \frac{(2-\theta)}{(1-\theta)^2} \exp^{(-2a\theta)}$
6.	Bockris-Devanathan and Muller (B.D.M.)	$\log C + \log \frac{\theta}{1-\theta} = C + b\theta^{3/2}$

where

$$b = e_{ads}^{-\Delta G} / RT$$

a = Interaction parameter

$a > 0$ = Atraction

$a < 0$ = Repulsion

Most of the organic inhibitors obey Langmuir on Temkin adsorption isotherm. The inhibitor is found to obey Langmuir, if a plot of log θ / (1-θ) Vs log C is linear. Similarly for Temkin a plot of θ Vs log C, for B.D.M. a plot of (log C - log θ/(1-θ)) Vs $\theta^{3/2}$ and for Frumkin a plot of log θ (1 – θ) C Vs θ will be linear.

Langmuir's Adsorption Isotherm

Langmuir put forward the first quantitative theory of the adsorption of gases and assumed that a gas molecule considering from gaseous phase would adhere to the surface for a short time before evaporating and that the condensed by layer is one atom or molecule thick. If θ is the fraction of the surface area covered by adsorbed molecules at any time, the desorption is to proportional to *p* and equal to *kd* θ, where kd is constant at constant temperature. Similarly, the rate of adsorption will be proportional to the area of bare surface and to the rate at which the molecule strikes on the surface. In equilibrium condition, the rate of adsorption is equal to the rate of desorption, *i.e.*

$$kd\ \theta = ka\ (1 - \theta)p$$

and the Langmuir isotherm can be expressed as

$$[\theta/1 - \theta] = [\mathrm{Kap/Kd}] = \mathrm{a.p}$$

It is of generally view that inhibition of metals in acidic solution results from the adsorption of molecules or ions of the inhibitor on the metal surface. The action of organic inhibitors depends on the type of interaction between the substance and the metallic surface. This could cause a change either in the electrochemical process mechanism or on the surface available to the process. The decrease in inhibition efficiency with increasing temperature, suggest weak adsorption interaction between zinc surface and the additives, which is physical in nature.

In order to further support the assertion that physical adsorption is proposed, the values of activation energy (E_a) were calculated using the integrated form of the Arrhenius equation.

$$\log\frac{K_2}{K_1} = \frac{E_a}{2.303R}\left[\frac{1}{T_1} - \frac{1}{T_2}\right]$$

where K_1 and K_2 are rate constants at T_1 and T_2 respecitvely. The low values recorded suggest physical adsorption.

From the corrosion rates or surface coverage (θ) for different inhibitor concentrations the respective adsorption isotherms can be obtained.

The surface coverage data fits into the Langmuir isotherm given as.

$$\frac{C}{a} = \frac{1}{b} \times C$$

where *C* is concentration of additives. The plots further suggest that both additives (*Nypa Fruticans Wurmb* extract and D.P.C.) Cover both the arodic and cathodic regions through general adsorption.

11

Synthesis of the Inhibitors

The inhibitors have been synthesized by adopting the known Wittig type of reaction methodology. They have been synthesized by following the experimental procedure described in Ullmann's *Encyclopedia of Industrial Chemistry*, Vol-A 19.

Triphenylphosphine has been mixed with the corresponding aromatic chloro compound in equimolar ratio. The mixture has been heated for about 2 hours in a sand bath and cooled. The solid product has been then filtered and dried. The crude sample obtained have been recrystallised from alcohol. The purity of the compounds has been identified through melting point determination and TLC.

When chlorobenzene has been taken as the reactant, the compound tetraphenylphosphonium chloride (TP) has been obtained.

$$(C_6H_5)_3P + C_6H_5Cl \longrightarrow [(C_6H_5)_4P]^+ Cl^-$$

Since tetraphenylphosphonium chloride has been an already reported compound and the other compounds have been prepared by the known Wittig type of reaction using triphenylphosphine with different p-substituted chlorobenzenes, it is sufficient that the presence of different groups in the compounds have been identified through FT-IR spectroscopic studies. The inhibitor (4-aminophenyl) triphenylphosphonium chloride has been obtained by taking 4-chloroaniline as the reactant.

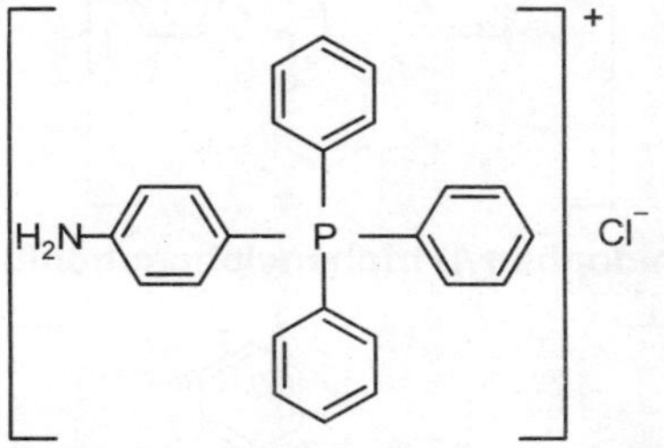

(4-Aminophenyl) triphenylphosphonium chloride

Similarly by changing the reactants, the different inhibitors cited below have been synthesized.

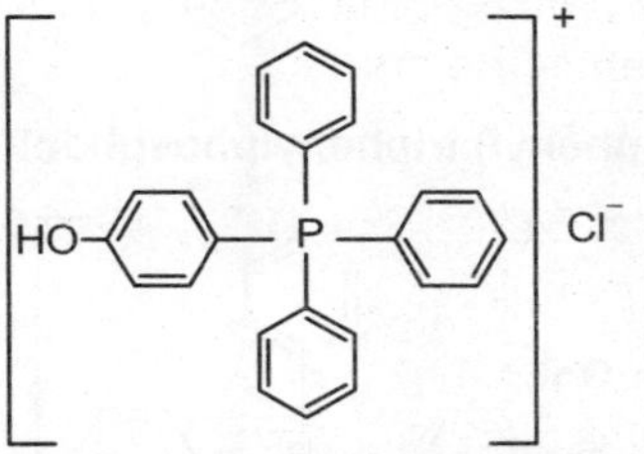

(4-Hydroxyphenyl) triphenyl phosphonium chloride

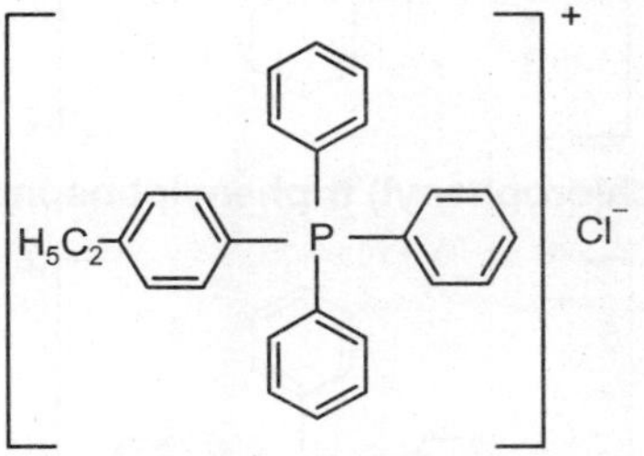

(4-Propylphenyl) triphenylphosphonium chloride

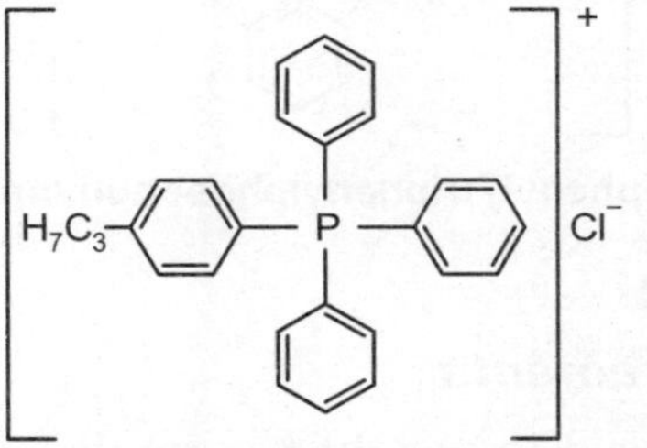

(4-Ethylphenyl) triphenylphosphonium chloride

$$\left[Cl-C_6H_4-P(C_6H_5)_3 \right]^+ Cl^-$$

(Acetamidophenyl) triphenylphosphonium chloride

$$\left[H_3COCHN-C_6H_4-P(C_6H_5)_3 \right]^+ Cl^-$$

(4-Chlorophenyl) triphenylphosphonium chloride

$$\left[(OHC)(Cl)C_6H_3-P(C_6H_5)_3 \right]^+ Cl^-$$

(3-Formyl-4-chlorophenyl) triphenylphosphonium chloride

$$\left[O_2N-C_6H_4-P(C_6H_5)_3 \right]^+ Cl^-$$

(4-Nitrophenyl) triphenylphosphonium chloride)

Techniques Adopted

Weight Loss Measurements

Mild steel specimens used in weight loss studies have been in the form of rectangular pieces of surface area 5 cm^2 and the thickness 0.02 cm. The specimens have been mechanically polished successively with 0/0, 1/0, 3/0 and 4/0 grades emery papers before each run and finally degreased with acetone. The samples have been then stored in desiccators. The initial weights of the specimens have been noted. The each specimen has been suspended through the holes punched at the top of the specimen in a conical flask containing 100 ml of the acid. The specimen has been immersed in the acid in each experiment for 2 hours. The temperature has been maintained at 30 ± 2°C. After two hours, the specimens have been taken out. They have been washed in running tap water and then in distilled water. They have been dried and reweighed. The loss in weight has been calculated. Each experiment has been duplicated to get good reproducibility. Weight loss measurements have been performed in 2M HCl and 2M H_2SO_4 with and without the addition of the inhibitors. The inhibitor concentration in these acids has been varied in the range of 0.0002 mM to 0.2 mM.

Percentage of inhibition of the inhibitors at various concentrations has been calculated using the formula.

$$\text{Inhibition efficiency (\%)} = \frac{W_0 - W_1}{W_0} \times 100$$

where

W_0 = Weight loss in plain acid

W_1 = Weight loss in inhibited acid

The experimental setup for the weight loss method.

Weight Loss Measurements at Different Temperatures

The same procedure adopted for weight loss studies at room temperature (30°C) has been followed here, except that the temperature of the study has been varied from 30°C to 60°C. At the end of the each experiment the specimens have been taken out, washed both in running tap water and in distilled water. They have been dried and their weights have been measured. The loss in weights has been calculated. Each experiment has been duplicated to get good reproducibility. Weight loss measurements have been performed in 2M HCl and 2M H_2SO_4 with and without the addition of the inhibitors at their best inhibiting concentrations. Percentage inhibition of the inhibitors at various temperatures has been calculated.

Synergistic Effect

The procedure adopted for weight loss studies at room temperature has also been followed here, but the only difference is that KI has been added with the inhibitor and the experiment has been carried out.

Gasometric Studies

Gasometric technique is another important non-electrochemical method for the determination the corrosion inhibition.

Mathur *et. al.,* have designed a gasometric unit. Corrosion rates could be monitored using this unit under controlled conditions of temperature and pressure without any aqueous tension correction.

The gasometric instrument consists of three parts. The first part consists of a thermostatic bath assembly in a glass through consisting of a relay and electrical heater and a thermometer. From the thermostatically maintained bath, water has been circulated through the experimental cell assembly and the vertical columns of the gas collector assembly.

The second part of the instrument consists of a reaction cell which is made up of cylindrical vessel of 250 ml capacity with a central ground joint opening through which the metal specimen can be inserted into the cell by means of a glass rod fixed to the central ground glass joint. It is also provided with a gas release stopper on one side through which excess gas pressure over the atmospheric pressure can be released. By gently opening the gas release stopper, the gas pressure of the vessel can be brought to atmospheric pressure. The cell has been placed in the glass beaker provided with an inlet and outlet for the circulation of water.

The third part consists of vertical column tubes made up of standard capacity graduated burettes surrounded by glass jackets, for the circulation of water from thermostat. Because of the circulation of water from the thermostat maintained at constant temperature, both the reaction and gas collection have been carried out at the same temperature with an accuracy of ± 1°C.

The gas has been collected over a solution of 20-25 per cent sodium chloride acidified with HCl or H_2SO_4 and coloured with methyl orange or methyl red. The dissolution of gases like CO_2 H_2, etc. are very low in sodium chloride solution.

The pressure reservoir bulb is surrounded by an outer glass jacket. The liquid in the reservoir bulb is also maintained at the same temperature of the bath, by the circulation of water from bath. The reservoir is fitted with a narrow bore glass tube at right angles to avoid parallax error during the adjustments of liquid level inside the burette and in the reservoir bulb. When the two levels are adjusted to be equal, the pressure of the gas inside the tube is at atmospheric pressure. As the liquid levels inside and outside the burette have been kept the same from the beginning of the experiment, the necessity for any pressure correction due to aqueous tension did not arise.

Mild steel specimens have been polished, degreased with acetone and stored in a desiccator. The specimens have been suspended from the hook. The volume of the acid used in each experiment has been 100 ml. The temperature and pressure have been maintained constant throughout the experiment. The duration of the experiment has been two hours. The volume of the gas evolved has been measured at regular time intervals of 20 minutes.

Gasometric studies have been made for both 2M HCl and 2M H_2SO_4 solutions with and without the addition of inhibitors of the best inhibiting concentration in each case. The percentage of inhibition has been obtained using the relation,

$$\text{I.E.}(\%) = \frac{V_0 - V_1}{V_0} \times 100$$

where, V_0 and V_1 are the volume of hydrogen liberated in the absence and in the presence of the inhibitors respectively.

Potentodynamic Polarisation Studies

Potentiodynamic polarisation studies have been performed for mild steel specimen both in the presence and the absence of the inhibitors.

The electrode used has been a mild steel rod of the same composion used for weight loss measurement. The specimen has been embedded in araldite with an exposed area of 1 cm^2. The polarisation cell used has been a three electrode assembly. A rectangular platinum foil has been used as the counter or auxiliary electrode. The counter electrode has a much larger area than the area of the working electrode. This will exert a uniform potential field on the working electrode. The reference electrodes have been Hg/ Hg_2Cl_2/2 M HCl for HCl solutions and Hg/Hg_2SO_4/2 M H_2SO_4 for H_2SO_4 solutions respectively.

The experimental set up of the electrochemical measurements has been shown in Figure 11.2 constant quantity of 100 ml of the test solutions has been taken in a polarisation cell. The working electrode has been polished with 0/0, 1/0, 2/0, 3/0 and 4/0 emery papers successively and degreased with acetone. The working electrode, reference and auxiliary platinum electrodes have been assembled and connections have been made.

Stirring has been provided to the test solutions to avoid the concentration polarisation before start of the experiment. A time interval of about 15 minutes has been given for the system to attain a steady state and the open circuit potential (OCP) has been recorded. Polarisation measurements have been carried out from 800 mV to –250 mV (Vs SCE) at a constant sweep rate of 50 mV/sec. The solution has not been deaerated to make the conditions identical to weight loss measurements.

Polarisation measurements have been made for mild steel specimens in 2 M HCl and 2 M H_2SO_4 in the presence and absence of the inhibitors. Current in mA and potential in mV have been plotted. From the graph, the Tafel slopes, corrosion current (in mA/cm^2) and the corrosion potential (in mV) have been calculated the inhibition efficiency has been obtained by making use of the relation.

$$\text{Inhibition Efficiency (\%)} = \frac{I_0 - I_1}{I_0} \times 100$$

where

I_0 = Corrosion current in plain acid

I_1 = Corrosion current in inhibited acid.

Impedance Measurements

A very effective approach to AC impedance measurements has been introduced by MIS EG and G Princeton Applied Research. The technique has been actually a combination of two methods: (*a*) The FFT (Fast Fourier Transform) technique for measurements from 0.1 Hz to 10 Hz and (*b*) Phase-sensitive lock in amplification for measurements from 1 Hz to 20 kHz.

In this way the optimum method can be applied to both high and low frequency experiments. Since the system includes a micro computer with dedicated software, it has been possible to merge the data from lock in amplifier and FFT measurements and display the impedance data over a wide range of frequencies.

The model 6310 AC impedance system has been used in this experiment. The system includes:

(*a*) The model 173 potentiostat/galvanostat connected with model 276 interface plug-in (1-3).

(*b*) The model 5206 computer controlled lock in system.

(*c*) Apple *R* 11e micro-computer with peripherals and the model 6310 AC impedance software system.

With this approach, the FFT excitation waveform is applied to the test system via the potentiostat and interface module. The interface also functions as a response measurement device. In the FFT mode, it transmits the raw data in digital form to the Apple computer for the subsequent reduction and display. In the lock-in mode, the total cell response signal is routed to the lock-in amplifier where it is resolved into its real and imaginary components.

The lock-in system then transmits its information to the micro computer for reduction and display. The entire experiment from definition to data display and evaluation is orchestrated by the model 6310 dedicated software package, which has been written in a convenient menu driven format. The three electrode-polarisation cell has been used in this technique. Mild steel specimen of area 1 cm^2 has been used as the working electrode. With the working electrode dipped in the electrolyte, it has been allowed 5-10 minutes time interval for the system to attain a steady state open circuit potential. Then the experiment has been guided with help of micro computer key board. After the experiment has been over, the real part of impedance (Z′) in ohms and the imaginary part of impedance (Z″) in ohms have been plotted on recorder as Z′ Vs Z″.

Impedance measurements of mild steel in 2 M HCl and 2M H_2SO_4 with and without the addition of inhibitors at four different concentrations have been carried out. The values of charge transfer resistance (R_t), double layer capacity (C_{dl}), inhibition efficiency (I.E.) and the surface coverage (θ) have been derived from impedance measurements and the inhibition efficiency of the compounds has been calculated by using the formula.

$$\text{Inhibition Efficiency (\%)} = \frac{R_{t(0)} - R_{t(1)}}{R_{t(0)}} \times 100$$

where

$R_{t(0)}$ = charge transfer resistance of plain acid

$R_{t(1)}$ = charge transfer resistance of inhibited acid.

Statistical Analysis

In the present study inhibitive efficiency of the inhibitors has been determined by making use of the methods namely weight loss, polarisation and impedance measurements. These are carried out under different concentrations of the inhibitors. Such studies provide data which may be statistically analysed. In this light, Analysis of Variance (ANOVA), a statistical data analysis, has been carried out.

ANOVA is a data analysis method of elegance, utility and flexibility and is the most effective method available for analyzing experimental data in which several treatments or factors are represented. In the simplest case of a one-way ANOVA in which the experiment consists of a number of independent treatments or groups, the first stage of the analysis is to carry out a variance ratio test (F-test) to determine whether all group means are the same. If treatment groups are few, a non-significant F-test would indicate no meaningful difference among the means and no further analysis would be required. However, a significant F-test suggests real differences among the treatment means and the next stage of the analysis would involve a more detailed examination of these differences.

There are various options available depending on the objectives of the experiment. Specific comparisons may have been planned before the experiment has been carried out, decided after the data have been collected, or comparisons between all possible combinations of the treatment means may be envisaged.

The experiments have been designed to test specific differences between the concentrations and parameters. Planned comparisons are hypotheses specified before the analyses commence whereas Post-Hoc tests are for further explanation after a significant effect has been found.

The basic strategy for planned comparisons is to divide up the treatments sums of squares among the various hypotheses, called 'contrasts', which are then analysed separately by F-test. When this procedure has been carried out for all possible comparisons between the means, then the sums of squares for all contrasts would be greater than the treatments sums of squares as a whole since the comparisons overlap and based on the same sources of variance. Such comparisons cannot be made independently of each other. As a result, comparisons must be constructed so that they are not overlapping. Hence, the sums of squares can be calculated for each contrast and a test of signficance made on each. The number of possible contrasts is equivalent to the number of degrees of freedom (DF) of the treatment groups in the experiment. Hence, when an experiment employs three or four groups, as in our scenario, then two contrasts can be validily tested. This approach has two advantages. First, there is no problem as to the validity of the individual comparisons, a problem present to some extent with all conventional Post-Hoc tests. Second, the comparisons provide direct tests of the hypotheses of the interest.

Surface Examinations

Surface examinations for the following mild steel specimens have been made using Scanning Electron Microscopic (SEM) studies.

1. Mild steel specimens dipped in 2 M HCl and 2M H_2SO_4.
2. Mild steel specimens dipped in acid solutions containing best protecting concentration of inhibitor ATP.

The experimental setup of the Scanning Electron Microscope has been shown.

REFERENCES

Aastrup, T, Wadsak M, Schreiner M and Leygraf C, 2000. *J. Electrochem. Soc.*, 147:2543.

Abbott, W.H, 1992. Proc. *16th Int. Conf, Electrical Contacts*, Loughborough, England.

Agrawal, Y.K., J.D. Talati, M.D. Shah, M.N. Desai, N.K. Shah. *Corrosion Science 46* 2004 633-651.

Alagta, Abdulmajed, Ilona Felhosi, Judit Telegdi, I. Bertoti, E. Kalman. Corrosion Science 49 2007 2754-2766.

Allam, I.M, Arlow J.S and Saricimen H, 1991. *Corros. Sci.*, 32:417.

Almeida, E, Morcillo M, Rosales B and Marrocos M, 2000 Mater. *Corros.* 51:859.

Alves, R.C.D. and Ferreira M.G.S, 1992. *J. Electrical Chem.*, 340:137.

Ananth, V, Subramanian G, Mohan P.S and Palraj S, 1986. *Bulletin of Electrochemistry.*, 2:541.

Anderson, F.A, 1956. ASTM STP 175 Philadelphia, PA.

Antonio, R.M and Corvo F, 2000. *Corros. Sci.*, 42:1123.

Arni, P.C, Cochrane G.C and Gray J.D, 1965. *Journal of Applied Chemistry*. 15:305.

Arroyave, C and Morcillo M, 1995. *Corros. Sci.*, 37:293.

Arroyave, C and Morcillo M, 1996. 13th Int. *Corros. Cong.*, Melbourne, Australia.

Arroyave, C, Lopez F.A and Morcillo M, 1995. *Corros. Sci.*, 37:1751.

Askey, A, Lyon S.B, Thompson G.E, Johnson J.B, Wood G.C, Cooke M and Sage P, 1933. *Corros. Soc.*, 34:233.

Baboian, R, 1991. *Corrosion* 91. Paper No.371, NACE.

Balsubramanium, R, Mungole M.N and Ramesh K.A.V, 2001. *J. Electrochem. Soc.* India, 50:107.

Barton, K and Bartonova Z, 1969. Proc. *3rd Int. Congr. Metallic Corros.*, 4:403.

Barton, K and Bartonova Z, 1970. *Werkst. Korros.*, 21:85.

Barton, K, 1972. *Protection Against Atmospheric Corrosion*, John Wiley, New York.

Barton, K, 1976. *Protection against Atmospheric Corrosion*, John Wiley and Sons, London.

Barton, K, 1976. *Protection Against Atmospheric Corrosion*, John Wiley and Sons, New York.

Bastidas, J.M and Mora E.M, 1998. *Can. Metall. Quart.*, 37:57.

Beck, L and Gunter J.R, 1984. *Thin Solid Films*, 117:131.

Black, H.L and Lherbier L.W., 1968. *Metal Corrosion in the Atmosphere,* ASTM STP, 435:3.

Blucher, B.D, Lindstrom R, Svensson J.E and Johansson L.G, 2001. *Journal of Electrochem. Soc.,* 148: B127.

Boulton, L.H, Miller N.A and Sanders M.C, 1988. *British Corrosion Journal.*, 23:117.

Brierly, W.B, 1965. J. Environm. Sci., 15.5.

Briggs, C.W, 1968. *Metal Corrosion in the Atmosphere*, ASTM STP; 435:271.

Brown, P.W and Masters L.W., 1982. *Atmospheric Corrosion*, Wiley, New York.

Brown, P.W. and Masters L.W., 1982. *Atmospheric Corrosion*, Wiley, New York.

Butcher, S.S, Charlson R.J, Orians G.H and Wolfe G.V, 1992. *Global Biogeochemical Cycles, Academic* Press, Inc., London.

Calvo, E.J and Schiffrin D.J, 1984. *J. Electrochem. Soc.*, 10:257.

Caruthers, W.H, 1986. *The Theory and Practice*, NACE, Houston, Texas, USA.

Cermakova, D and Vlchkova Y, 1966. *Proc. 3rd Int. Cong. Metallic Corros.*, Moscow, 497.

Chawla, S.K and Payer J.H, 1990. *J. Electrochem. Soc.*, 137.60.

Chawla, S.K. and Payer J.H., 1990. *Corros.* 46:860.

Clarke, S.G. and Longhurst E.E, 1961. J. *Appl. Chem.*, 11:435.

Cohen, H.M, 1988. *Aluminium*, 35:197.

Corvo, F and Leon I, 1988. *Rev Iberoamericana de Corrosion Proteccion*, 5:19.

Corvo, F. 1984. *Corros*, 40: 4-15.

Cuesta, O, 1993. Ph.D. Thesis, Royal Institute of Technology, Stockholm, Sweden.

Dermaj, A., N. Hajjaji, S. Joire and others Electrochemica Acta 52(2007) 4654-4662.

Divers, E and Mellor J.W, 1952. *Comprehensive Treatise on Inorganic and Theoretical Chemistry*, Longmanns, London, 3:94.

Donchenko, M.I and NKO T.V, 1979. *Metall.*, 15:96.

Donovan, P.D and Stringer J, 1971. *Br. Corros.* J., 6:132.

Donovan, P.D and Stringer J, 1972 *Proc. 4th Int. Cong. Metallic Corros.*, NACE, Houston, Texas, 537.

Donovan, P.D, 1986. *Protection of Metals from Corrosion in Storage and Transit*, Ellis Horwood, Chichester, England, 78.

El Warraky, A.A. and A.E. *Meleigy British Corrosion Journal 37* (2002). No. 4.

Ericsson, P and Johansson L.G, 1986. Proc. *10th Scandinavian Corrs.* Cong., Stockholm.

Ericsson, R. 1978. Werks. Korros., 29:400.

Eriksson, P, Johansson L.G and Strandberg H, 1993. J. Electrochem Soc., 140: 53.

Eriksson, P, PhD Thesis. 1992. *Chalmers University of Technology*, Goteborg, Sweden.

Espada, L, Merino P, Gonzalez A and Sanchez A, 1987. *10th Int Cong. Metallic Corros.*, Madras, India, 3.

Evans, T.E, 1972. *Proc. 4th Int. Cong. Metallic Corros.*, Texas, 408.

Evans, U.R, 1951. *Chem. Ind.*, 706.

Evans, U.R, 1981. *An Introduction to Metallic Corrosion*, Arnold, U.K.

Evans, U.R. 1976. The *Corossion and Oxidation of Metals: Second Supplementary* Vol. 8, Edward Arnold, London.

Evans, U.R. and Hoar T.P, 1932 *Proc. Roy. Soc.* (A), 137-343.

Evans, U.R. and Taylor C.A 1972., *J, Corros. Sci.*, 12:227.

Falk T, Svensson J.E and Johansson L.G, 1988. *Journal of Electrochem. Soc.*, 147; 1751.

Feitnecht, W, 1952. *Chimia*, 6:3.

Felhosi, Ilona and Erika Kalman, *Corosion Science 47*, (2005) 695-708.

Feliu, S, Morcillo M and Feliu Jr. S, 1993. *Corros, Sci.*, 34:403.

Feliu, S, Morcillo M and Feliu Jr. S, 1993. *Corros. Sci.*, 34:415.

Flinn, D.R, Cramer S.D, Carter J.P, Hurwitz D.M and Linstrom P.J, 1986. *Materials Degradation Caused by Acid Rain, American.*

Fontana, M.G., 1987. *Corrosion Engineering*, 3rd Ed. McGraw-Hill Book Company Inc. New York.

Forslund, M and Leygraf C, 1993. *The Electrochem.Soc. Proc. Series*, Pennington, New Jersey, 486.

Fouda, A.S., A.A. El-Bindary, A.A. Al-Sarawy and E.E.El=Katori. *Bulletin of Electrochemistry*, vol. 21, no. 11. November 2005, pp 481-487.

Franey, J.P, Graedel T.E and Kammlott G.W, 1982. *Atmospheric Corrosion*, J. Wiley and Sons, Inc.

Fukuda, Y. Fukushima T, Sulaiman A, Musalam I, Yap LC.Chotimongkol L, Judabong S, Potjanart A, Keowkangwal O, Yoshihara K and Tosa M, 1991. *J. Electrochem. Soc.,* 138:1238.

Fyfe D, 1994. Corrosion, Oxford, Butterworth-Heinemann, London.

Galloway, J.N. and Likens G.E, 1976. *Water Air Soil Poll.*, 6:241.

Garrels, R.M, 1954. Geochim. *Cosmochim. Acta*, 5:153.

Godard, H.P, Jepson W.B and Bothwell M.R, 1967. *The Corrosion of Light Metals*, John Wiley and Sons Inc., New York, 170.

Goodwin, F.E, 1990. *Metallurgy and Performance*, TMS, Warrendale, 183.

Gourbeyre, Y., B. Tribollet, C.Dagbert and L. Hyspecka. *Journal of the Electrochemical Society*, 153(5) B 162-B168 (2006).

Graedel, T. E. McGroy-Joy C and Franey J.P, 1986. *J. Electrochem. Soc.,* 133:452.

Graedel, T.E and Frankenthal R.P, 1990. *J.Eiectochem.* Soc., 8:137.

Graedel, T.E, 1986. *J. Electrochem. Soc.,* 133:2476.

Graedel, T.E, 1987. *J. Electrochem. Soc.,* 134:109.

Graedel, T.E, 1989. *J. Electrochem. Soc.,* 136:193.

Graedel, T.E, Franey J.P and Kammlott G.W, 1984. *Corrosion Science.*, 224:599.

Graedel, T.E, Franey J.P, Gualtieri G.J, Kammlott G.W and Malm D.L, 1985. *Corros. Sci.,* 25: 1163.

Graedel, T.E, J. 1989. *Electrochem. Soc.*, 136:204C.

Graedel, T.E, Nassau K. and Franey J.P, 1987. *Corros. Sci.,* 27:639.

Graedel, T.E., 1996. *Corros. Sci.,* 38:2153.

Grossman, P.R., 1987. Atmospheric Factors Affecting Engineering Metals, ASTM STP, 646.

Hatch and John E, 1984. *Aluminium: Properties and Physical Metallurgy ASM OHIO*, 256.

Hatch, J.E, 1984. *Aluminium: Properties and Physical Metallurgy*, Metral Park, OH, ASM, Int., 200.

Haynie, F.H, 1980. *ASTM STP 691 Philadelphia*, PA:ASTM, 157.

Haynie, F.H, 1988. *ASTM STP 965 Philadelphia*, PA:ASTM, 282.

Horng, Y.T, Yiang I and Chang T.C, 1987. *10th Int. Cong. Metallic Corros.*, Madras, India.

Hu Cheng, Changbao Zhu, Bin Huang, Mi Lu, Yong Yang. *Electrochimica Acta 52* (2007) 5789-5794.

Indira, C.J, Prasad K.V, Syamala Kumari V.S, Namboodiri P.N.N, Natesan M, Palaniswamy N and Raghavan M, 2000. *10th Nat Cong. Corros Cont.*, Madurai, India, 148.

Joel, P.S. and Karl W, 1992. *Mater. Perf.,* 31:46.

Johansson, E, 1984. *KI report*, Swedish Corrosion Institute.

Jovic, V.D., M.W. Barsoum, B.M. Jovic, A Ganguly, T.El-Raghy. *Journal of Electrochemical Society*, 53 (7) B 238-B234, (2006)

Julve, E. and Gustems L.L, 1993. *Corros. Sci.,* 35:1273.

Karlsson, A, Moller P. J and Vagn *J, 1990. Corros. Sci.*, 30:153.

Kawamura, K and Kaplan I.R, 1984. *Anal. Chem.* 56:1616.

Keene, W.C, Galloway J.N and Holden J.D, Jr., 1983. *Journal of Geophys.* Res., 88:5122.

Keene, W.C. and Galloway J.N. 1984. *Atmos Environ.,* 18:2491.

Knotkova-Cermakova, D and VLchkova Y, 1971. *Br. Corros.* J., 6:17.

Kok, G.L, Darnall K.R, Winer A.M, Pitts J.N, Jr and Gay B W, 1978. *Environ. Sci. Technol.*, 12:1077.

Leest, R.E.v.d, 1986. *Werkst. Korros.*, 37:629.

Lenglet, M. Lopitaux J, Leygraf C, Odnevall !, Carballeria M, Noualhaguet J.C, Guinement J. Gautier J and Boissel J, 1995. *Journal of Electrochem.* Soc., 142:3690.

Lipfert, F.W, 1987. *Mater. Perf.,* 26:12.

Lobnig, R.E, 1996. *J. Electrochem. Soc.,* 143:1539.

Lobnig, R.E, Frankenthal R.P, Siconolfi D, J and Sinclair J.D, 1993. *Journal of Electrochem. Soc.,* 140; 1902.

Lobnig, R.E., Frankenthal R.P., Siconolfi J.D, Sinclair J.D and Stratmann M, 1994. *J. Electrochem. Soc.,* 141:2935.

Lobnig, R.E., Siconolfi D.J, Maisano J, Grundmeier G, Streckel H, Frankenthal R.P., 1996. Stratmann M and Sinclair J.D., *Journal of Electrochemical Soc.*, 143:1175.

Lopez-Delgado, A, Cano, E, Bastidas J.M and Lopez F.A, 1998. *Journal of Electrochem Soc.,* 145:4140.

M. Lebrini, F. Bentiss, H. Vezin, M. Lagrenee Corrosion Science 48 (2006) 1279-1291.

Manning, M, 1988. *Air pollution, acid rain and the environment. Report by Watt Committee on Energy* HMSO, U.K.

Mansikkamaki, K., P. Ahonen, G. Fabricius, L. Murtomaki and K. Kontturi. *Journal of the Electrochemical Society*, 152(1) B 12-B16 (2005).

Mardar, A.R., 1997. ASM Handbook, ASM*, Metais Park*, Vol. 20, 470.

Marsh, G.P, Taylor K.J, Bryan G and Worthingus S.E, 1986. *Corrosion Science*, 26:971.

Mattson, E, 1985. *Chemtech*, 15:234.

Mayne, J.E.O, and Burkill J.A, 1986. *Br. Corros. J.,* 21:20.

Mohan, P.S, Natesan M, Sundaram M and Balakrishnan K, 1996. *Bulletin of Electrochem.*, 12:91.

Mohan, P.S, Sundaram M and Guruviah S, 1987. *10th Int. Cong Metallic Corros.*, Madras, India. 179.

Money, K.L, 1987. Metals Handbook Corrosion, Metals Park, Ohio, ASM International, 204.

Morcillo, M, 1995. *Atmospheric Corrosion,* ASTM STP 1239, ASTM, Philadelphia, 257.

Morcillo, M, Chico B, Otero E and Mariaca L, 1999. *Mater. Perf.*, 24:72

Morcillo, M. Chico B, Mariaca L and Otero E. 1999. *Corros. Sci.,* 41:91.

Moskivin, L.N, Efimov A.A, Teterin V.F and Tomilov S.S, 1982. *Teploenergetika* (Moscow), 9:12.

Naeemi, A.H and Albrecht P, 1984. Int. Cong. Metallic Corros., Toronto, Canada, 418.

Naixin, X, Zhao L, Ding C, Zhang C, Li R and Zhong *Q, Corros Sci.,* (2002). 44-163.

Natesan, M, Palaniswamy N, Rengaswamy N.S., Rajesh Kumar S and Raghavan M, 2002. 7th. *Int. Symp. Advance in Electrochem, Sci. and Technol.* Chennai, India.

Notoya, T, 1991. *J. Mater. Sci. Lett.*, 10:389.

Nriagu, S.O, 1978. *Sulfur in the Environment.* Part II. *Ecological Effects*, John Wiley, New York.

Odnevall, W.I and Leygraf C., *Corrosion. Science*, 43(2001) 2379.

Oesch, S and Faller M, 1997. *Corros. Sci.*, 39:1505.

Parkinson, A.R, 1980. Anti-Corros., *Methods. Mater.*, 37:11.

Patterson, W.S. and Wilkinson J.H, 1938. *J. Soc. Chem. Ind.*, 57:445.

Pawar, Pritee, A.B. Gaikwad and P.P. Patil. *Electrochimica Acta* 52 (2007) 5958-5967.

Pearson, E.C, 1952. Huff H.J and Hay R.H, *Can. J. Technol.*, 30:311.

Petrova, T.I, Kharitonova N.L and Popova A.I, 1982. *Tr. Mon Energ. Inst.*, 575:86.

Pourbaix, M and Pourbaix A, 1989. *Corros.*, 45:71.

Raynor, G.S, Smith M.E and Singer I.A, 1974. *Journal of. Air Poll Contr. Assoc.*, 24:586.

Rice, D.W, Peterson P, Rigby E.B, Phipps P.B, Cappell R.J and Tremoureus R, 1981. *J. Electrochem.* Soc., 128:275.

Roberge, P.R, 1999. *Handbook of Corrosion Engineering,* McGraw-Hill, USA. 58.

Rozenfeld, I.L, 1961. Proc. *1st Int. Cong. Metallic Corros.*, Butterworth, London, 243.

Santucci, S and Picozzi P, 1984. *Thin Solid Films*, 113:243.

Sanyal, B and Bhadwar D.V, 1962. *J. Sci. Ind. Res.*, 21D: 243.

Sastry, T.P. and Rao V.V, 1981. J. *Electrochem. Soc. India*, 30:289.

Sawant, S.S and Wagh A.B, 1991. *Corros. Prev. Cont.*, 6:75.

Scendo, M., *Corrosion Science* 47 (2005) 2778-2791.

Schikorr, G, 1961. *Werkst. Korros.*, 12:1.

Schikorr, G, 1964. Werkst. *Korros.*, 15:457.

Schikorr, G, 1967. *Werkst. Korros.*, 18:514.

Schmid, G.H, Z. 1959. *Electrochem*, 63: 1183.

Scully, J.C., 1990. *The Fundamentals of Corrosion* 3rd Edn., Pergamon Press, New York.

Seinfeld, J., 1986. *Atmospheric Chemistry and Physics of Air Pollution*, Wiley, New York.

Seinfeld, J.H, 1986. *The Atmospheric Chemistry and Physics of Air Pollution*, Wiley, New York.

Sharma, S.P, 1980. J. *Electrochem. Soc.*, 127:21.

Shetty, S. Divakara, Prakash Shetty and H.V.S. Nayak, *Indian Journal of Chemical Technology*, Vol. 12, July 2005 pp 462-465.

Shreir, L.L, Jarman R.A and Burstein G.T, 1994. *Corrosion* Vol. 1, Butterworth-Heinemann, Ltd. Great Britain, 2:35.

Simon, D, Mollimard D, Perin C and Bardolle J, 1988. *Proc. 14th Int. Conf. Electric* Contacts, Paris.

Sinclair, J.D and Psota-Kelty L.A, 1984. *Proc. 9th Int. Cong. Metallic Corros.*, Ottawa, Canada, 8:296.

Sinclair, J.D, 1988. *J. Electrochem. Soc.*, 135:89C.

Sinclair, J.D, 1993. *The Electrochem. Soc. Proce. Series*, Pennington, New Jersey, 93:325.

Sinclair, J.D, Psota-Kelty L.A and Peins G.A, 1992. *Atmos. Environ.*, 26A:871.

Sinclair, J.D, Psota-Kelty LA, Weschler C.J and Shields H.C, J. 1990. *Electrochem. Soc.*, 137:1200.

Sinclair, J.D. and Psota-Kelty L.A, 1990. *Atmos. Environm.*, 24A:627.

Skorchelletti, V.V and Tukachinsky S.E, 1955. *J.Appl. Chem.*, 28:615.

Speller, F.N., 1951. *Corrosion (Causes and Prevention)*, McGraw-Hill Book Company Inc., New York.

Speller, F.N., *Corrosion Cause and Prevention*, New York, London (1935).

Spence, J.W, Haynie F.H, Lipfert F.W, Cramer S.D and McDonald L.G. 1992. *Corros.*, 48:1009.

Stevenson, C.M and Roy Q.J, 1968. *Mateorol. Soc.*, 94:56.

Stiles, D.C and Edney E.O, 1989. *Corros*, 45:896.

Stroosnijder, M.F., C. Brugnoni, G. Laguzzi, L.Luv, N.De Cristofsro. *Corrosion Science* 46 2004 2355-2359.

Sundaram, M, Mohan P.S and Ananth V, 1987. *10th Int. Cong. Metallic Corros.*, Madras, India, 143.

Svensson, J.E and L.G. Johansson, 1993. *J. Electrochem. Soc.*, 140:2210.

Syed, S. Abd El Rehim, hamdi H. Hassan, Mohammed A. Amin. *Corrosion Science* 46 (2004) 5-25.

Thomas, H.E and Alderson H.N., 1968. *Metal Corrosion in the Atmosphere*, ASTM STP; 435:83.

Tidblad, J and Leygraf C, 1995. J. Electrochem.Soc., 142:749.

Tidblad, J, Leygraf C and Kucera V, 1991. *J. Electrochem.* Soc., 138:3592.

Trimgham, T.C.E., 1958. Causes and Prevention of Corrosion in AIR Craft, SIR ISAAC, Pitman & Sons, Ltd.

Uhligh, H.H, 1985. *Corrosion and Corrosion Control*, John Wiley and Sons, New York.

Van, V, C. C, Luria M, Ray J.D, Gunter R.L, Wellman D.L. and Boatman J.F, 1987. EOS-Trans. AGU, 68:1212.

Vashi, R.T and Patel H.G, 1997. *Bull. Electrochem.*, 13:343.

Vashi, R.T, Malek G.M, Champaneri V.A and Patel R.N, 2002 Bulletin of Electrochemistry., 18:91.

Vassie, P.R., 1987. *Br. Corros. J.*, 22:37.

Vasudevan, T., S. Muralidharan, S. Al and S.V.K. Iyer. *Corrosion Science 37* (1995) 1235-1244.

Vernon W.H.J, 1931. Trans. Far. Soc., 27:255.

Vernon, W.H.J, 1934. J. *Chem. Soc.*, 1853.

Vernon, W.H.J, 1935. *Trans. Far. Soc.*, 31:1668.

Vilche, J.R, Varela F.E, Acuna G, Codaro E.N., Rosales B.M, 1995. Fernandez A and Moriena G, *Corros. Sci.*, 37:941.

Walters, G.W, 1991. *Corros. Sci, 32:* 1353.

Walters, G.W, 1991. *Corros. Sci., 32:* 1331.

Zakipour, S, Leygraf C and Portnoff G, 1986. *J. Electrochem.* Sco., 135:873.

Zakipour, S, Tidblad J and Leygraf C, 1995. *J. Electrochem. Soc.*, 142:757.

Zika, R, Saltzman E., Chameides W.L and Davis D.D, 1982. *Journal of Geophys. Res.*, 87:5015.

12

Corrosion Testing

Base Case

In order to obtain a relative ranking of the corrosion resistance of steel materials for underbody structural components, the Auto/Steel Partnership is conducting laboratory tests at ACT Laboratories, Inc. in Hillsdale, Ml. Eight materials are being tested in the as delivered (*i.e.*, without post-coatings) condition. The sheet steel materials are:

- 1010 Hot Rolled,
- 1008 Galvanneal 45A45A,
- 1008 Hot Dip Galvanized G60,
- Hot Dip Galvanized G90.
- 350 MPa Hot Rolled,
- T1-25 Aluminized.
- 409 High Chrome Hot Rolled and
- 700 MPa NUCu Hot Rolled.

The 1010, 1008 and 350 MPa materials are all commonly used to manufacture current underbody structural components. The T1-25, 409 and 700 MPa materials have been included because of their potential to offer improved corrosion resistance. The T1-25 and 409 materials are in curent production. The 700 MPa NUCu material is currently under development at Northwestern University in Chicago, IL. With 1.60 per cent Cu and 0.90 per cent Ni, it has excellent atmospheric corrosion resistance and may prove useful for underbody components.

The SAE J2334 Lab Test Cycle (Figure 12.1) is being used to determine the relative perforation resistance and the relative weight loss of the eight test materials. A detailed description of this test method is given in Reference 6.2. Perforation resistance is being evaluated using the speciman geometry shown in *(Figure 12.2 on page 178)*. Three sets of specimens are being tested. After 40 SAE J2334 cycles, one set of specimens is removed from the test cabinet and pit depths are measured. Pit depths on the second set are measured after 80 cycles and on the third set after 160 cycles.

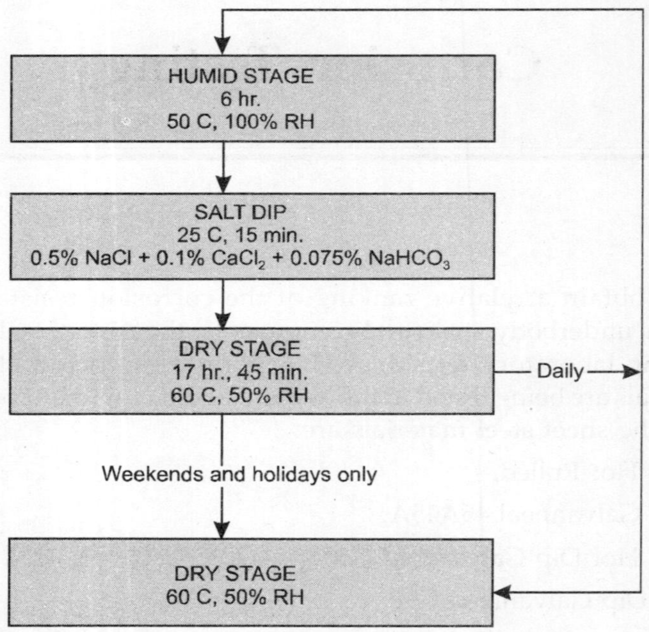

Fig. 12.1 : Perforation Specimen

Weight loss is being determined using the speciman geometry shown in (*Figure 12.3*). Again, three sets of specimens are being tested. After 40 SAE J2334 cycles, one set is removed and each specimen weighed to determine weight loss. The weight loss on the second set of specimens is determined after 80 cycles and on the third set after 160 cycles.

It is anticipated that the Auto/Steel Partnership's base case corrosion testing will be completed in early 2000. Following analysis by the Light Truck Frame Project Team, the results will be issued as a revision to this publication.

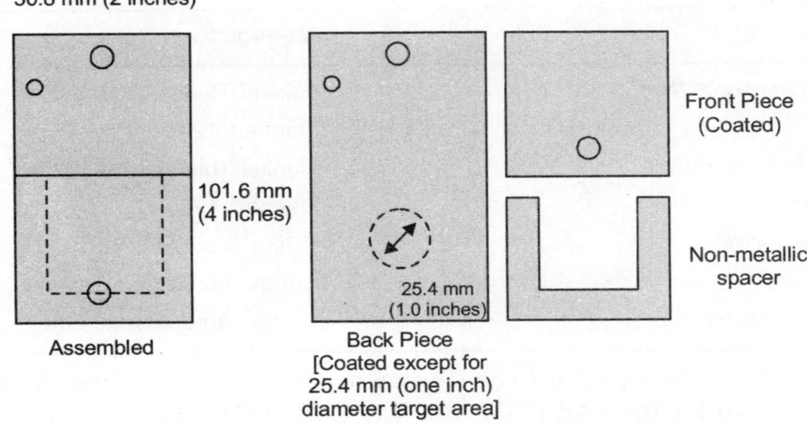

Fig. 12.2 : Weight Loss Specimen.

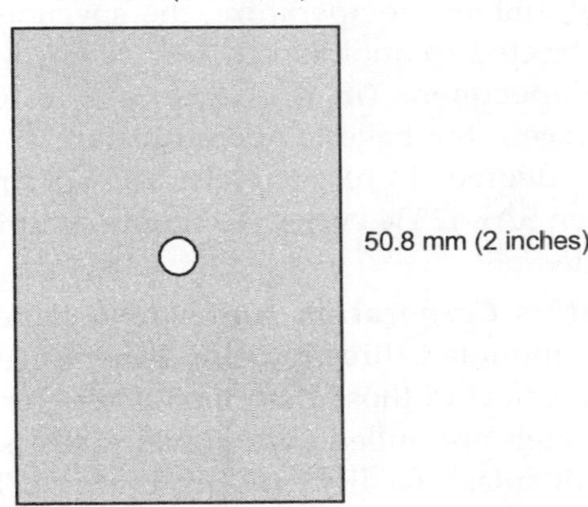

Fig. 12.3 : Weight Loss Specimen.

Coated Case

The Auto/Steel Partnership is also evaluating the relative performance of post-coatings applied to the base steel materials used for underbody structural components. The coatings under evaluation are shown in Table 12.1.

Three tests are being used to evaluate the post-coatings:

- ***SAE J2334:*** The seven coatings are being tested in triplicate up to 80 cycles. A cycle is defined in *(Figure 12.1)*. The specimens are made from SAE 1010 hot rolled sheet, 2.54 mm (0.100 inches) thick. Each specimen is a 101.6 mm × 304.8 mm (4 inches × 12 inches) rectangle, diagonally scribed after the coating has been applied. After every ten SAE J2334 cycles, the specimens are evaluated.

Table 12.1 : Pre-Coating for Underbody Structural Components

Coating	Manufacturer
Conventional Wax	Henkel Thiemelt 89-5200
	Daubert 1200
High Temperature	Henkel Thiemelt 89-5260HT
Wax	Daubert 1280HT
Electrocoat	PPG CR 590-CP 534
Polymer	Sentry Paint Alkyd Enamel
Autodeposition	Henkel Autophoretic 800

- ***SAE J2334 modified:*** The specimens are identical to those described above for the SAE J2334 test. The SAE J2334 cycle, outlined *(Figure 12.1)*, is being used. However, after every ten cycles, the specimens receive a bake and shot blast. One set of specimens (the seven coatings in triplicate) are baked for30 minutes at 149°C (300 degrees F). After two hours at ambient temperature, the specimens are shot blasted and then subjected to another ten SAE J2334 cycles. A second and third set of specimens (in triplicate) are tested using the same proce-dure except the bake temperatures are 121 and 93 degrees C (250 and 200 degrees F) respectively. The specimens are evaluated after every ten SAE J2334 cycles. Testing is continued up to 80 cycles if appropriate.
- ***General Motors Corporation trailer test:*** Panels, with the seven coatings, are mounted directly behind the wheels on a trailer. The panels are identical to those described above for the J2334 test. The trailer and panels are pulled over gravel roads (stone chipping) and through a salt splash facility (salt application). The panels are also exposed, in a booth, to high temperature/high humidity soaks. The stone chipping severity in the test is roughly representative of average customer usage in a rural environment. The test continues for ten cycles. Each cycle takes 24 hours to complete and has three phases:
- an eight hour road test plus ambient temperature soak,
- an eight hour booth soak and
- an eight hour ambient temperature soak/dry off.

ACT Laboratories, Inc. is conducting the SAE J2334 and SAE J2334 Modified tests. General Motors is conducting the Trailer Test at its Milford, Ml Proving Grounds. It is anticipated the coated case corrosion testing will be completed early in 2000. Following analysis by the Light Truck Frame Project Team, the results will be issued as a revision to this publication.

Lessons Learned-Review Questions

The following lists of questions may be used as checklists to ensure that corrosion concerns are properly addressed. The lists are based on "lessons learned" with respect to material, design, processing, testing and environmental exposure. While not all-inclusive, if the questions are addressed early in the development of an under-body structural component, the chances of success are greatly increased. If material, design, processing and test engineering groups pursue these questions individually as well as across disciplines, optimized component corrosion retarding will result.

Material Issues

1. Has the substrate material selection process included corrosion resistance as a criterion?
2. What are the corrosion mechanisms to which the substrate material will be subjected?
3. Are there any unique properties associated with the substrate material that make it susceptible to specific corrosion mechanisms (*e.g.*, higher carbon content and hardness typically result in a material being susceptible to stress corrosion cracking and embrittlement)?
4. Has the substrate material been used in other applications? Were these applications successful? Can the successful applications serve as a benchmark?
5. Will the substrate material be coated? Will the coating be applied prior to fabrication or after fabrication? What type of coating will be used (*e.g.*, metallic, wax, paint, E-coat, etc.)?
6. Is the coating selected susceptible to any unique corrosion mechanisms?
7. What factors other than the corrosion process might affect corrosion resistance (*e.g.*, chip resistance, heat resistance, dirt retention, ozone degradation, etc.)?

Design Issues

1. Does the design selected result in the component, or specific areas of the component, being susceptible to particular forms of corrosion (*e.g.*, crevice corrosion, galvanic corrosion, etc.)?
2. Has the design selected (or specific portions of the design) been utilized before? If so, are "lessons learned" readily available for review? Has a benchmarking study been conducted for previous, similar designs?

3. Does the design selected facilitate proper processing?
4. If E-coating is used, are adequate processing holes provided for current flow, and material access and egress? (For current flow, 25 mm diameter holes are typically spaced every 300 mm).
5. Does the design selected allow materials (*e.g.*, phosphates, paints, waxes, etc.) to drain properly between process stages and/or at the end of the process?
6. Are drain holes shielded or oriented to avoid direct road splash? Are the number, size and location of the drain holes adequate to provide drainage of any contaminates?
7. Have poultice (mud, debris, etc.) traps been identified and minimized?
8. Are ample air escapes (bleed holes) provided for closed sections during processing? Are these bleed holes oriented such that they complement the intended process (*e.g.*, to minimize air bubble size and location)?
9. Have the number of joints and exposed seams in the design selected been minimized?
10. Have stone impingement areas been eliminated or minimized?

Processing Issues

1. Does the design dictate specific processing techniques (*e.g.*, if adequate E-coat processing holes cannot be provided because they reduce component strength, then must a wax, paint or autophoretic coating be used)?
2. Has the proposed processing technique been utilized before? If so, how does it impact corrosion resistance?
3. What impact will fabrication processes have on pre-coated material or coatings applied after fabrication? Will fabrication damage pre-coated material? Does any fabrication process create hard to clean areas?
4. Does any fabrication process leave behind processing fluids or contaminates that are incompatible with a post-coating process?
5. Has the coating process been optimized to assist in coating coverage (*e.g.*, proper attitude of parts during the process, porpoising of frames as they proceed through tanks of paint or wax, etc.)?

Testing/Environmental Exposure Issues

1. Have corrosion validation tests been conducted on all components and sub-systems of an assembly? (A laboratory cyclic corrosion test

is highly recommended. It should be modified to cover other factors such as cyclic stress, if relevant.)

2. What is the intended service life? Is the test selected to evaluate corrosion resistance appropriate for this length of service?
3. What are the in-service environmental conditions (*e.g.*, high temperature, stone chipping, road splash, road poultice)? Have all of these environmental conditions been incorporated into a comprehensive validation plan? Has each condition been investigated individually as well as in combination with the other conditions?
4. Are specific design or material requirements dictated by the potential field environment?
5. Does customer use/maintenance have an impact on component performance (*e.g.*, frequent underbody washing, compatibility with engine fluids, etc.)?

REFERENCES

Autodeposition, Parker-Amchem Corp., 1995.

Automotive Adhesives and Sealants, Henkel Corp., 1997.

Automotive Steel Design Manual, American Iron and Steel Institute, 2000 Town Center, Suite 320, Southfield, MI 48075-1199, Revised 1998.

Categorization and Properties of Dent-Resistant, High-Strength and Ultra High-Strength Automotive Sheet Steel, SAE J2340, Society of Automotive Engineers, Inc., 400 Commonwealth Drive, Warrendale, PA, 15096-0001.

Categorization and Properties of Low-Carbon Automotive Sheet Steels, SAE J2329, Society of Automotive Engineers, Inc., 400 Commonwealth Drive, Warrendale, PA, 15096-0001.

Chemical Compositions of SAE Carbon Steels, SAE J403, Society of Automotive Engineers, Inc., 400 Commonwealth Drive, Warrendale, PA, 15096-0001.

Cracking Down on Corrosion, American Iron and Steel Institute, 2000 Town Center, Suite 320, Southfield, MI, 48075-1199, 1992.

Electrodeposition Finishes, PPG Industries Inc., 1994.

Fontana, M.G. and Greene, N.D., Chapter 4, *Corrosion Engineering,* McGraw-Hill Book Co., New York, 1978, p. 116.

Fontana, M.G. and Greene, N.D., *Corrosion Engineering,* McGraw-Hill Book Co., New York, 1967, p. 32.

High-Strength Steel Bulletin, Edition 17, Auto-Steel Partnership, 2000 Town Center, Suite 320, Southfield, MI, 48075-1123.

Jordon, D.L., Franks, L.L. and Kallend, J.S., *Relative Contributions of Several Cathodic Reactions to the Anodic Dissolution of Electrogalvanized* Steel, Paper No. 391, Proceedings of Corrosion and Corrosion Control of Aluminum and Steel in Lightweight Automotive Applications, sponsored by NACE T-14 and SAE ACAP Committees, edited by Simpson, T.C., Moran, J.P. and Soepenberg, E.N., Published by NACE, Houston, TX, 1985.

Lubrizol Hot Melt Rustproofing, The Lubrizol Corp., 1979.

Neville, R.J. and Melbourne, S.H., *Corrosion of HSLA and Mild Steels Beneath Automobiles,* Metals Performance, January 1975.

Neville, R.J., *A First Look at Coatings on HSLA Steel Under Cars,* Technical Report 76-49, American Society for Metals, Metals Park, OH, 44073, 1976.

Neville, R.J., *HSLA and Low Carbon Steel: Same Corrosion Resistance,* Metal Progress, May 1975.

Selection of Galvanized (Hot Dipped and Electrodeposited) Steel Sheet, SAE J1562, Society of Automotive Engineers, Inc., 400 Commonwealth Drive, Warrendale, PA, 15096-0001.

Sheet Steel Availability and Property Guide, insert to *High-Strength Steel Bulletin,* Edition 10, Auto/Steel Partnership, 2000 Town Center, Suite 320, Southfield, MI, 48075-1123.

Steel, High Strength, Hot Rolled Sheet and Strip, Cold Rolled Sheet, and Coated Sheet; SAE J1392, Society of Automotive Engineers, Inc., 400 Commonwealth Drive, Warrendale, PA, 15096-0001.

Townsend, H.E., Davidson, D.D. and Ostermiller, M.R., *Development of Laboratory Corrosion Tests by the Automotive and Steel Industries of North America,* Proceedings, Fourth International Conference on Zinc and Zinc Alloy Coated Steel Sheet, Tokyo, 1998.

13

Sample Research Work on Corrosion

SOME SULPHATED WATER SOLUBLE NATURAL POLYMER (CARRAGEENANS) COMPOUNDS AS CORROSION INHIBITORS FOR DISSOLUTION OF IRON IN HYDROCHLORIDE ACID SOLUTION

K.S. Khairou and I. Zaafarany

Chemistry Department. Faculty of Applied Sciences, Umm Al-Qura University, Makkah Al Mukaramha P.O. Box - 118 (Saudi Arabia)

ABSTRACT

The effect of some sulphated water soluble polymer (carrageenan) compounds on the corrosion behaviour of iron electrode in 1M hydrochloric acid solution as corrosive medium has been investigated using galvanostatic polarization technique. Some corrosion parameters such as anodic and catholic Tafel slope, corrosion potential, corrosion current density, surface coverage and inhibition efficiency was calculated. The polarization measurements indicated that the inhibitors are mixed type. The inhibition efficiency was found to increase with increasing concentration and number of sulpher atom per molecules. Inhibition was explained on basis of parallel adsorption of these compounds on the iron electrode. The adsorption process follows Langmuir adsorption isotherm.

Key words: Iron, corrosion inhibitors, adsorption, Carrageenans compounds.

Introduction

The study of corrosion is of high practical and technological interest. Acids find applications in industrial acid cleaning, acid pickling, acid descaling and oil well acidizing, inhibitors are commonly employed in these environments to minimize the base metal corrosion by the acids. The selection of appropriate inhibitors mainly depends on the type of acid, its concentration, temperature, velocity, presence of dissolved solids and the type of metallic materials involved. The important prerequisites for a compound to be an efficient inhibitor are: (*i*) it should form a defect free, compact barrier film; (*ii*) it should chemisorb on to the metal surface; (*iii*) it should be polymeric polymerize in sites on the metal; and (*iv*) the barrier thus formed should increase the inner layer thickness.

Most of the well-known inhibitors used for inhibition of iron in acidic medium are organic compounds containing nitrogen, sulpher and/or oxygen atoms. It has been observed that most of the organic inhibitors act by adsorption on the metal surface. This phenomenon is influenced by the nature and surface charge of metal, by the type of aggressive electrolyte and by the chemical structure of inhibitors.

The aim of the present work in to study the effect of there compounds of sulfated water soluble natural polymer (carrageenan) compounds as corrosion inhibitors on the corrosion of iron in 1M HCl using galvanostatic polarization technique.

Carrageenans Compounds

Carrageenans are linear polymer of about 2500 galactose derivates with regular but imprecise structure dependent on the source and extraction conditions. The structural unit of these compounds are as follows:

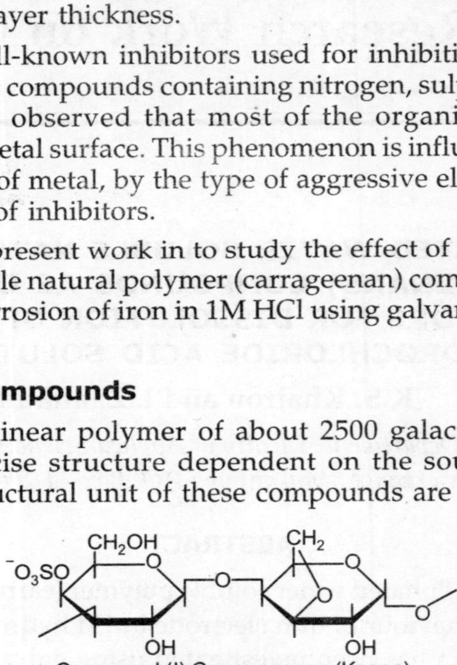

Compound (I) Carrangeenan (Kappa)

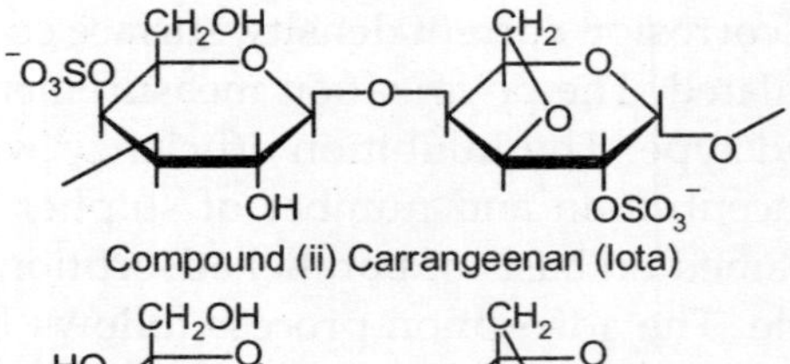

Compound (ii) Carrangeenan (Iota)

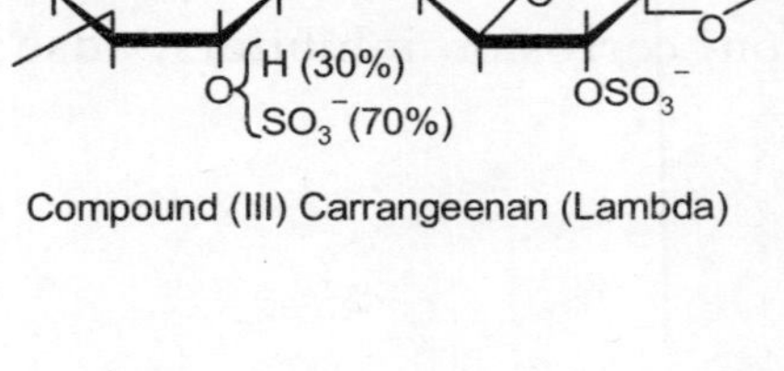

Compound (III) Carrangeenan (Lambda)

Experimental

Iron electrode having the chemical composition (%) 0.052C, 0.189 Mn, 0.008P, 0.011 S. 0.011 Si, 0.012 Cr, 0.029 Ni, 0.04 Cu, 0.039 Al and the remainder is Fe, provided by the "Saudi Iron and Steel Company" was used in the present study. The bottom end of the rod specimen with mean surface area of 1 cm^2 was successively abraded with 1-0 and 00-emery paper, degreased with acetone and dried between filter paper then immersed in 100 ml of the test solution.

Galvanostatic polarization measurements were carried out using Mensberg potentiostat/galvanostat PS6 with controlling software (PS remote) was used for accurate measurements of potential and current density. Three compartment cell with a saturated calomel reference electrode (SCE) and a platinum foil auxiliary electrode was used.

Results and Discussion

Addition of different concentrations of carrageenans compounds on the galvanostatic polarization of iron electrode was studied in 1M HCl. Figure 13.1 shows that the effect of compound III as a typical example. Similar curves were obtained for other compounds (not shown). From these curves one can observe that at first transition region in which the potential increases (anodic polarization) or decreases (cathodic polarization) slowly with current density followed by a rapid linear increase of potential (Tafel region).

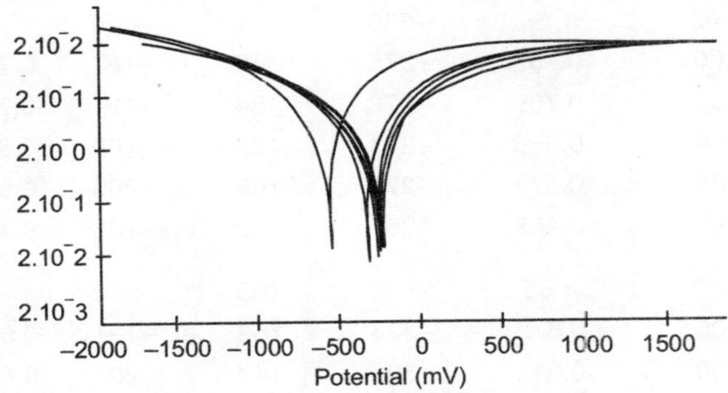

Fig. 13.1 : Galvanostatic Polarization Curves for Iron Electrode in 1M HCl in absence and presence of different concentration of compound III

(1) 0.00 ppm (2) 100 ppm (3) 200 ppm (4) 300 ppm (5) 400 ppm (6) 500 ppm.

Transition region which starts from the free corrosion potential and extends to the beginning of the Tafel region is characterized by the simultaneous occurrence of cathodic hydrogen evolution and anodic dissolution of metal. At the end of transition region there is a metal dissolution and the current becomes purely anodic (anodic polarization) or hydrogen evolution takes place with suppressing the metal dissolution and the current is purely cathodic (cathodic polarization).

The values of corrosion current density ($I_{corr.}$) was determined by the intersection of the extrapolated of the cathodic and anodic Tafel lines with the stationary corrosion potential ($E_{corr.}$). The percentage inhibition efficiency (I.E.) was calculated using the following equation.

$$\text{I.E.} = \left(1 - \frac{I_{add}}{I_{free}}\right)100 \qquad ...(13.1)$$

where, I_{add} and I_{free} are the corrosion current densities in the absence and presence of the inhibitors, respectively.

Table 13.1 shows the effect of inhibitor concentrations on the corrosion kinetic parameters such ad anodic and cathodic Tabel slops (β_a and β_c) E_{corr}, I_{corr}. surface coverage θ and I.E.

An inspection of the results obtained from Table 13.1 reveals that, the increasing in concentrations of the additives compounds show the following:

Table 13.1 : Corrosion Parameters obtained from Galvanostatic Polarization Technique of Iron Electrode in 1M HCl Containing different Concentrations of Carrageenas Compounds

	Inhibitor conc., ppm	I_{corr}, (μAcm^{-3})	E_{corr} mV (sec)$^{-1}$	b_a mV dec^{-1}	β_c	θ	I.E
Compound I	0.00	1.65	–530	163	–200	–	–
	100	0.755	–276	166	–197	0.755	54-24
	200	0.705	–278	154	–191	0.705	57.27
	300	0.656	–274	157	–189	0.656	60.24
	400	0.573	–270	166	–200	0.573	65.27
	500	0.468	–261	160	–203	0.468	71.64
Compound II	0.00	1.65	–530	163	–200	–	–
	100	0.672	–320	153	–191	0.593	59.27
	200	0.612	–305	147	–206	0.629	62.88
	300	0.572	–295	161	–216	0.653	65.33
	400	0.513	–282	154	–216	0.689	68.91
	500	0.435	–268	165	–207	0.736	73.64
Compound III	0.00	1.65	–530	163	–200	–	–
	100	0.606	–315	165	–206	0.633	63.27
	200	0.570	–306	158	–196	0.654	65.43
	300	0.524	–297	164	–215	0.682	68.24
	400	0.453	–281	156	–208	0.725	72.54
	500	0.342	–278	160	–212	0.793	79.27

(*i*) The corrosion potential (E_{corr}) is shifted to more positive values and the corrosion current density (I_{corr}) decrease with increasing inhibitor concentration indicates the inhibiting effect of the compound.

(*ii*) The values of anodic and cathodic Tafel slopes (β_a and β_c) are approximately constant which suggest the simple blocking of the available surface area of the metal by the inhibitor molecules. In other words, the adsorbed inhibtor molecules decreases the surface area available for the both metal dissolution and hydrogen evolution reaction without affecting the reaction mechanism. Therefore, it could be concluded that the carrageenans compounds affect on both anodic and cathodic reaction (*i.e.*) mixed inhibitors.

(*iii*) The values of IE was found to increase with increasing the inhibitor concentration. The inhibition achieved by these compounds decreases in the following order:

compound III > compound II > compound I

The inhibition effect of these compounds can be attributed to their parallel adsorption at the metal solution interface. The parallel adsorption is owing to the presence of one or more active centre for adsorption.

Adsorption Isotherms

Carrageenan compounds inhibit the corrosion process by the adsorption on metal surface. Theoretically, the adsorption process can be regarded as a single substitution an "*x*" number of water molecules adsorbed on the metal surface *viz.*

$$I_{(aq)} + xH_2O \rightarrow I_{(sur)} + xH_2O_{(sq)} \quad ...(13.2)$$

where *x* is known as the size ratio and simply equals the number of adsorbed water molecules replaced by a single inhibitor molecules. The adsorption depends on the structure of the inhibitor, the type of the metal and the nature of its surface, the nature of the corrosion medium and its pH value, the temperature and the electrochemical potential of the metal solution interface. Also, the adsorption provides information about the interaction among the adsorbed molecules themselves as well as their interaction with the metal surface. Actually an adsorbed molecules may make the surface more difficult or less difficult for another molecules to become attached to a neighbouring site and multilayer adsorption take place. Finally, various surface sites could have varying degrees of activation. For these reasons a number of mathematical adsorption isotherm expression have been developes to take into consideration some of non-ideal effects.

The respect inhibitive action of polymer compounds due to adsorption of its compounds on the iron surface among a barrier for change and mass transfer between the metal and corrosive environment. As the concentration of polymer compounds increases the fraction of iron surface covered by adsorbed molecules (θ) increases resulting in higher inhibition efficiency.

The degree of surface coverage (θ) was calculated using the following equation:

$$\theta = \frac{I_{add}}{I_{free}} \qquad \text{...(13.3)}$$

where I_{free} and I_{add} are the corrosion current densities in the absence and presence of the additive compounds, respectively. The value of θ are reported in Table 13.1. The degree of surface coverage θ was found to increase with increasing the concentration of additives.

Attempts were made to fit θ values to various isotherms *e.g.* (Frumkin, Temkin, Freundlich and Langmuir). The best fit was obtained with Langmuir isotherm according to the following equation:

$$\frac{\theta}{1-\theta} = KC \qquad \text{...(13.4)}$$

and rearranging it gives:

$$\frac{C}{\theta} = \frac{1}{K} + C \qquad \text{...(13.5)}$$

where (C) is the concentration of additive is the equilibrium constant of adsorption.

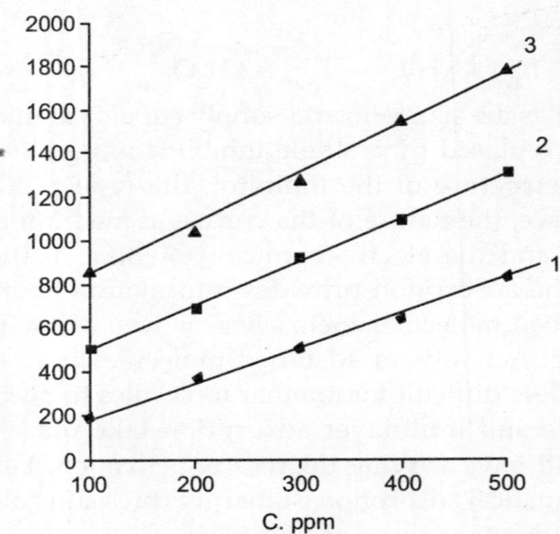

Fig. 13.2 : Langmuir Adsorption Isotherm (1) compound I (2) compound II (3) compound III.

The plot of $\frac{C}{\theta}$ against C gives a straight lines of intercept $\frac{1}{K}$. The plots are shown for polymer compounds additives in Figure 13.2. The resulted straight lines from the above relation have almost the unit slopes. This indicates that, the adsorption of polymer compounds on the iron surface follows Langmuir adsorption isotherm and consequently, there is no interaction between the molecules adsorbed at the iron, surface.

The equilibrium constant of adsorption (Ka) in related to the standard free energy of adsorption (ΔG^*_{ads}) by the relation.

$$K_a = \frac{1}{55.5}\exp\left[\frac{-\Delta G^*_{ads}}{RT}\right] \quad ...(13.6)$$

where R is universal gas constant, the value 55.5 is the concentration of water in the solution in mole.

The values of Ka and ΔG_{ads} of the inhibitors adsorbed on the iron surface were calculated and listed in Table 13.2.

Table 13.2 : The Equilibrium Constant of Adsorption and the Standard Free Energy of Adsorption of the Carrageenas Compounds on the Surface of Iron at 25°C

Inhibitors	Ka	ΔG_{ads} KJ mole^{-1}
Compound I	5.57×10^{-3}	–2.939
Compound II	2.08×10^{-3}	–5.445
Compound III	1.54×10^{-3}	–6.092

The standard free energy of adsorption is associated with water adsorption/desorption equilibrium which forms an important part in the overall free energy change of adsorption. It is clear that ΔG^*_{ads} increases with increasing the size of molecules. The negative values of ΔG^*_{ads} obtained here indicated that the adsorption process of these compounds on the iron surface is spontaneous one.

Conclusions

1. Carrageenans compounds act as an inhibitor to corrosion of iron in 1M HCl solution.
2. The inhibition efficiency increases with the increasing the inhibitor concentrations.
3. The inhibition process is due to the adsorption of the inhibitor molecule on the iron surface.
4. The adsorption of carrageenans compounds on the iron surface follows Langmuir adsorption isotherm.

REFERENCES

Abd El-Maksoud, S. A., *Corros. Sci.*, 44, 803 (2002).

Abd El-Maksoud, S.A., *Corros. Sci.*, 44 (4) 803 (2002).

Abd, El. Maksound, S.A. *Appl. Surf. Sci.*, 206, 129 (2003).

Abdallah, M., *Materials Chem. and Phys.*, 82, 786 (2003)

Abdallah, M: *Bull of Electrochem.* 16 (6) 258 (2000).

Abdel, Rehim, S.S, Khaled, K.F. and Abd El-Shafi, N.S., *Electrochim Acta.* 51(16), 3269 (2006).

Blomgern, E., Bockris, J.O.M. and Jesech, C: *J. Phys. Chem.*, 65, 200 (1961).

Chebabe, D., Ait Chikh, Z., Hajjaji, N., Srhiri, A and Zucchi, F., *Corros. Sci.*, 45 (2) 309 (2003).

Chetouani, A., Harmouti, B., Benhadda, T. and Daoudi, M., *Appl. Surf. Sci.*, 249 (1-4), 375 (2005).

Emergil. K.C. and Atako, O., *Materials Chem. and Phys.*, 82 (2-3), 373 (2004).

Epelbion, I., Morel, P. and Tokenout, H: *J. Electrochem Soc.*, 118, 1282 (1971).

Jeyaprabha, C., Sathiyanarayanan, S. and Venkatachari, *G., Electrochim Acta,* 51 (19), 4080 (2006).

Khaled, K.F., *Appl. Surf Sci.*, 230, 307 (2004).

Khaled. K.F., *Electrochim Acta,* 48 (17), 2493 (2003).

Kliskic, M., Radosevic, J. and Gndic: *J. Appl. Electrochem.* 27, 947 (1997).

Lu, BT., Chen, Z.K., Luo, J.L. Patchett, B.M. and Xu, ZH: *Electrochim Acta,* 50 (6) 139 (2005).

PITTING CORROSION OF PURE IRON ELECTRODE IN OH/ CL SOLUTIONS AND ITS INHIBITION BY SULPHATED WATER SOLUBLE NATURAL POLYMER

K.S. Khairo and I. Zaafarany*

Chemistry Department, Faculty of Applied Science, Umm Al-Qura University, Makkah Al-Mukaramaha, P.O. Box-118 (Saudi Arabia)

ABSTRACT

Pitting corrosion of an iron electrode in 0.1 M NaOH solution containing increased addition of NaCl solutions was studied. As the concentrations of NaCl increases the pitting potential was shifted to more negative direction indicating the acceleration of pitting corrosion. The pitting corrosion potential changes, with the concentrations of Cl ion according to sigmoid S-shaped curves. This behaviour was explained on the basis of the formation of passivatible active and continuously propagated pits. Addition of sulphated water soluble natural polymer (carrageenan compounds) caused a shift of the pitting potential in the noble direction accounting for increased to a pitting attack.

Key words: Iron, pitting corrosion, inhibition, carrageenan compounds.

Introduction

Some aqueous solutions containing certain ions particularly Cl, Br, I can cause a localized attack resulting in a destruction of the metal. Various metals (*e.g.* Fe, Al, Mg, Zn, Cu, Cd and Co) and their alloys are susceptible to pitting corrosion. The pitting potential, E_{pitt}, characterizes the resistance of the metal to pitting corrosion and, therefore, it can be used as a measure of the susceptibility of the different metals and alloys to pitting corrosion in aggressive environments. The nobler the value of E_{pitt}. The greater the resistance of the alloy to pitting attack.

Unfortunately, most of the corrosion inhibitors are expensive synthetic chemical having hazards properties to living creatures and environments. So, it is very important to choose cheap and safely handled compounds to be used as corrosion inhibitors. The recent research by the electrochemists and corrosion engineers tried to find naturally organic substances or biodegradable organic materials to be used as inhibitors.

The aim of the present study is to investigate the ability of some naturally occurring compounds known as carrageenans which produced from certain species of seaweeds to inhibit the pitting corrosion of iron electrode in OH/ Cl solutions using potentiodynamic anodic polarization techniques.

Experimental

The test electrode was made of pure iron obtained from Saudi Iron and Steel Company and having the following chemical compositions (%) (C 0.052, Mn 0.189, S 0.011, P 0.008, Si 0.011, Al 0.039, N 0.0001, Cr 0.0128, Cu 0.04, Mo 0.024, Ni 0.0293 and the remainder is Fe).

The bottom end of the rod specimen with a mean surface area of 1 cm^2 was successfully abraded with 1-,0- and 00-emery paper, degreased with acetone and dried between two filter paper and then immersed in 50 ml of the test solution. All chemical used were of AR quality. The solutions were prepared using bidistilled water. No attempts were made to deaerate them. The electrolytic cell was all pyrex glass and is described elsewhere.

Potentiodynamic anodic polarization of the iron electrode was performed at a scanning rate of 1mV sec^{-1}, using a Wenking potentioscan type POS-73. The current density-potential curves were recorded on X-Y recorded type PL-3. All experiments were carried out a 25 ± 1 °C.

Results and Discussion

Susceptibility of Iron Electrode to Pitting Corrosion by Chloride Ions

Figure 13.3 shows the potentiodynamic anodic polarization curves of an iron electrode in 0.1M NaOH solution with and without the addition of NaCl as pitting agent at scan rate 1mV s^1. The slow scan rate permits that the pitting initiation occurs at less positive potential. It is clear from the results that in the concentrations range of NaCl studied the metal does not exhibit an active-passive transition. However, increasing the concentrations of Cl ion, there is

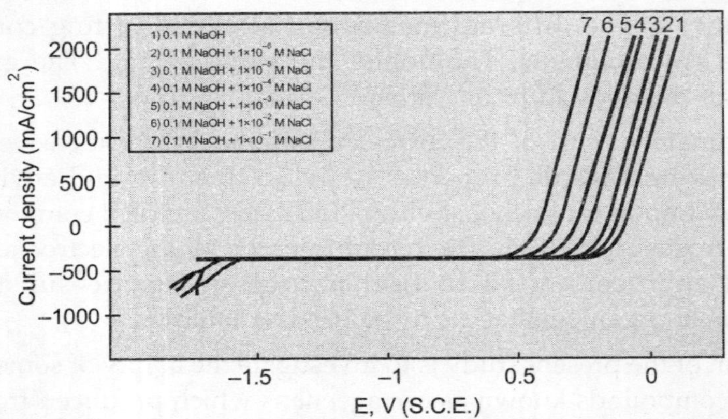

Fig. 13.3 : Potentiodynamic Anodic Polarization curves of pure Iron Electrode in 0.1 M NaOH containing different concentrations of NaCl.

a sudden and marked increase of current density at a definite potential indicating the passivity breakdown and initiation of pitting corrosion. The potential at which the sudden rise takes place is defined as the pitting potential (E_{pitt}). The higher concentration of Cl ion, the higher is the shift of pitting potential towards the active direction. The breakdown of passivity could be attributed to the adsorption of chloride ions on the passive film formed on the iron surface, which create an electrostatic field across film/solution interface. Thus, when the electrostatic field reaches a certain value, the adsorbed anions begin to penetrate into the passive film and the pitting corrosion is initiated.

Figure 13.4 represents the relationship between the pitting potential, E_{pilt} and the logarithm of the molar concentrations of the Cl^- ion. The sigmoidal S-shaped curve was obtained indicated that:

(*i*) At low Cl^- ion concentrations the pitting potential shifts slightly in a negative direction because the Cl^- ions are not sufficient to destroy completely the passivating film on the metal surface.

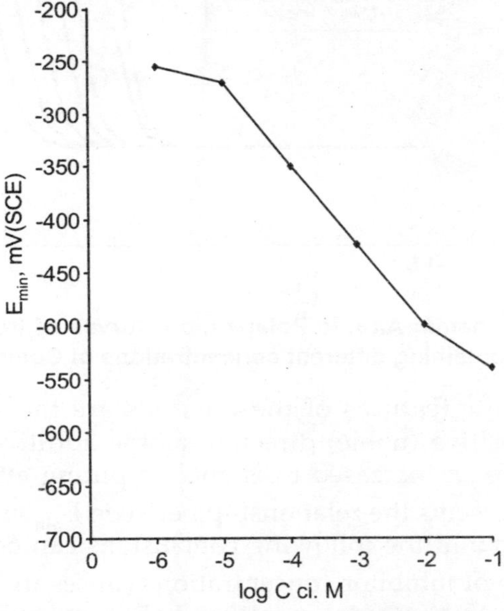

Fig. 13.4 : The Relationship between Pitting Potential of pure Iron Electrod and Logarithm the Molar concentrations of NaCl.

(*ii*) At relatively higher Cl^- ion concentrations, E_{pitt} varies with log C_{cl}^- according to straight line relationship in the form.

$$E_{pitt.} = X_1 - Y_1 \log C_{Cl}^- \qquad ...(13.7)$$

where X_1 and Y_1 are constants which depend on both the nature and the type of the aggressive anion and of the electrode. This behaviour is to be attributed to the destruction of the passive film formed on the metal surface and the pits formed continuously propagate and cannot undergo repassivation.

(*iii*) At higher Cl^- ions concentrations, it is to be expected that film breakdown showed far exceed film formation. Pits continuously propagate in a limited range of pitting potential.

Inhibition of Pitting Corrosion by Carrageenan Compounds

The effect of increasing addition of carrageenan compounds namely, compounds I, II and III on the potentiodynamic anodic polarization curves of an iron electrode in 0.1M NaOH + 0.1M NaCl solutions was studied. The curves in (Figure 13.5) represent the behaviour reported in the presence of compound III as an example of these compounds. Similar curves were obtained for other compounds I and II not shown.

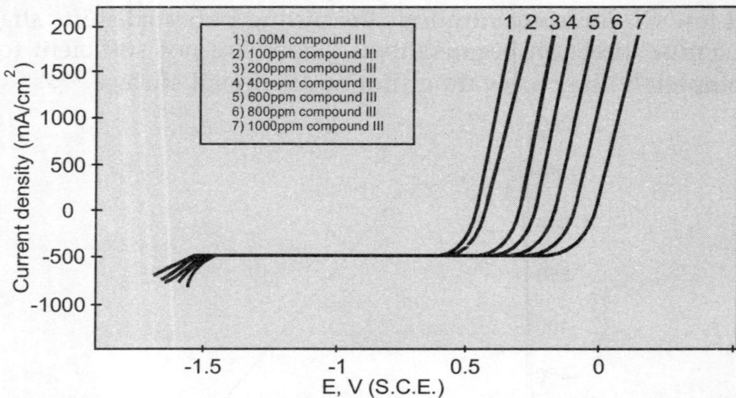

Fig. 13.5 : Potentiodynamic Anodic Polarization Curves of Iron Electrode in 0.1M NaOH + 0.1 M NaCl containing different concentrations of Compound (III).

The characteristic features of these curves are the shift of the pitting potential in the positive (noble) direction as the additive concentrations is increased indicating an increased resistance to pitting attack.

Figure 13.6 represents the relationship between E_{pitt} and log $C_{inh.}$ Straight lines were obtained and the following conclusions can be drawn:

(*i*) An increase of inhibitor concentrations causes the shift of the pitting potential into the more positive values in accordance with the following equation:

$$E_{pitt} = X_2 + Y_2 \log C_{add} \quad ...(13.5)$$

where X_2 and Y_2 are constants which depend on both nature of the electrode and the type of additives used.

(*ii*) At one and the same inhibitor concentrations, the degree of resistance to pitting corrosion attack decreases in the following order: III > II > I.

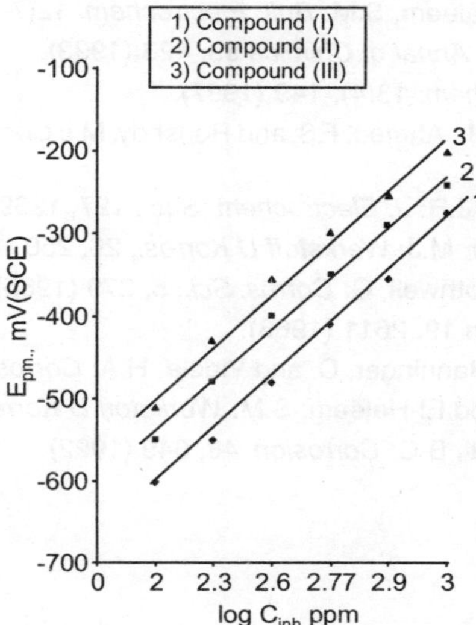

Fig. 13.6 : The Relationship between Pitting Potential and Logarithmic of Molar Concentrations of the Inhibitors.

The inhibition action of these compound, could be explained by their strong horizontal, adsorption on the electrode surface. The adsorbed layer isolate the metal from the pitting corrosive medium and increases the resistance to pitting attack.

Conclusions

1. NaCl solution accelerate the pitting corrosion of iron electrode in 0.1 M NaOH.
2. The pitting potential iron electrode varies with the logarithm of the molar concentrations of NaCI according to segmoidal S-shaped curve.
3. Carrageenan compounds inhibit the pitting corrosion of iron.
4. The inhibition action of carrageenan compounds is attributed to its horizontal adsorption on the iron surface.

REFERENCES

Abd El-Haleem, S.M. and Abd. El-Aal, A: *J. Chem. Soc of Japan:* 43, 18 (1980).

Abd El-Haleem, S.M., Abd El-Fattah, A.A. and Tayor, W: *Res. Mechanica,* 15, 97 (1985).

Abd El-Haleem, S.M., Abd El-Paheem, S.S. and Azzam, A.M., *Workstoff U Korros.* 27, 630 (1976).

Abd El-Rehim, S.S., Abd El-Wahab, S.M. and Fouad, E.E., Hassan, H.H: *Mater, Corros.,* 46, 633 (1995).

Abdallah, M, Helal, E.A. and Fouda, A.S: *Corros. Sci.,* 48, 1639 (2006).

Abdallah, M. and Abd El-Haleem, S.M: *Bull. Electrochem.* 12(7-8), 449 (1996).

Abdallah, M. and Mead, A: *Annal di Chimica* 93, 423 (1993).

Abdallah, M: *Bull, Electrochem.* 13(4), 149 (1997).

Abdel Fattah, A.A., Atia, K.M., Ahmed, F.S. and Ronshdy, M.I: *Corros. Prev. & Control,* 33, 67 1986.

Alvarez, M.G. and Galvele, J.R: *J. Electrochem. Soc.,* 127, 1239 (1980).

Foroulis, Z.A. and Thubriker, M.J: *Werkstoff U Korros.,* 26, 250 (1975).

Hoar, T.P., Mears, D. and Rothwell, G: *Corros. Sci.,* 5, 279 (1965).

Ja, M. Kolotyrkin: *Corrosion* 19, 2611 (1963).

Moreno, D.A., Ibars, J.R., Ranninger, C. and Videla, H.A: *Corros Sci.,* 48(3), 225 (1992).

Shams El-Din, A.M. and Abd El-Haleem, S.M: *Werkstoff U Korros* 24, 389 (1973).

Thompson, N.G. and Syretti, B.C: *Corrosion,* 48, 649 (1992).

POTENTIAL-MODULATED REFLECTANCE STUDY OF THE IRON IN ALKALINE SOLUTION

K.S. Khairou and I. Zaafarany

Chemistry Department, Faculty of Applied Sciences, Umm Al-Qura University, Makkah Al Mukarammah P.O. Box: 118 (Saudi Arabia).

ABSTRACT

Cyclic voltammetry and potential modulated reflectance techniques have been used to study the growth of surface films on iron electrodes in alkaline solution. There are still uncertainties about the structure of the passive film or iron. In this article, it is possible to clearly see the relationship between electrode potential and the change of the surface layer structure-particularly when using modulation spectroscopy. It has been suggested, from the results obtained, that in sweeping from hydrogen evolution to oxygen evolution a number of processes take place, altering the composition of the surface film; the composition of the surface film being a combination of Fe(II), Fe (III) and Fe(VI) in the transpassive region.

Key words: Iron, passivity, potential-modulated reflectance.

Introduction

The nature of the passivating film on iron at different pH values has been studied for many years by classical electrochemical techniques like cyclic voltammetry or impedance analysis[1-5]. Recent studies include both *ex situ* and *in situ* techniques, such as: XPS[6-15], AES[15], X-ray diffraction Mossbauer spectroscopy[8], ellipsometry[9-11], 3-parameter reflectometry[12], unenhanced Raman spectroscopy[13-14] and potential-modulated reflectance[15-22]. Many models for the passive film have been proposed, but no clear picture of it has emerged yet.

Potential-modulated reflectance (PMR) spectroscopy is a moderately priced *in situ* technique. In it the (usually minute) changes, ΔR, produced in the monochromatic light reflected from an electrode, R, by a periodic (usually sinusoidal) modulation of its polarization potential are detected by a lock-in amplifier. PMR spectroscopy is very sensitive (changes in $\Delta R/R$ as low as 10^6 are easily measured) but has the drawback that interpretation of the spectra is far from straightforward. In recent years, PMR has been used in several studies[15-22] of iron passivation, as a result of which different iron compounds were postulated to be present in the passivating layer. Here we report PMR results over a pH 14, and at all polarization potential regions where measurement was possible.

Experimental

Pure iron disk, 5 mm thick and 6 mm diam, were obtained from SABEC, main impurities were 0.15 per cent Cu and 0.1 per cent (C + P + Mn + Si). The iron disk was polished with successively finer (down to 0.05 μm) alumina powders and then degreased with acetone in an ultrasonic bath. All solvents and reagents were of p.a. quality. Ultrapure water was obtained, Solutions were deoxygenated by N_2 bubbling with vigorous magnetic stirring[23] for 10 min just before use. The Pyrex electrolytic cell had two Spectrosil flat windows set at 90°, so that the angle of incidence of the light on the electrode was 45°. Either polypropylene or Plexiglas electrode holders were used. The geometrical area of the iron electrode exposed to the solution was 1.3 cm^2. A Luggin capillary with a tap was used in order to minimize the ohmic drop and to avoid diffusion of chloride ions from the calomel reference electrode into the electrolytic solution.

A schematic diagram of the PMR setup is shown in Figure 13.7. Oriel 150W Xe and OSRAM 150W halogen lamps, Instrumatic B102 and PTI 01-001 monochromators, Hamamatsu 1P28 and R928 photomultiplier tubes, a Wenking POS 73 potentiostat, a Levell TG 200 DMP oscillator, and an EG & G-PAR 9503 lock-in amplifier were used.

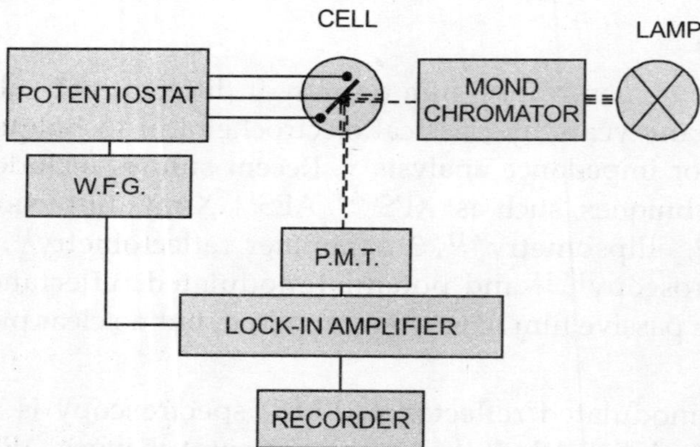

Fig. 13.7 : Schematic diagram of the setup for Measurement of Potential-modulated Reflectance (WFG: wave-function generator, PMT: Photo-multipllayer tube).

The substitution of the Xe lamp by a halogen one improved five times the signal-to-noise ratio. A servo device that kept constant the anode current, while the wavelength was swept, by changing the high voltage supplied to the photomultiplier tube allowed the direct recording of PMR spectra. The halogen lamp could be used down to 300 nm in the best cases. Special care had to be taken with the Xe lamp in the UV region, because stray light could contribute from more than 10 per cent to near 100 per cent of the total radiation, even at monochromator settings as high as 300 nm in the most unfavourable cases. This stray light may cause the appearance of false PMR maxima. Schott glass filters were used to check the level of stray light and to avoid unwanted diffraction orders. Some experiments were conducted with a diffraction grating blazed at 300 nm, instead of that blazed at 300 nm usually employed, in order to check the presence of possible artifacts caused by "ghosts" in the diffraction grating. A 50 mV rms sinusoidal wave was used to modulate the electrode potential at a frequency of 9-270Hz.

In each experiment, the PMR spectra were recorded at different polarization potentials, varying them in either the anodic or the cathodic direction. The DC and AC currents were measured with a digital voltmeter at the current out-put of the potentiostat in order to detect a possible change in the electrode during recording of spectra. After each spectrum, the inphase and quadrature components of the AC current were measured with the lock-in amplifier so that we could estimate the actual amplitude modulation applied to the double layer by a vectorial subtraction of the electrolyte ohmic resistance. Prior to recording the PMR spectrum, the inphase and quadrature components of the PMR signal, $\Delta R/R$, were measured in order to choose the higher one. We follow the usual convention for the sign of $\Delta R/R$, according to which an increase in reflectance upon a positive increase of the polarization potential is considered as positive.

Results and Discussion

Passivation of iron in NaOH solution was studied by cyclic voltammetry, sweeping from H_2 to O_2 evolution. The voltammogram in 1M NaOH is given in Figure 13.8.

For anodic peaks ($A_1 - A_4$) and two cathodic ones (C_1 and C_2) were found, in agreement with Burke. Only the peaks A_3 and C_2 grow with cycling. After several cycles and electrochromic effect was observed, the color changing from transparent to brown at low and high potentials, respectively. In the transpassive region, it is suggested that Fe (III) disappears, owing to its oxidation to an iron compound in an oxidation state higher than 3. Beck and Rangel were able to detect an anodic peak prior to oxygen evolution (FeOOH + 50H $\rightarrow FeO_4^2 + 3H_2O + 3e-$), and a cathodic reduction peak for the process ferrate (VI) to ferrate (III), using concentrated NaOH solutions. The results presented in this work demonstrated that OH concentration marked by influence the production of FeO_4^{-2}. These Fe (VI) species "FeO_3" undergo two competing chemical follow up reactions, namely:

1. Hydrolysis to yield ferrate (VI) ions, which are transported in to the bulk of solution;
2. Splitting off O_2 molecules

$$4FeO_4^{-2} + 2H_2O4FeO^2 + 3O_2 + 4OH.$$

The reflectogram, Figure 13.9-13.14 now the plot of AR vs. E in 1M NaOH at 400 nm wavelength. There is a close similarity in the positions of the peaks in comparison with Figure 13.9. The peaks at -0.6V are clearly related to the oxidation and reduction of the Fe (II)/Fe (III) couple. In each case a large peak is observed in the forward-anodic sweep. The response at +0.8V in the reflectogram correspond to the formation of Fe(VI).

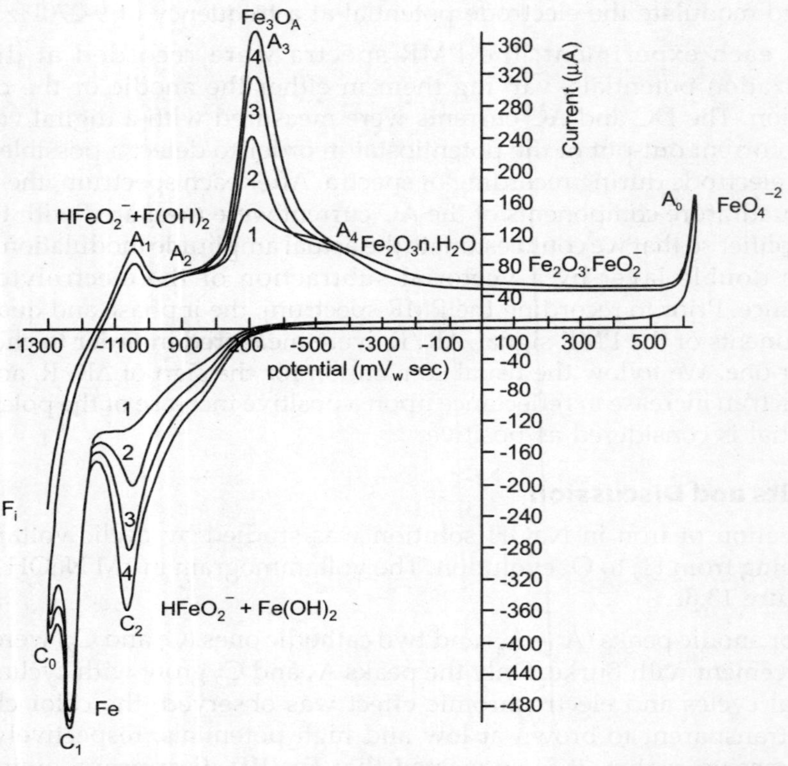

Fig. 13.8 : Cyclic Voltammetry of iron in 1M NaOH with Pourbaix information Concerning the Thermodynamic behavior of Iron Compounds.

Both reactions have a rate constant of about $1s^{-1}$. Homogeneous decomposition of FeO_4^{-2} is slower by factor of 105, yielding ferrate (*iii*) therefore an increase in the change of the peak corresponding to the reduction of Fe (III) to Fe (II), As Fe (VI) readily dissolves into the electrolyte, an etched surface is left behind, i.e., at very positive potentials the electrode starts to dissolve. As the Fe (VI) dissolves into solution, the film continues to grow. The film thickness at any time depends on the growth rate, and the rate of dissolution. Both the dissolution rate and the formation of the film depend on potential. We measured the PMR spectra.

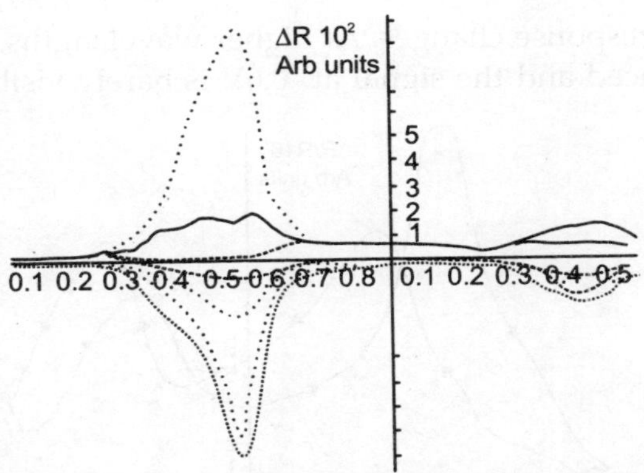

Fig. 13.9 : A plot of ΔR/R against E in 1M NaOH at a Wavelength of 400 nm Frequency 9Hz (>), 27Hz (>>) and 90Hz (>>>).

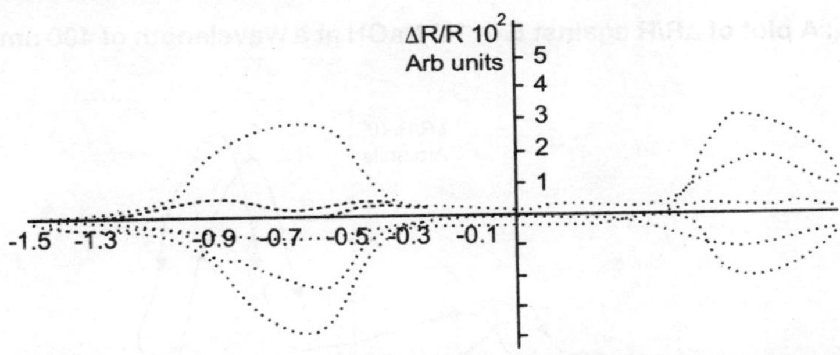

Fig. 13.10 : A plot of ΔR/R against E in 1M NaOH at a Wavelength of 500 nm Freuqncy 9Hz (>), 27Hz (>>) and 90Hz (>>>).

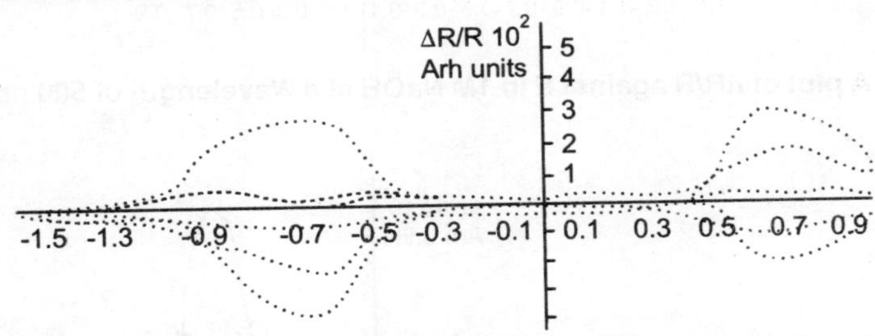

Fig. 13.11 : A plot of ΔR/R against E in 1M NaOH at a Wavelength of 600 nm Frequency 9Hz (>), 27Hz (>>) and 90Hz (>>>).

On increasing the wavelength from 400 nm to 600 nm the signals in the Fe(Il)/Fe(VI) peak region decrease, whereas the signal in the more anodic region becomes quite large in comparison. At the beginning of O_2 evolution, the oxidation of Fe(lll) to Fe(VI) occurs. Fe(VI) absorbs in the red light, and therefore a much bigger signal is seen at 600 nm, Figure 13.14.

Reflectograms of ΔR/R vs. potential were also recorded at varying wavelengths, Figure 13.12-13.14, it can be clearly seen that on increasing the wavelength the response changes. At higher wavelengths, the peak at +0.8V is more pronounced and the signal at -0.6V is barely visible.

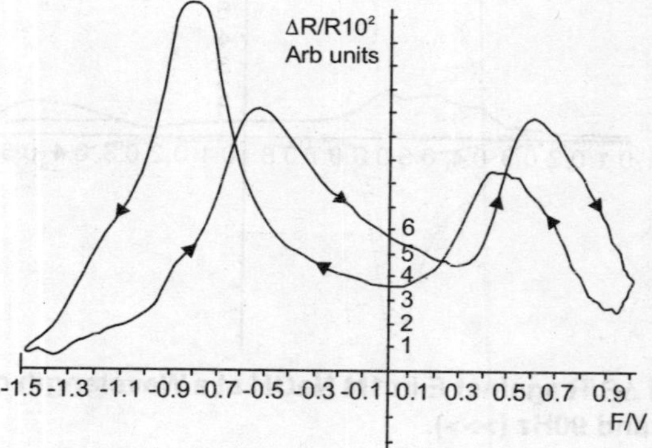

Fig. 13.12 : A plot of ΔR/R against E in 1M NaOH at a Wavelength of 400 nm Frequency 270Hz.

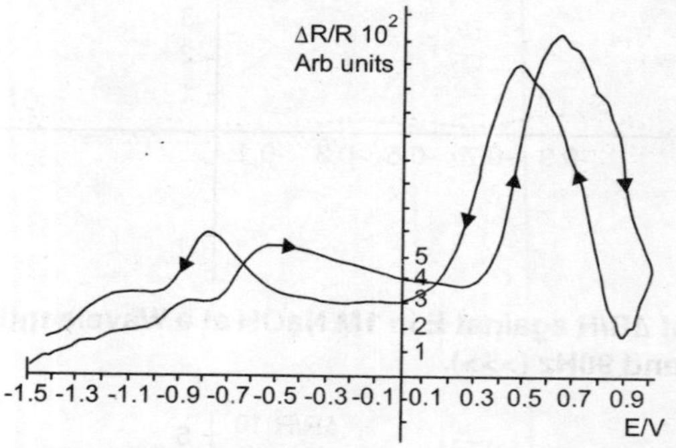

Fig. 13.13 : A plot of ΔR/R against E in 1M NaOH at a Wavelength of 500 nm Frequency 270Hz.

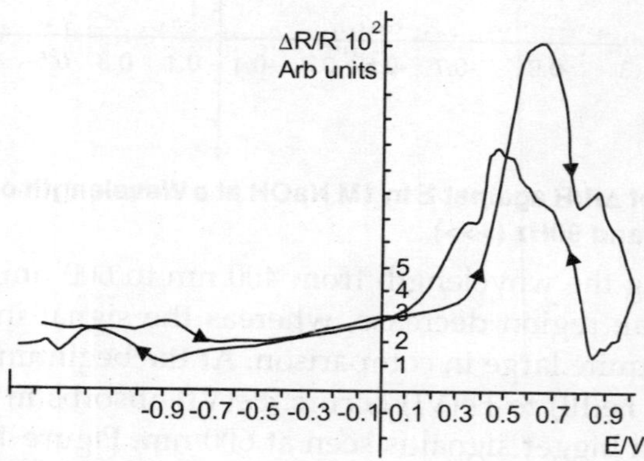

Fig. 13.14 : A plot of ΔR/R against E in 1M NaOH at a Wavelength of 600 nm Frequency 270Hz.

In 0.1M NaOH the general shape of the reflectogram was the same as in 1M NaOH. The modulated reflectance signal ΔR/R was found to be proportional to the modulation voltage. The magnitude of ΔR/R was also found to depend on the modulatic frequency as can be see in Figure 13.9-13.11. The inphase and quadrature components of the PMR signal ΔR/R, were measured in order to establish the phase shift between ΔR/R and the modulation. Figure 13.9, for example, shows that the inphase 0° and quadrature 90° component of ΔR/R are almost equal at low frequencies 9Hz. At higher frequencies, however, the 90° component in the range -0.9 to -0.5V is larger than the 0° component. This corresponds to a charge in phase angle from 45° at low frequencies to about 90° at higher frequencies 90Hz.

We considered a surface reaction involving the oxide layer. Potential modulation causes partial oxidation and reduction to occur and as a result the optical transmission of the film varies. At low frequencies the relationship between potential, current, charge and absorption are as shown in Figure 13.11. It can be seen that the reflectance signal ΔR/R should be in phase with the modulation.

At high frequencies the oxidation an reduction process are not completed on the time scale of the modulation. Consequently, the ΔR/R signal will be smaller. It is clear that the absorption is now shifted by 90° with respect to the modulation The experimental results showed that alternation does occur at high frequencies and that the phase angle tends towards 90° as expected. However, low frequencies the phase angle reached 45° rather than zero.

This showed that the processes of oxidation and reduction are relatively slow so that they are not complete even at 9Hz. It is very likely that in the passive region the PMR signal is due to electro reflectance of the oxide film and not to faradic reaction. This is supported by the fact that ΔR/R is independent of frequency, in the active and transpassive regions due to faradic reaction dependent on frequency.

Absorption Edges

FeO: has its absorption edge at about 280 nm, γ-Fe_2O_3: has its edge at 490 nm, and α-Fe_2O_3 at 570 nm. All three of the ox hydroxides α, β and γ-FeOOH have the edge at 380-420 nm. Fe_3O_4 spectra do not show a defined absorption edge in the UV region, as Fe_3O_4 is a black metallic compound, and as a result, absorption occurs in the infrared. No spectroscopic data has been found for $Fe(OH)_2$; but, as its white color appears, it has an edge in the UV region, as many Fe (II) compounds do. The soluble species, has an absorption band at 510 nm. Larramona and Gutierrez[28], assuming that the absorption edges of the compounds present in the surface film corresponded to the maxima in the PMR spectra, were able to distinguish many iron compounds from one another.

Conclusion

This part includes the results of Potential modulated reflectance. The only conclusions reached were that a number of iron compounds were present in the passivating layer. The peaks at –0.6V represent the oxidation and reduction of the Fe(II)/Fe(III) couple. In each case a large peak is observed in the forward-anodic sweep. The response at + 0.8V corresponds to the presence of Fe(Vl). The following steps are considered:

1. As far as the PMR results are concerned, the composition of the passive film on iron does not depend on pH.
2. The PMR maxima of the passive film correspond to the absorption edges of compounds in the passive layer and that the absorption edge is independent of sample crystallinity. This assumption has been able to assign the maxima in the PMR spectra of an iron electrode over a wide potential range.
3. According to the assignments of the PMR maxima, an Fe(II) compound is present at all polarization potentials, from the beginning of H_2 evolution up to the beinning of O_2 evolution, FeOOH is formed at the beginning of the passive region, and progressively dehydrates into α and γ Fe_2O_3 with increasing anodic potential, α Fe_2O_3 is oxidized to another compound at the beginning of O_2 evolution in alkaline media. The film in the active region in alkaline and borax solutions has a variable composition of Fe(II) and Fe (III).
4. More spectroscopic data, especially for $Fe(OH)_2$ and Fe_3O_4, must be obtained for more reliable assignments to be possible.

REFERENCES

Akimov, A.G., I.L. Rozenfel'd, and M.G. Astaf ev, *Zashch. Met.*, 12, 167 (1976).

Albani, O.A., J.C. Zerbino, J.R. Vilche, and A.J. Arvia, *Electrochim. Acta,* 31, 1403 (1986).

Beck, F., *Electrochimica Acta,* 30, 173 (1985).

Brett, M.E., K.M. Parkin, and M.J. Graham, *This Journal.* 133, 2031 (1986).

Burke, L.D. and M.E.G. Lyons, *This Journal,* 133, 347 (1986).

Burke, Z.D. and M.E.G. Lyons *J. Electronal. Chem.* 198, 347 (1986).

Cahan, B.D. and C.-T. Chen, *This Journal,* 129, 474 (1982).

Carrington, A., D. Schonland, *J. Chem. Sec* 659 (1957).

Chen, C.-T. and B.D. Chahan, *ibid.,* 129, 17 (1982).

Froelicher, M., A. Hugot-Le Goff, and V, Jovancicevic, A. Hugot-Le Goff, and V. Jovancicevic, in "Passivity of Metals and Semiconductors," M. Forment, Editor, p. 85, Elsevier Publishing Co., New York (1983).

Gutierrez, C. and M.A. Martinez, *This Journal,* 133, 1873 (1986).

Haupt, S., C Calinski, V. Collisi, H.W. Hoppe, H.D. Speckmann, and H.-H. Strehblow, *Suri, Interface Anal.,* 9, 357 (1986).

Hopfner, W. and W.J. Plieth, *Werkst. Korros.,* 36, 373 (1985).

Hugot-Le Goff, A. and C. Pallota, *This Journal,* 132, 2805 (1985).

Kara, N. and K. Sugimoto, This Journal, 126 1328 (1979); N. Kara and K. Sugimoto, in "Passivity of Metals and Semiconductors", M. Froment, Editor, p-211, Elsevier Publishing Co., New York (1983).

Keddam, M. and C. Pallota, *This Journal,* 132, 781 (1985).

Kolotyrkin, Ya M., R.M. Lazorenko-Manevich, and L.A. Sokolva, *J. Electroanal. Chem.,* 228, 301 (1987).

Larramona, G. and C. Gutierrez, *Electrochem. Soc.* 136, 2171 (1989).

Lorenz, W. J. and I.Mansfeld, *Electrochim Acta,* 31, 467 (1986).

Navarro, A. and C. Gutierrez, *J. Electroanal. Chem.,* 109, 361 (1980).

Ohtsuka, T., K. Azumi, and N. Sato, in "Passivity of Metals Semiconductors" , M. Froment, Editor, p. 199. Elsevier Publishing Co., New York (1983).

Ojetors, L., *Electropchim, Acta,* 21, 263 (1976).

Paaisch, W., *Surf. Sci.,* 37, 59 (1973).

Rangel, C.M., *Electrochmica Acta,* 34, 255 (1989).

Thanos, I.C.G., *Electrochim, Acta.* 31, 811 (1986).

T-Zakroczymski, C.J. Fan, and Z.Szklarska-Smialowska, *This Journal,* 132, 2862 (1985).

Vela, M.E., J.R. Vilche, and A.J. Arvia. *J. Appl. Electrochem.,* 160, 490 (1986).

Wheeler, D.J., B.D. Cahan, C.T. Chen, and E. Yeagor, in "Passivity of Metals," R.P. Frankenthal and J. Kruger, Editors, 456. The Electrochemical Society Softbound Proceedings Series, Princeton, NJ (1978).

CYCLIC VOLTAMMETRIC BEHAVIOUR OF IRON ELECTRODE IN SODIUM HYDROXIDE SOLUTIONS

I. Zaafarany

Department of Chemistry, Faculty of Applied Science, Umm Al-Qura University, P.O. Box 118, Makkah Al Mukaramha (Saudia Arabia).

ABSTRACT

The electrochemical behaviour of iron electrode in different concentrations and sweep rate of NaOH solution were studied using cyclic voltammograms. Four anodic peaks (A_1 – A_4) were observed in the anodic scan of cyclic voltammograms where as two cathodic peaks (C_1 and C_2) were observed in the cathodic scan of cyclic voltammograms. The four anodic peaks due to the formation $Fe(OH)_{ads}$ peak(A_1), $Fe(OH)_2$, peak (A_2), Fe_2O_3 (peak A_3) and formation of more stable Fe(III) species (peak A_4) and the cathodic scan due to the reduction of species formed on the anodic scan.

Key words: Iron electrode, NaOH, Cyclic voltammograms, Electrochemistry.

Introduction

Iron is one of the metal used in several fields of industry. Iron and similar metals are exposed to corrosion in connection with environmental conditions. The corrosion rate varies subject to structure of ions and molecules, kind and concentration of ions, nature of solution and type of materials.

Oxidation and reduction process taking place on iron electrode in alkaline media are important from the point of view of alkaline accumulators, and many authors have dealt with the reaction mechanism and influence of additives, etc.

Extensive studies of the iron electrodes in alkaline solution have been presented in numerous publications. Two main reasons of this great interest can be given: On one hand, iron electrodes in alkaline solution could be appropriate for various accumulator applications (Fe/NiOOH, Fe/air etc). On the other hand, iron is one of the most important metal in modern technology. Corrosion problems cover the whole range of pH in aqueous systems from acidic to basic, solutions.

Iron electrodes for batteries are normally placed in concentrated alkali solution 5M KOH. The charged state of the battery in Fe (O) gained by electrochemical reduction (discharge). The discharge reaction first leads to Fe(II), which is found to be $Fe(OH)_2$. Prolonged discharge leads to the formation of a sludge which was identified by *in situ* Mossbouer spectroscopy during cyclic galvanostatic oxidation-reduction of iron and found to be mainly Fe(OOH) and unreacted $Fe(OH)_2$ on numerous occasions, it has been pointed out that the formation of oxides involves soluble Fe(II) and Fe(III) species.

Experimental

Methods: The test electrode was made up of pure Iron obtained from Saudi Iron and Steel Company and having the following chemical composition (wt%) (C, 0.052, Mn 0.189, S0.011, P 0.008, Si 0.011, Al 0.039, N 0.001, Cr 0.012, Cu 0.04, Mo 0.024, Ni 0.029, and the remaining is iron). A cylindrical iron rod embedded in aralidite with exposed surface area of 0.5 cm^2. Prior to each experiment, the surface of iron specimen were mechanically polished with different grades of emery paper, degreassed with acetone and rinsed in distilled water. No attempts were made to deareate them. The electrolytic cell was all Pyrex and described elsewhere.

Cyclic voltammograms curves (CVs) were performed using auto lab (ECO Chemie) combined with the software package GPES (General Purpose Electrochemical System). This is a computer controlled electrochemical measurement system. It consists of data acquisition system are potentiostat-galvanostat. CV's were used to study the electrochemical behaviour of iron in different concentrations of NaOH solutions sweeping from hydrogen evolution to oxygen evaluation. A measurements were taken at 25 ± 1°C.

Results and Discussion

Cyclic voltammogram behaviour of iron Electrode in NaOH solutions

The concentration range investigated was 0.1-5M NaOH (pH = 13-14). Typical voltammograms are shown in Figure 13.15 to 13.17. All the curves correspond to multicycling. The obtained voltammograms and similar to that published by Burke and Lyons, who used solutions of NaOH, four anodic peaks (A – A_4) and two cathodic peaks (C_1 and C_2) were observed; at lower concentrations, the peaks A_2 and A_4 decrease. The current of peaks A_3 and C_2 increase with the number of cycles; their dependence on the NaOH concentration passes through a maximum in the region 1M, corresponding to the maximum charge delivered by the electrode during one cycle. By a suitable choice of the limiting anodic potential it can be shown that the peak C_2 is related to A_3 and the peak C_1 is related to both A_1 and A_2 Figure 13.15. Thus, the couple C_2–A_3 belongs to one redox system and the triad C_1-A_1, A_2 to another, couple.

Table 13.3 : The Charge Density and Film Thickness Results from the Cyclic Voltammograms of an Iron Electrode in 1M NaOH

Sweep rate (mV/s)	Total anodic density (Q_a) (C/cm^2)	Peak height (I_p) A_3	Peak Potential (E_p) A_3	Charge density of A_2 of A_3 (C/cm^2)	Film thick ness (nm)
1	1.858e-3	1.24e-5	-0.747	5.813e-4	10.35
5	2.102e-3	1.471e-5	-0.702	7.631e-4	10.01
10.	2.606e-3	2.942e-5	-0.672	9.618e-4	9.14
30	2.434e-3	6.919e-5	-0.628	9.691e-4	8.54
50	3.268e-3	0.932e-3	-0.623	6.505e-3	7.93
100	4.536e-3	1.863e-3	-0.612	7.318e-3	4.2
150	5.891e-3	2.768e-3	-0.608	9.656e-3	4.06

Table 13.4 : The Multicycles Effect on the Film of an Iron Electrode in 1M NaOH

Number of cycles	Total anodic charge density (Q_a) (C/cm^2)	Peak height (I_p) A_3	Peak Potential (E_p) A_3	Charge density of A_3 (C/cm^2)
1	4.536e-3	1.201e-3	-0.620	3.286e-3
2	4.289e-3	1.225e-3	-0.618	3.414e-3
3	4.273e-3	1.244e-3	-0.6 16	3.521e-3
4	4.295e-3	1.261e-3	-0.614	3.610e-3
5	4.326e-3	1.275e-3	-0.614	3.682e-3
6	4.360e-3	1.275e-3	-0.612	3.738e-3
7	4.394e-3	1.300e-3	-0.612	3.781e-3

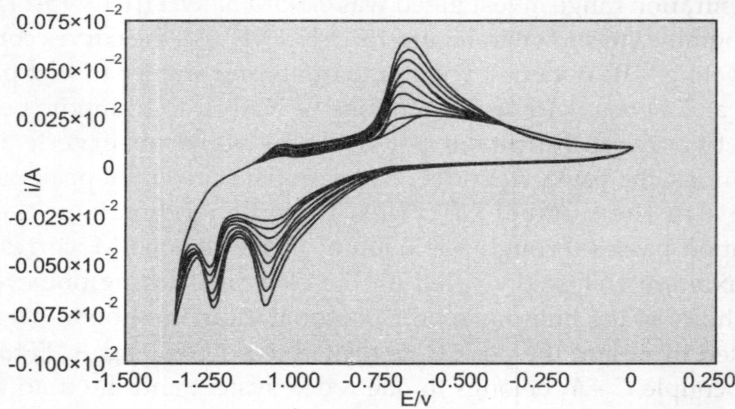

Fig. 13.15 : Cyclic Voltammetry of iron in 2M NaOH at sweep rate 1mV/s, (SCE).

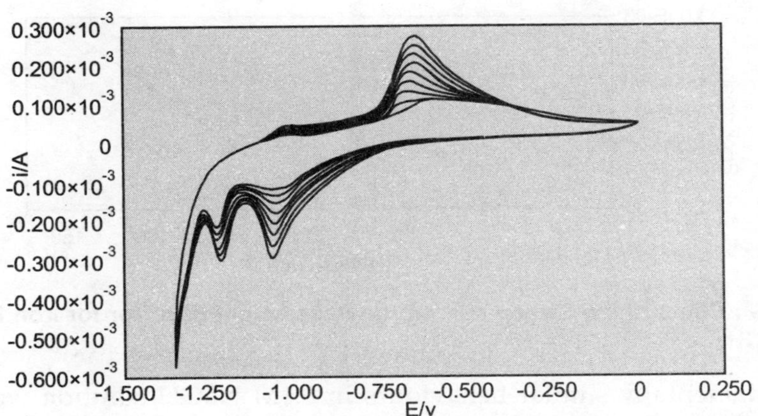

Fig. 13.16 : Cyclic Voltammetry of Iron in 0.1M NaOH at sweep rate 30m V/s, (SCE).

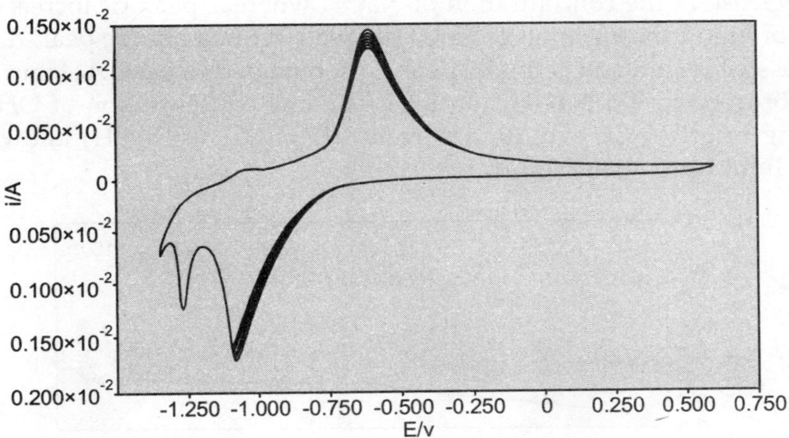

Fig. 13.17 : Cyclic Voltammetry of Iron in 5M NaOH at sweep rate 100m V/s, (SCE).

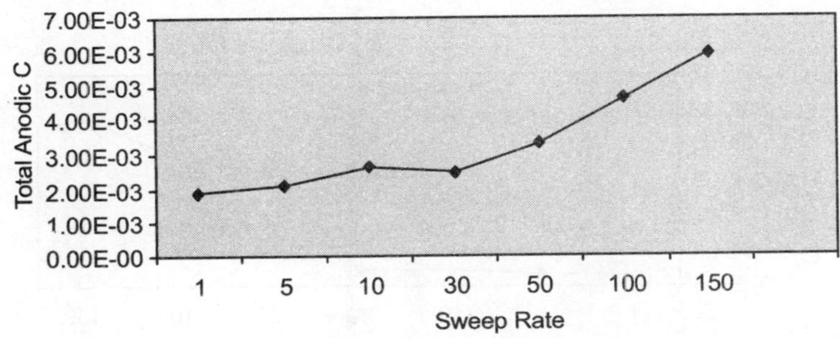

Fig. 13.18 : Effect of the Sweep rate on the total Anodic charge Density for Iron Electode in 1M NaO.

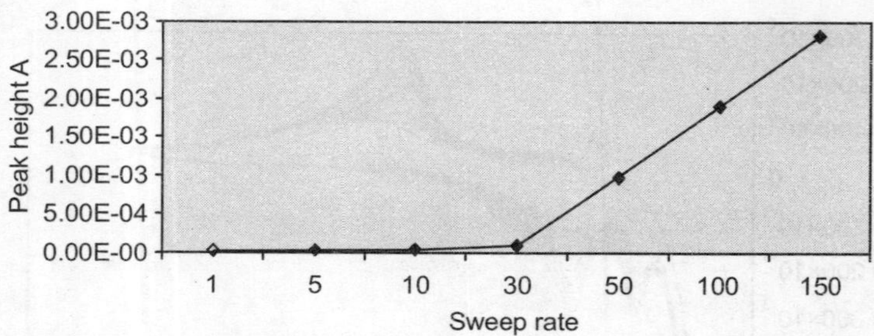

Fig. 13.19 : Effect of the Sweep rate on the Peak height of A³ for for Iron Electode in 1M NaOH.

Fundamentally similar behaviours in 0.1M NaOH solution were also obtained for 1M NaOH solution, Figure 13.15-13.17 but it was recognized from these results that especially, peak A_3 and peak C_2 decreased in accordance with increase in the concentration of NaOH whereas peak C_1 increased in a region of high concentration of NaOH. A well defined anodic peak A_5 in the transpassive region and cathodic peak C_3 conjugated to peak A_5 Figure 13.15 were observed in 2M NaOH solutions. The low concentration of OH- ions, resulting in a low O_2 evolution current, (E^{ϕ} = 1.23-0.059 PH) allowed the anodic limit to be increased.

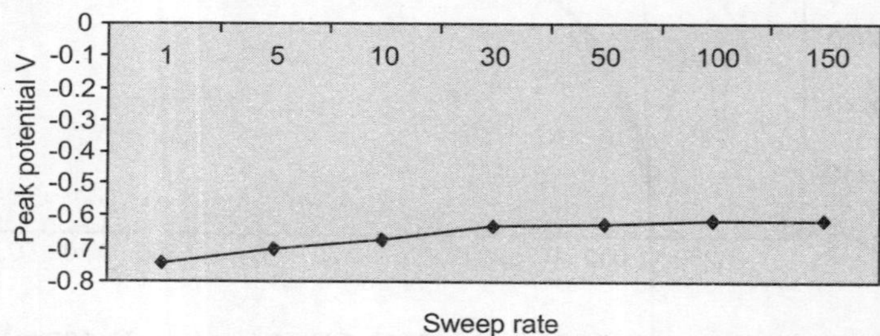

Fig. 13.20 : Effect of the Sweep Rate on the Peak Potential A³ for for Iron Electode in 1M NaOH.

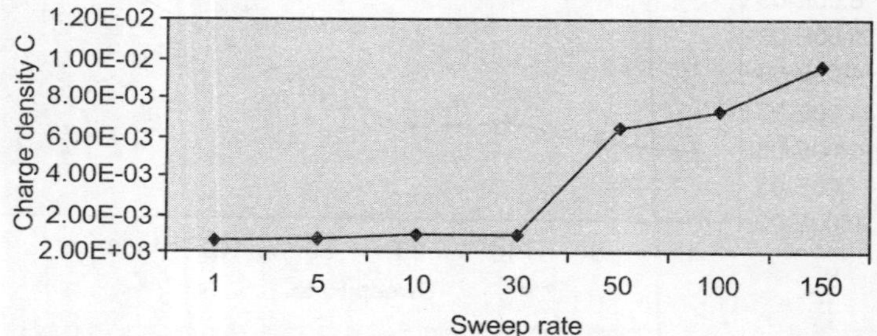

Fig. 13.21 : Effect of the Sweep Rate on the Charge Density A³ for Iron Electode in 1M NaOH.

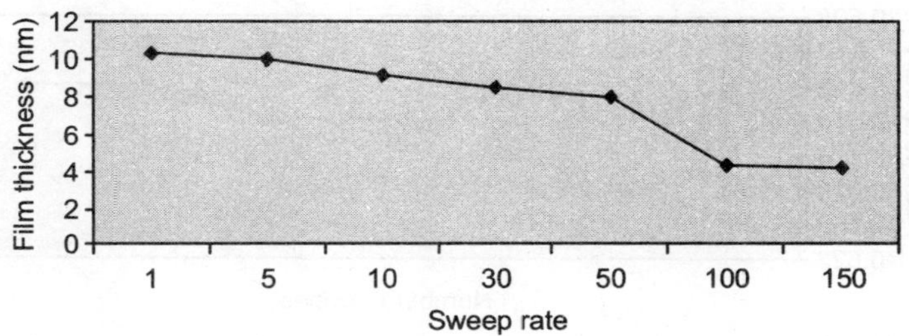

Fig. 13.22 : Effect of the Sweep rate on the Film thickness for Iron Electode in 1M NaOH.

The general shape of the cyclic voltammograms, however, was similar to that obtained in 2M NaOH, suggesting that the composition of the film, both in the passive and in the active region is the same in hydroxide. The peak A_0 at the upper end of the potential corresponds to the oxygen gas evolution reaction and the peak C at lower end of the potential corresponds to hydrogen gas evolution reaction (Figure 13.15). With increasing sweep rate, the peak potential.

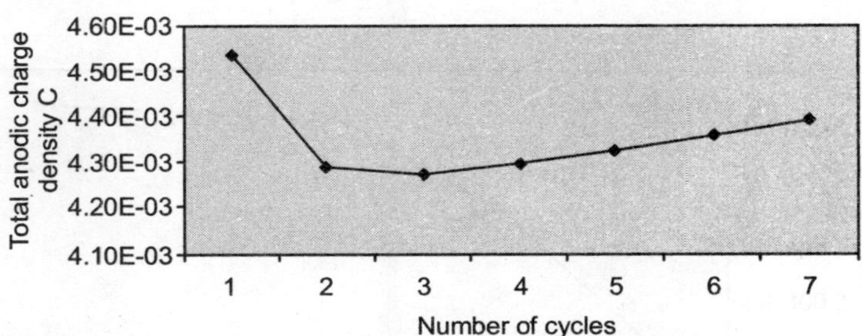

Fig. 13.23 : Effect of the Multi cycles on the total Anodic charge Density (*Qa*) (C/cm²) for Iron Electode in 1M NaOH.

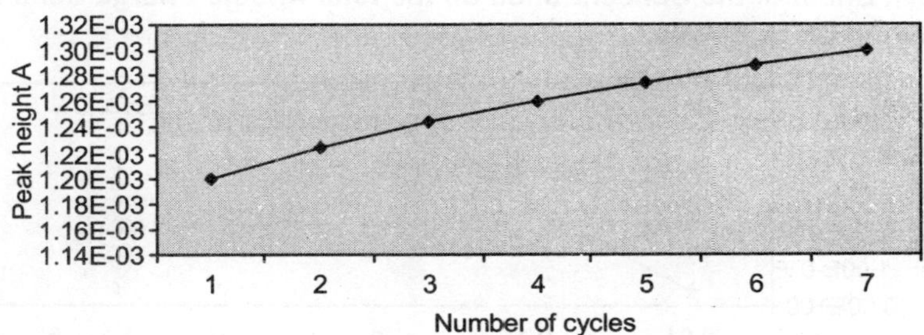

Fig. 13.24 : Effect of the Multi cycles on the Peak height A^3 for Iron Electode in 1M NaOH.

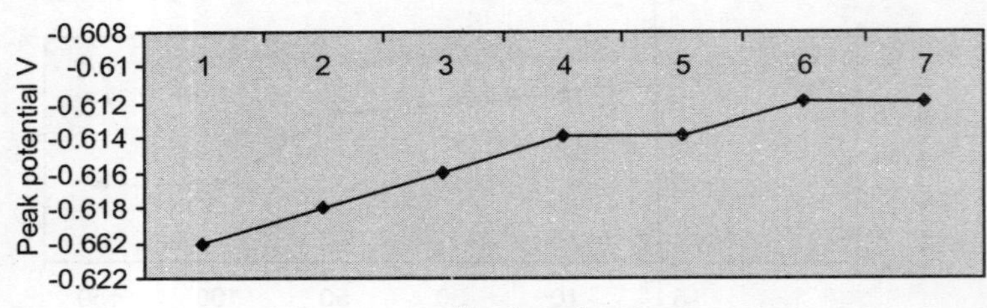

Fig. 13.25 : Effect of the Multi cycles on the Peak potential A^3 for Iron Electode in 1M NaOH.

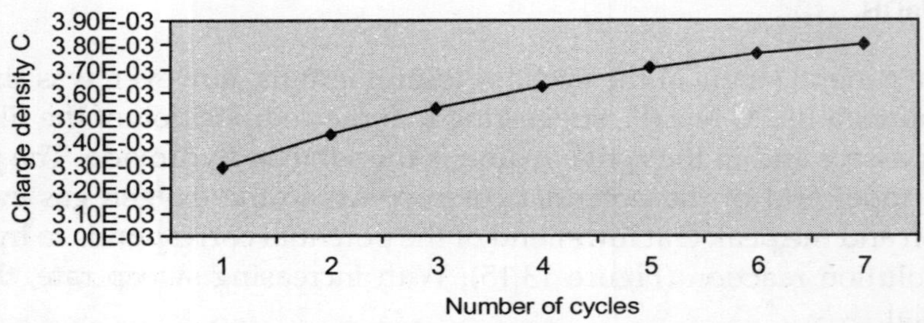

Fig. 13.26 : Effect of the Multi cycles on the Charge Density A^3 for Iron Electode in 1M NaOH.

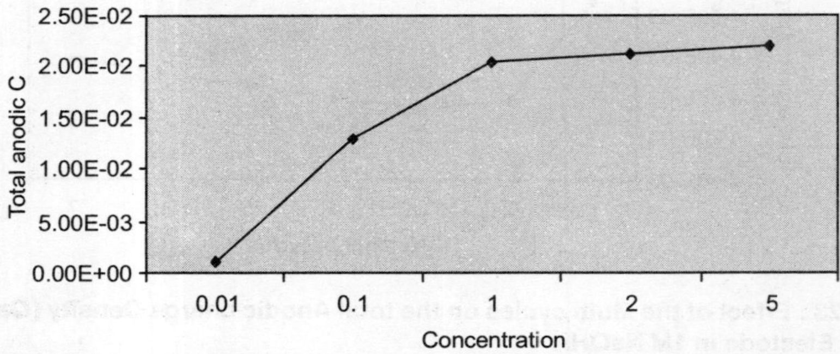

Fig. 13.27 : Effect of the Concentration on the total Anodic Charge Density for Iron Electode in NaOH Solutions.

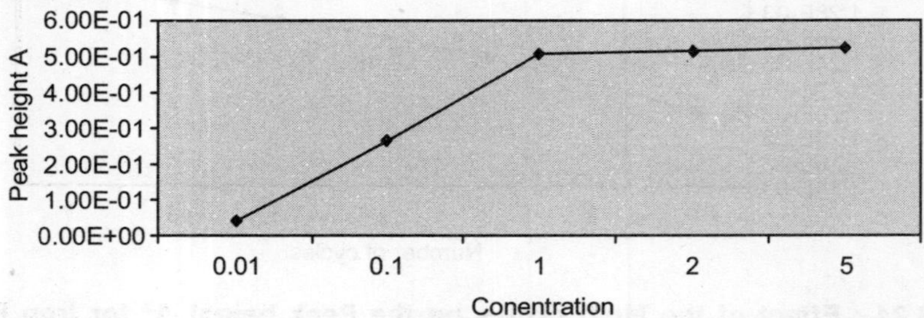

Fig. 13.28 : Effect of the Concentration on the Peak height A^3 for Iron Electode in NaOH Solutions.

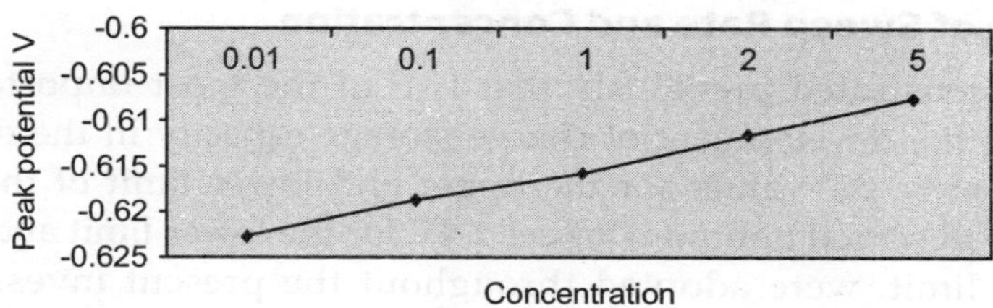

Fig. 13.29 : Effect of the Concentration on the Peak potential A^3 for Iron Electode in NaOH solution.

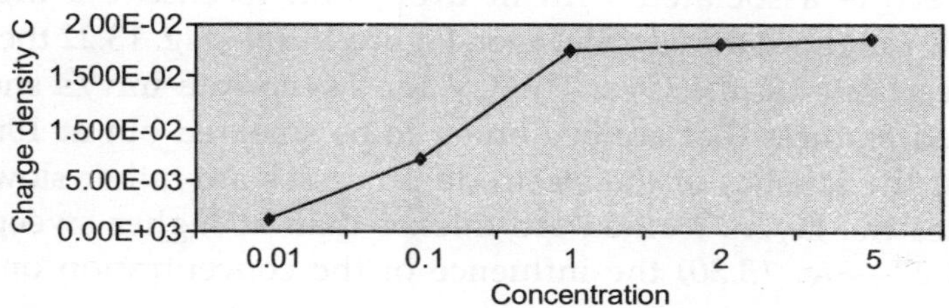

Fig. 13.30 : Effect of the Concentration on the Charge Density A^3 for Iron Electode in NaOH solutions.

of A_2 and A_3 are shifted to more positive values, whereas those of the C, and C_2 are shifted in the negative direction. The best curve shape was obtained at sweep rate 40-50 mVs^{-1}. The positions of the peaks on the potential scale, their relative orders of magnitude, and their behaviour during cycling as observed are shown in *(Figure 13.15-Figure 13.17)*. There is general agreement that the voltammograms of iron in strongly alkaline media involve two conspicuous peaks, an anodic and a cathodic one (A_3 and C_2) their current increase with increasing number of cycles up to a limit. Their potentials vary appreciably (anodic from –0.67 to –0.40V, cathodic from –1.15 to –0.85V). The reasons why the peak potentials vary are not always clear. The peaks A_3 and C_2 *(Figure 13.15)*, appear relatively small on the first cycle, but they increase with number of cycles, evidence for thickening of the formed oxide film.

Table 13.5 : The Concentration Effect on the Film of an Iron Electrode in NaOH

Concen-tration	pH	Total anodic charge density (Q_a) (C/cm²)	Peak height (I_p) A_3	Peak Potential (E_p) A_3	Charge density of (C/cm²)
0-01	12	1.23e-3	38e-3	-0.623	1.236e-3
0.1	13	12.805e-3	260e-3	-0.619	7.125e-3
1	14	20.161e-3	500e-3	-0.616	17.354e-3
2	14	20.919e-3	505e-3	-0.612	17.996e-3
5	14	21.677e-3	510e-3	-0.608	18.524e-3

Influence of Sweep Rate and Concentration

It was demonstrated previously that two of the most important factors influencing the development of charge storage capacity in the case of iron electrodes were the values for the upper and lower limit of the potential sweep. The observed optimum values 1.4V for the lower limit and + 0.6V for the upper limit, were adopted throughout the present investigation. A relatively small number of ixide growth cycles were used in most experiments in order to maintain reasonably small current values (and hence, minimize potential errors associated with iR drop) and to ensure a high level of reactivity throughout the surface layer. Figure 13.18—Fig. 13.22 the influences of the sweep rate on the CVs. The CV for sweep rate Imv/s shows rather complicated features that are beginning to be smeared out at 10mv/s. This shows that the kinetics of the electrode processes are rather slow. At lower sweep rates the layers formed are thicker than at higher sweep 'rates. In *(Figure 13.27—Fig. 13.30)* the influence of the concentration on the CV is shown.

Development of Charge Capacity

Charge measurements were performed on the voltammograms by two methods, the first one by using computer integration for the relevant area of interest (peak A_3), and the second by photocopying the results, cutting out the relevant area and weighing it relative to an area of known dimensions.

The charge was calculated as being the area/sweep rate and subsequent division by the area of the electrode (0.1964 cm^2) gives the charge density, Q. The charges obtained by the two methods were quite similar; for peak A_3 = 6.02 ± 0.5 mC/cm^2 by weighing and 7 ± 0.5 mC/cm^2, by computer integration. The total anodic charge. density 14.626 mC/cm^2 is larger than the cathodic charge density 10.632 mC/cm^2 ± 0.53 (was found to be about 25%). The influence of different factors on the charge density, peak height and film thickness are presented in *(Tables 13.3—Fig. 13.5).*

Under multicycle conditions the charge density and the film thickness increase with cycle number as shown in *(Figure 13.23—Fig. 13.26)*. The film is reported to be more stable at room temperature and in concentrated alkaline solution *(Figure 13.27—Fig. 13.30).*

The dependence of peak height on sweep rate appears to be linear *(Figure 13.21)*. A detail analysis of the sweep rate dependence would require more measurements over a wider range of sweep rate. At low sweep rates it is likely that there is dissolution occurs in the Fe^{2+} region *i.e.* Fe.$(OH)_2$ is soluble to a certain extent then the thickness is overestimated. The film thickness is about 4nm, *(Figure 13.22)*, which agree with other methods like ellipsometry.

A marked dependence of charge capacity development on the oxide growth sweep rate was calculated from *(Figure 13.18 and Fig. 13.22)*. The nature of this dependence is influenced by the layer thickness, which is usually decreasing of higher sweep rates. Figure 13.22 and Table 13.3 show that Q_A decreases with the increase of the sweep rate and finally is attaining a constant value.

The variation of charge capacity development with increasing number of oxide growth cycles are outlined in *(Figure 13.23 and 13.26)* Table 13.4 page 207. The anodic charge, Q_A, consumed in the potential range 1.4V < E < 0.6V. Q_A increase almost linearly with oxide thickness and pH *(Figures 13.17 and Fig. 13.30 Table 13.5)*.

REFERENCES

Anderson, B. and L. Ojefors: *J. Electrochem. Soc.* 123: 814 (1976).

Beck, F., R. Kaus and M. Oberst: *Electrochim Acta* 30(2): 173 (1985).

Burke, Z.D. and M.E.G. Lyons: *J. Electroananic Chem.* 198: 347 (1986).

Casto, E.B., *Electrochim. Acta,* 14: 2117 (1994).

Cerny, J. and K. Micka: *J. of Power Sources* 25: 111 (1989).

El-Sayed, A. Revue Roumaine *de chimie:* 38(2): 139 (1993).

Geronov, Y., I. Tonvo and S. Georgiev: *J. Appendix Electrochem.,* 5:351 (1974).

Hurlen, T., *Electrochim, Acta,* 8: 609 (1963)

Macdonald, D.D. and D. Owen: *J. Electrochem. Soc.,* 120: 317 (1973).

Ojefors, L. *J. Electrochem. Soc.* 123: 1691 (1976).

Shams, A.M. El-Din and S.M. Abd El-Haleem Werkst Korros., 24: 389 (1973).

Silver, H.G. and E. Leaks: *J. Electrochem. Soc.,* 117: 5 (1970).

Zor, S., B. Yazici and M. Erbil: *Corros. Sci.,* 47: 2700 (2005).

Zor, S., Turkish: *J.Chem.* 26: 403 (2002).

ELECTROCHEMICAL BEHAVIOUR OF IRON ELECTRODE IN SODIUM SULPHIDE SOLUTIONS

I. Zaafarany

Department of Chemistry, Faculty of Applied Science, Umm Al-Qura University, Makkah Al-Mukaramah (Saudi Arabia).

ABSTRACT

The electrochemical behaviour of iron electrode in sodium sulphide solutions was studied using cyclic voltammograms technique. The morphology of the surface before and after immersion of iron electrode in Na_2S solution was also studied using scanning electron microscope (SEM) and energy dispersive analysis of X-rays (EDAX). Two anodic peaks were observed in the anodic scan due to the formation of FeS_2, converted to FeS on the surface of electrodes. On the other hand one cathodic peak occurred due to the reduction of FeS_2 in the cathodic branch of cyclic voltammograms. The formation of iron sulphide was supported by SEM photograph and increase of sulphur counts observed in EDAX analysis. The current for peaks (A and B) increases with increasing sodium sulphide concentration and voltage scan rate but the values of peak potential remains unchanged.

Key Words: Iron, sodium sulphide, cyclic voltammogram, SEM, EDAX.

Introduction

The electrochemical behaviour of iron in sulphide solutions has been studied both from a fundamental and a practical point of view, especially in relation with the corrosion problems in the pulp and paper industry. The electrochemical behaviour of iron in sulphide solution has extensively studied. The first anodic peak in voltammetric sweeps at 0.1V versus a reversible hydrogen electrode (RHE) was attributed to the formation of FeS, although others have assigned it to the formation of an iron oxide with FeS being formed in a second anodic peak after dissolution of the oxide film. Perhaps these differences may be due to the different pH values and/or Na_2S concentrations. Salvarezza *et al.* have explained the behaviour of iron in alkalina sulphide solutions on the basis of an initial competitive adsorption between OH, SH and H_2O with the nature of the products formed and increasing on the concentration of both OH and SH.

Aim of the work is to study the electrochemical behaviour of iron electrode in sodium sulphide using cyclic voltammogram technique. The film formed was investigated by scanning electron microscope (SEM) and energy dispersive analysis of X-ray (EDAX).

Experimental

Iron electrode having the chemical composition (%) 0.052C, 0.189 Mn, 0.008 P, 0.011 S, 0.011 Si, 0.012 Cr, 0.029 Ni, 0.04 Cu, 0.039 Al and the remainder is Fe, provided by the "Saudi Iron and Steel Company" was used in the present study. The bottom of the rod specimen with a mean surface area 0.52 cm^2 was successively abraded with 1-,0- and 00-emery paper, degreased with acetone and dried between two filter papers and then immersed in 50 ml of the test solution. All chemicals used were of Analar quality. The solutions were prepared using double distilled water. No attempts were made to deareate them. The electrolytic cell was all Pyrex and described elsewhere.

Cyclic voltammetry curves (CVs) were performed using autolab (ECO Chemic) combined with the software, package, GPES (general purpose electrochemical system) was used. It consists of data acquisition system and potentiostat-galvanostat.

Scanning electron microscope (SEM) of the type (XL-30) was used to examine the surface iron electrode in absence and presence of sulphide solution. All micrograph of corroded specimens were taken at a magnification of (X-500). Energy dispersive analysis X-ray (EDAX) examination using a Traktor TV-2000 energy dispersive spectrometer was used in this work.

Results and Discussion

Cyclic Voltammogram of Iron in 0.03 M Na_2S solution

The cyclic voltammetry technique is useful for identifying the steps involved in the overall reactions resulting in the formation of various films on metallic surface. It is particularly useful for distinguishing between products resulting from chemical, electrochemical reactions. Its main limitation is that, it is only useful for examining very thin film formed in relatively short time.

Figure 13.31 represents the cyclic volta mograms curves of iron electrode in 0.03 M Na solution at sweep rate of 50 mV sec^{-1}. From the inspection of the curves in Figure 13.31. It is clear that there are two anodic peaks (A and B) and passive region. The first anodic peak (A) located at -0.87V and the second anodic peak (B) located at -025V. The anodic peak was attributed to formation of terrous sulphide FeS which thicken an anodic polarization. This process can be looked upon as occurate through the ionization of iron metal followed combination of ferrous ions and sulphide ions why the precipitation of a porous black scale of ferrous sulphide on the iron surface.

$$Fe \rightleftharpoons Fe^{2+} + 2e^- \quad ...(13.1)$$

$$2Fe^{2-} + S^- \rightarrow Fe_2S \quad ...(13.2)$$

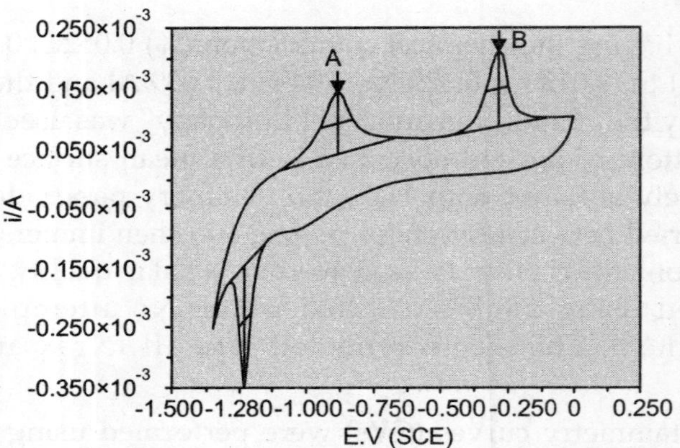

Fig. 13.31 : Cyclic voltammograms of Fe in 0.03 MNa_2 rate of 50mV/sec.

The mechanism of film formation under peak (A) can be readily account for on the basis of specific adsorption of OH and S^{2-} or (HS) on the metal surface.

The second peak (B) appears at about 0.25V is thought to correspond to the parts transformation of the thick corrosion product Fe_2S formed under peak A to FeS (pyrite) according to the following reaction.

$$Fe_2 + S + S^{2+} \rightleftharpoons Fe^{-}S \qquad ...(13.11)$$

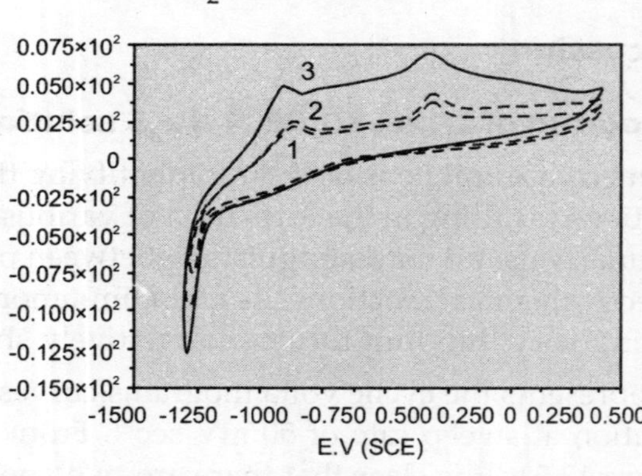

Fig. 13.32 : Different cyclization of cyclic voltammograms of Fe in 0.1 MNa_2S solution at voltage scan rate of 50mV/sec.

Some FeS may also be formed by the select combination between Fe^{2+} ions and sulphide ores which could black some pores in the sulphide ore film.

$$Fe + S^{2+} \rightleftharpoons FeS + 2e^{-} \qquad ...(13.12)$$

On the reversing scan, there is only one combined cathodic (reduction) peak. This peak was attributed to the reduction of ferrous sulphide.

Effect of Cyclization

Figure 13.32 represents the cyclic of iron electrode in 0.1M Na_2S solution recorded in three successive sweeps-1, 2 and 3 at voltage scan rate of 50 mV/sec. The numbers on the curves correspond to the sweep number. The observed difference in the curves can be attributed to different initial states of the electrode surface and can be recognized along both the anodic and cathodic branches of the cyclic voltammograms. The initial state of the electrode surface determines to an important extent the shape of the resulting cyclic voltammograms. It is of interest to remark that the second and third sweeps give essentially similar voltammograms.

The quantity of electricity integrated under the whole anodic branch of the voltammogram is relatively highly enlarged in value with the increasing the number of sweep. This behaviour could be attributed to the activation of the metal surface and the continuous formation of different ferrous sulphide species along the whole anodic-branch of cyclic voltammograms. It is note-worthy that the presence of (OH′) ions may bring about partial activation of the formed sulphide layer possibly due to the formation of hydroxyl complex ion through the interaction of OH ions with the metal in the pores of sulphide layer.

In summary, one concludes that pre-condition of the metal surface in the second sweep (activation) interferes with normal formation

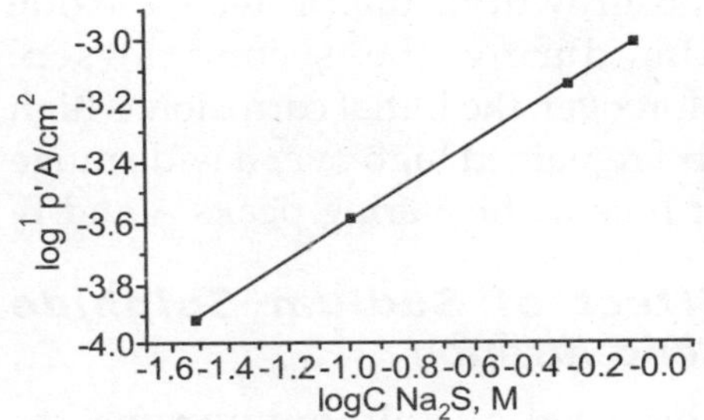

Fig. 13.33(a): The relation between the dissolution current density for peak (A) vs. the molar concentrations of Na_2S solution on a double logarithmic scale.

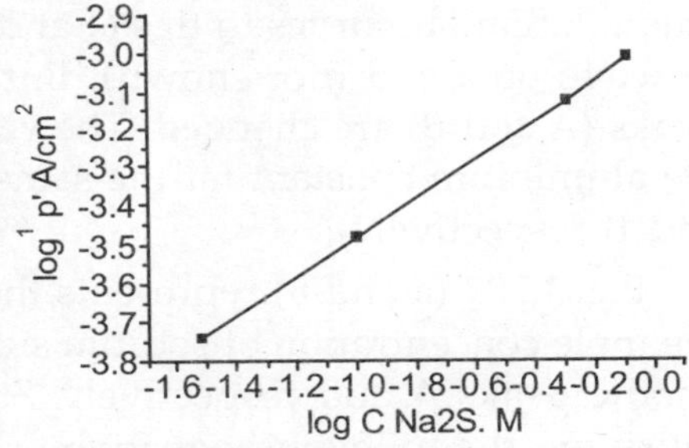

Fig. 13.33(b) The relation between the dissolution current density for peak (B) vs. the molar concentrations of Na_2S solution on a double logarithmic scale.

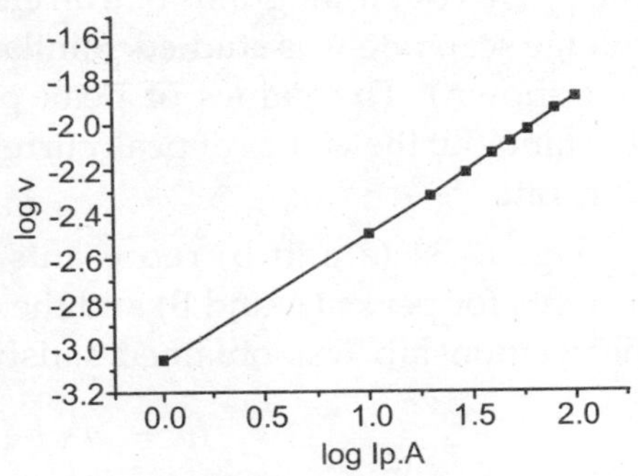

Fig. 13.34(a): The relation between the dissolution current for peak (A) vs. the voltage scan rate (v) on a double logarithmic scale.

and growth of the protective oxide film during the second swsep. Moreover, the initial corrosion is high and remained high over a wide range of potential covering peaks A and B.

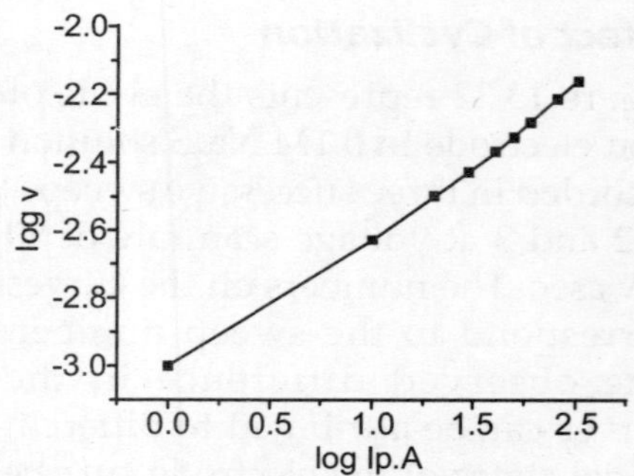

Fig. 13.34(b) The relation between the dissolution current for peak (B) vs, the voltage scan rate (v) on a double logarithmic scale.

Effect of Sodium Sulphide Concentration

The cyclic voltammograms of electrode in different concentrations of its electrode in different concentrations of sodium sulphide at voltage scan rate of 50mV/sec rate studied. Similar curves to tigs (1 and 2) wave obtained (not shown). But the values of peak current density of peaks (A and B) are changed. The value of peak potential for peaks A and B are aluminium constant (at the same potential -0.87V and -0.25 for peaks A and B respectively).

Fig. 13.33 (a and b) represents the plot between the peak current up and the mole concentration of sodium sulphide on a double logarithmic scale for anodic peaks A and respectively. Straight lines relationship was obtained satisfying the following equation.

$$\log Ip = a + b \log C_{Na_2S} \qquad ...(13.13)$$

where, a and b are constants depend on the type of electrode used.

Effect of Voltage Scan Rate

The cyclic voltammograms of iron electrode in 0.8M Na_2S solution at different voltage scan rate was studied. Similar curves to figures 1 and 2 were obtained (not shown). The values of peak potential for peaks A and B are almost constant. But the values of peak current (Ip) increases with increase the voltage scan rate.

Fig. 13.34 (a and b) represents the relation between the anodic peak currents for peaks (A and B) and the square root of voltage scan rate. Straight the relationship was obtained satisfying the following equation.

$$Ip = a + b\sqrt{v} \qquad ...(13.14)$$

where *a* and *b* are constants depending the type electrode and sulphide concentration.

The linear dependence of the anodic current for peaks A and B on the square root of the sweep rate suggests the diffusional characteristics of the corresponding voltammetric peaks. Thus, the deposition of a thin film of sulphide is controlled by diffusion of S^2 ion toward the electrode surface.

Surface Analysis

The layer formed after immersed the iron electrode in 0.03M Na_2S solution was investigated using scanning electron microscope (SEM) and energy dispersive analysis of X-rays (EDAX).

Fig. 13.35 (a and b) show SEM micrograph examination of the iron electrode surface before and after immersion in a solution of 0.03M Na_2S at 50 mV/sec, respectively. The electrode was acid-etched prior to the experiment. The consequence of this treatment is the nucleation of a greater number of more randomly distributed sulphide centers than in case of a polished electrode. The growth of the patches is also faster. The formation of sulphide on the surface iron is supported by EDAX analysis.

Fig. 13.36 (a and b) show the EDAX analysis of iron electrode before and after immersed in 0.03M Na_2S solution at a voltage scan rate of 50 mV/sec. EDAX of the various area shows no detectable sulphur on the etched electrode (before immersion of Fe in Na_2S) (Figure 13.36a). But in Fig. (13.36b) shows a marked increase in the sulphur counts. The presence of sulphur emphasizes the formation of iron sulphide on the surface of iron.

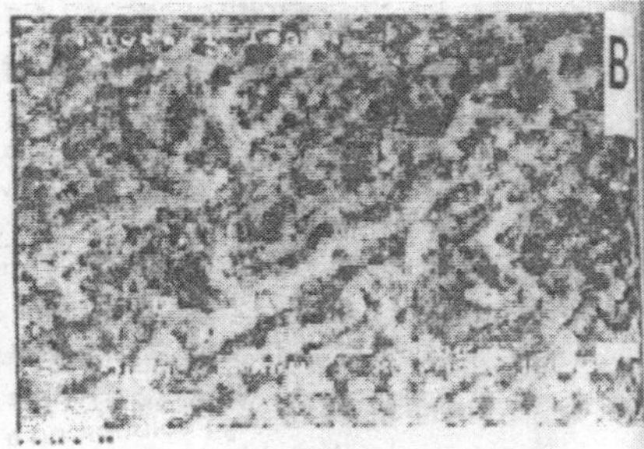

Fig. 13.35. SEM of of Fe before (A) and after (B) immersed In 0.03M Na_2S solution at voltage scan rate of 50mV/sec.

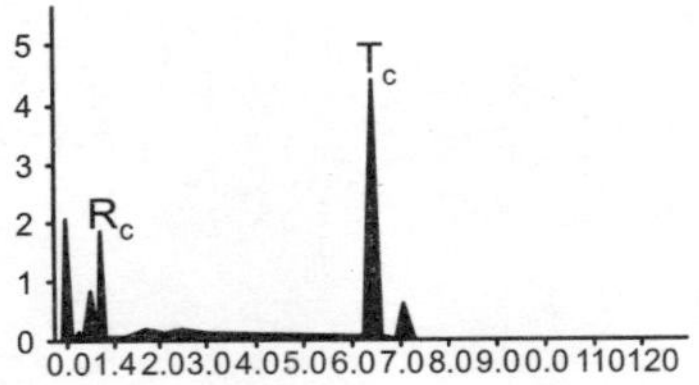

Fig. 13.36(a): EDAX of of Fe before immersed in 0.03M Na_2S solution

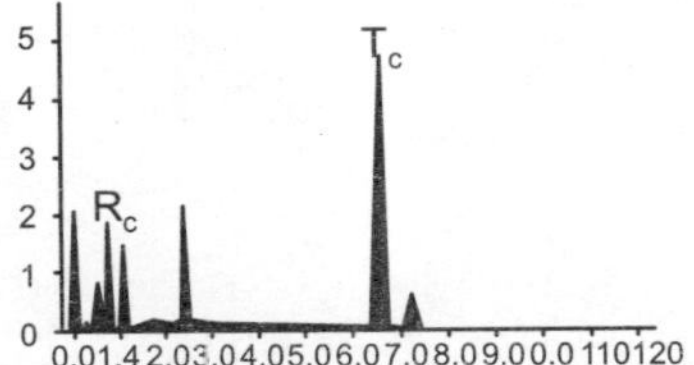

Fig. 13.36(b): EDAX of of Fe after immersed in 0.03M Na_2S solution at voltage scan rate of 50mV/sec.

Conclusion

1. Two anodic peaks were observed in the cyclic voltammograms of iron electrode in 0.03M Na_2S solution.
2. The first anodic peak is due to the formation of FeS_2 while the second anodic peak is due to the transformation of FeS_2 to FeS.
3. The peak current for peaks A and B increases with increasing Na_2S concentration and voltage scan rate, but the peak potential remain unchanged.
4. SEM and EDAX analysis emphasizes the formation of sulphide ion on the surface of iron electrode.

REFERENCES

Abdullah, M. and H.E. Megahed: *Monasthefte fur chemie* 126: 519 (1995).

Bolmer, P.W., *Corrosion* 21: 69 (1956).

Khairy, M.E. and A.N. Darwish: *Corros. Sa,* 13: 149 (1973).

Salvarezza, R.C., H.A. Videla and AJ. Ariva. *Corros Sci.* 22(9) 815 (1982).

Shoesmith, D.W., P. Taylor, M.G. Bailey and Ikeda: *Electrochim. Acta* 23:903 (1978).

Sury, R., *Corros, Sci.,* 16:879 (1976).

Tayior, P. and D.W. Shoesmith: *Can. J. Chem.* 56 2797 (1979).

Vera, J., S. Kapusta and N. Hackerman: *J. Electrochem. Soc.* 133: 461 (1986).

Vera, J., S. Kopusta and N. Hackerman: *J. Electrochem. Soc.,* 133(3): 462 (1986).

CYCLIC VOLTAMMETRIC BEHAVIOUR OF COPPER ELECTRODE IN SODIUM SULFIDE SOLUTIONS

I. ZAAFARANY[1] and H. BOLLER[2]

[1]*Chemistry Department Faculty of Appllied Science, Umm Al-Qura University,*

[2]*Makkah Al Mukaramha, P.O. Box: 118 (Saudi Arabia). Institute of Inorganic Chemistry, Johannes-Kepler-Universitat Linz, A-4040 Linz (Austria).*

ABSTRACT

The cyclic voltammograms of the copper electrode in Na_2S solution was studied using cyclic volammogram's technique.Three anodic peaks were observed in the anodic branch of the voltammogram's.The peaks may be attributed successively to the formation of Cu_2S, CuS and Cu_2O. On the other hand, the cathodic branch shows four peaks. These peaks correspond to the reduction of copper oxide and copper sulfide formed in the anodic branch.

Key words: Copper electrode, sodium sulfide, cyclic voltammetry.

Introduction

The sulfidation of metals is a process of practical importance on well as of theoretical interest as oxidation. From the theoretical point of view, sulfidation reactions afford important parallels and contrasts with the corresponding oxidation reactions. On reaction films of solid were formed on metals and alloys consist in general, field of study of great importance in electrochemistry, which is still open for investigations on the electrochemical behaviour of copper in sulfide solutions and the formation of sulfide films on copper are relatively scare despite their importance in many areas of applied chemistry and electrochemistry. Stoichiometric and non-stoichiometric copper sulfide films have been widely used in dielectric metallization, in solar cell technology and as ion specific electrode, when soluble sulfides are present in potable water or seawater, a thick black, poorly adherent scale forms on copper or brass surface. This scale is composed mainly of Cu_2S although CuS, Cu_2O and non-stoichiometric copper sulfide species such as $Cu_{1.8}S$ have also been reported.

Cu_2S has been formed as an insoluble film on Cu electrode in aqueous sulfide solutions according to the equations:

$$2Cu + HS^- + OH^- \rightleftharpoons Cu_2S\ (film) + H_2O + 2e^- \qquad ...(13.15)$$

The aim of the present work aims to give new lights on the characteristics of the reaction products performed on the copper surface in sodium sulfide solution using cyclic voltammogram technique.

Experimental

The working copper electrode was prepared from high purity (99.98 %) copper rod. A small piece of copper rod, diameter 6 mm, length 6 mm was placed in a "Kel-F" shield. This was fixed to a borosilicate glass tube with epoxy resin. Electrical contact was achieved through a copper wire soldered to the end of the electrode, not exposed to the solution. Before being used, the electrode surface was polished with different grade emery papers until it appeared free of scratches and other defects. Then, it was rinsed with acetone and finally washed twice with distilled water. All chemical used were of A.R. quality. The electrolytic cell was madeup of pyrex glass and is described elsewhere.

Cyclic voltammogram curves (CV's) were performed using autolab [ECO Chemie] combined with the software package GPES (General Purpose Electrochemical System) was used. This is a computer-controlled electrochemical measurements system. It consists of data-acquisition system and a potentiostat/galvanostat. CV was used to study the corrosion of copper in sodium sulfide solutions (Na_2S) sweeping from -1.25V to 0.025 V. All measurements were taken at 25 ± 1°C.

Results and Discussion

Cyclic Voltammetry

Figure 13.37 represents the CV's of a copper electrode in 0.8 M Na_2S recorded in three successive sweeps at 25°C and at a voltage sweep rate of 50mV/sec. The observed difference in the curves can be attributed to different initial states to the electrode surface and can be recognized along both the anodic and cathodic branches of the cycle voltammograms. It is of interest to remark that the second and third sweeps give essentially similar voltammograms which differ from that the film sweep in some significant characteristics.

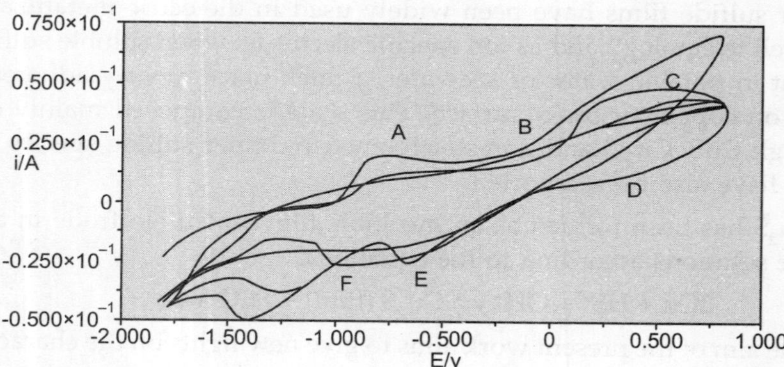

Fig. 13.37 : Cyclic voltammogram of copper in 0.8M Na_2S at sweep rate 50mV/s.

Obviously the initial state of the electrode surface determine the shape of the resulting cyclic voltammograms to an important extent. There are three peaks (A, B and C) in the anodic branch of the voltammograms and four peaks in the cathodic branch (D, E, F and G). No passivation is observed as the current flown steadily.

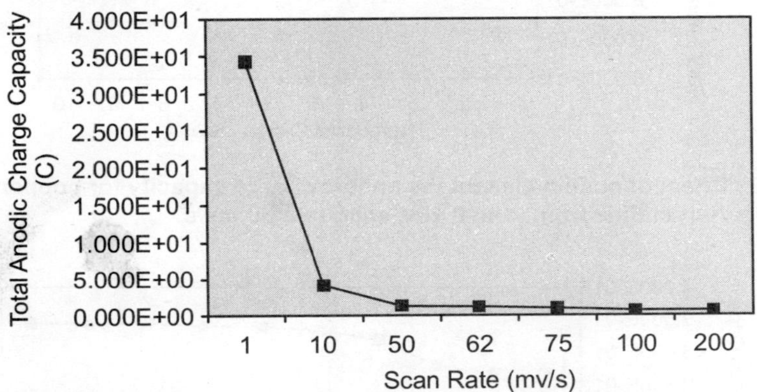

Fig. 13.38 : Effect of sweep rate on the anodic charge capacity for copper electrode in 0.8-sodium sulfide from-1.2 to 0.1v

Peak A is composite, as can be seen from the fine structure in the first sweep and the three reduction peaks E, F, and G. Other possible reactions belonging to peak A are the formation of Cu(I) oxide or hydroxide and the oxidation of HS to elemental sulfur. There is an interesting interplay between the reduction peaks F and G while Peak F only appears at the first cycle and disppears in the following cycles while the new peak G is appearing. Peak F may be attributed to an oxide reduction while peak G to sulfide, reduction to metallic copper.

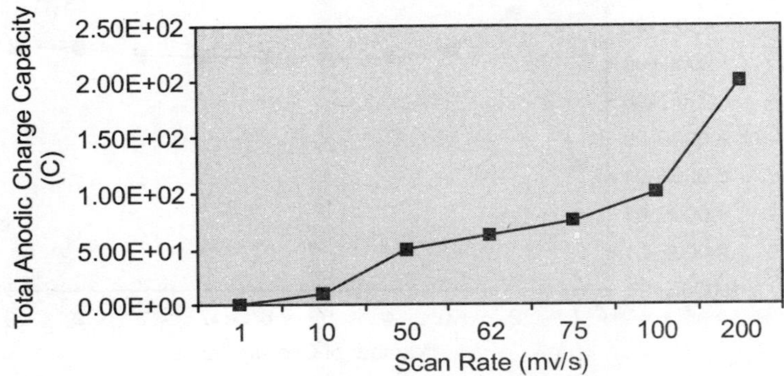

Fig. 13.39 : Effect of sweep rate on the cathodic charge capacity for copper electrode in 0.8M-sodium sulfide from –1.2 to 0.1 V.

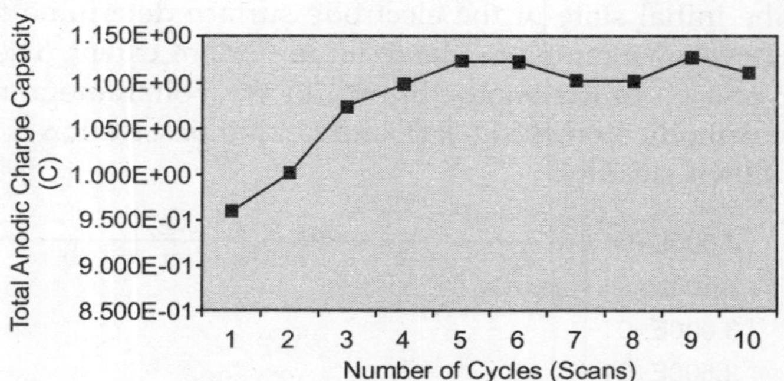

Fig. 13.40 : Effect of multicycles on the anodic charge capacity for copper electrode in 0.8M-sodium sulfide from -1 to 0.25V, scan rate 50 mv/s.

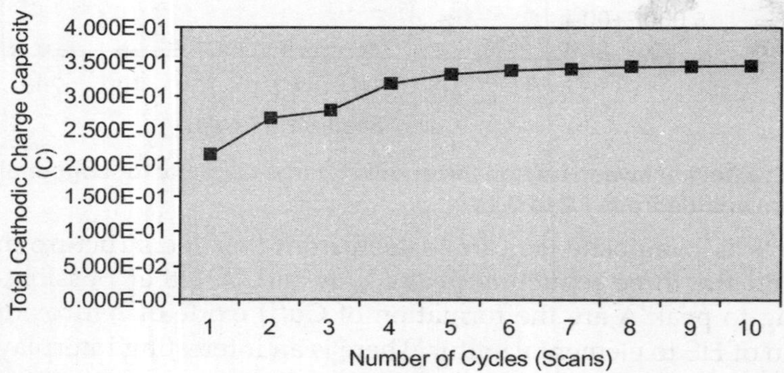

Fig. 13.41 : Effect of multicycles on the cathodic charge capacity for copper electrode in 0.8M-sodium sulfide from -1 to 0.25V, scan rate 50 mv/s.

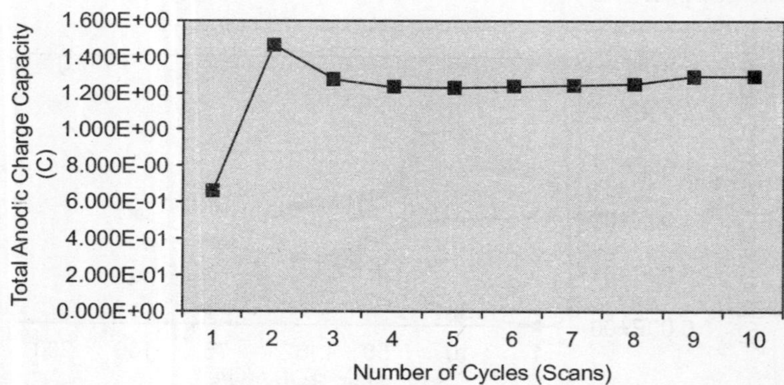

Fig. 13.42 : Effect of multicycles on the anodic charge capacity for copper electrode in 0.8 M-sodium sulfide from -1.8 to 0.8V, scan rate 200 mv/s.

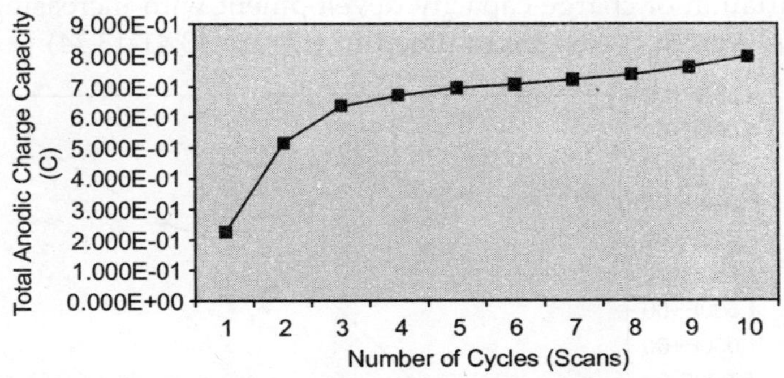

Fig. 13.43 : Effect of multicycles on the cathodic charge capacity for copper electrode in 0.8M-sodium sulfide from -1.8 to 0.8V, scan rate 200 mv/s.

Influence of Sweep Rate and Concentration

It was demonstrated previously that two of the most important factors influencing the development of charge storage capacity in the case of copper electrodes were, the values for the upper and lower limit of the potential sweep. The observed optimum values 1.8V for the lower limit and + 0.8V for the upper limit, were adopted throughout the present investigation. A relatively small number of sulphide growth cycles were used in most experiments in order to maintain reasonably small current values (and hence, minimize potential errors associated with iR drop) and to ensure a high level of reactivity throughout the surface layer. Figs. 13.38-13.44 show the influences of the sweep rate on the CVs. The CV for sweep rate 1mv/s shows rather complicated features that are beginning to be smeared out at 10mv/s. This shows that the kinetics of the electrode processes are rather slow. At lower sweep rates the layers formed are thicker than at higher sweep rates. In Figs. 13.45-13.48 the influence of the concentration on the CV is shown.

Development of Charge Capacity

A marked dependence of charge capacity development on the sulphide growth sweep rate was calculated from Figs. 13.38 to 13.39. The nature of this dependence is influenced by the layer thickness, which is usually decreasing with higher sweep rates.

Figs. 13.38 to 13.39 shows that QA decreases with the increase of the sweep rate and finally is attaining a constant value and show that QC is rising with increasing sweep-rate however, QC stays always smaller than QA within the range of the experiments.

The variation of charge capacity development with increasing number of sulphide growth cycles are outlined in (Figure 13.41-13.44).

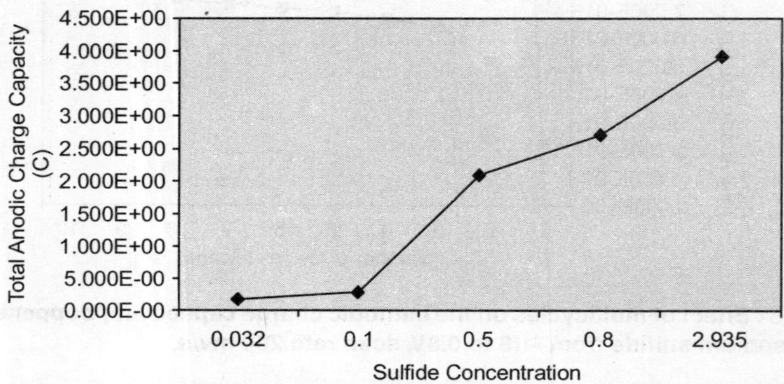

Fig. 13.44 : Effect of sulfide concentration on the anodic charge capacity for copper electrode in sulfide solution from—1.8 to 0.8V, scan rate 50 mv/s.

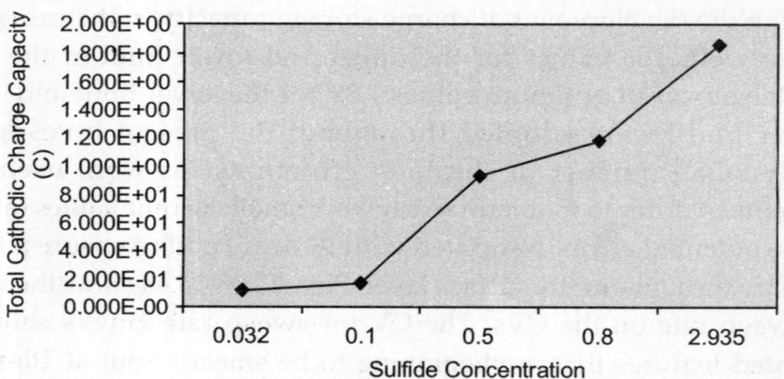

Fig. 13.45 : Effect of sulfide concentration on the cathodic charge capacity for copper electrode in sulfide solution from –1.8 to 0.8V, scan rate 50 mv/s.

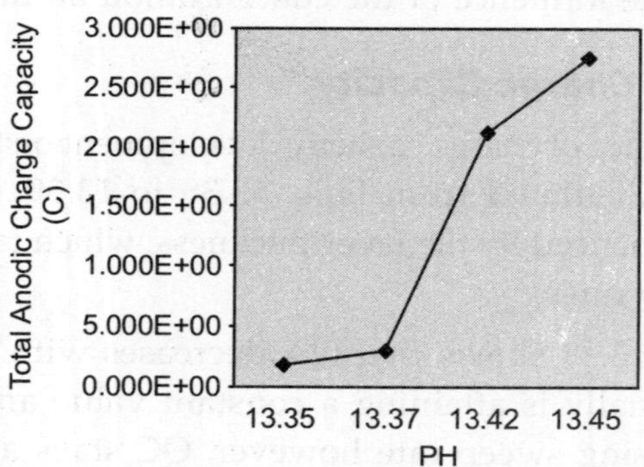

Fig. 13.46 : Effect of pH on the anodic charge capacity for copper electrode in sodium sulfide solution from –1.08 to 0.8V, scan rate 50 mv/s.

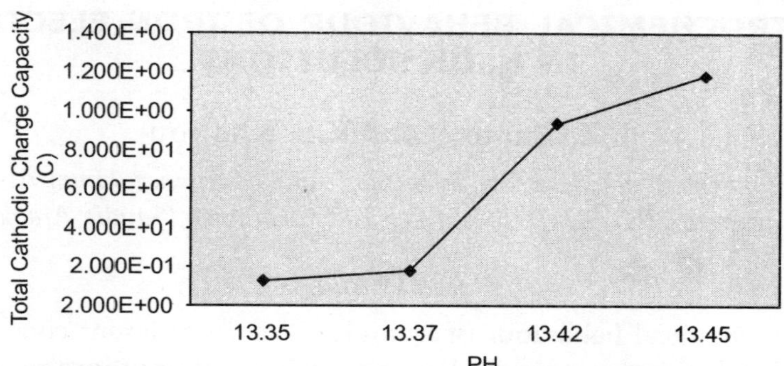

Fig. 13.47 : Effect of pH on the cathodic charge capacity for copper electrode in sodium sulfide solution from –1.08 to 0.8V, scan rate 50 mv/s.

The anodic charge, QA, consumed in the potential range 1.8V ≤ E ≤ 0.8V, and the cathod charge, QC, recovered during the stripping of the deposited sulphur layer change not very much as function of multicycling. QC is always smaller that QA, indicating incomplete reduction of the anodical formed layer. QA and QC increase almost linear with sulfide concentration and pH (Figures 13.44-13.47).

REFERENCES

Gennerode, M.R., De Chialvo and A.J. Arvia: *J of Appl. Electrochem.* 15: 685 (1985).

Jacobs, S., M. Edwards: *Water Res.* 34: 2798 (2000).

Lkeda, B., *et al., Electrochimica Acta,* 23: 903-916 (1978).

McNeil, M.B., A.L. Anos, T.L. Woods *Corrosion,* 49: 755 (1993).

Peter, L.M., *Electrochim. Acta* 23: 1073 (1978).

Rand, D.A.J., *J. Electroanal. Chem.* 83: 19 (1977).

Schimmel, M.I., N.R. De Tacconi, K. Rajesnwars, *J. Electronal. Chem.* 453: 187 (1998).

Shams, A.M., El-Din and S.M. Abd El-Haleem Werkstoffe Korros. 24: 389 (1973).

Stepanova, L.I., T.V. Mazolevskaya, O.G. Purovskaya: *Met. Finish,* 101: 18 (2003).

Velasquez, R., D. Leinen, J. Pascual, J.R. Ramos-Barrodo, R. Cordova, H. Gomez, R. Schrebler: *J. Electroanal. Chem.* 510: 20 (2001).

Zirino, A., R. De Marco, I. Rivera, B. Pejcic: *Electroanalysis.* 14: 493 (2002).

ELECTROCHEMICAL BEHAVIOUR OF IRON ELECTRODE IN NaOH SOLUTIONS

I. Zaafarany* and K.S. Khairou

Department of Chemistry, Faculty of Applied Science, Umm Al-Qura University, P.O. Box 118, Makkah Al Mukaramah (Saudia Arabia).

ABSTRACT

The electrochemical behaviour of iron electrode in different concentrations of NaOH solution was studied using cyclic voltammograms and A.C. Impedance techniques. Four anodic peaks (A_1 –A_4) were observed in the anodic scan of cyclic voltammograms where two cathodic peaks (C_1 and C_2) were observed in the cathodic scan of cyclic voltammograms. The four enodic peaks due to the formation $Fe(OH)_{ads}$ peak (A_1), $Fe(OH)_2$, peak (A_2), Fe_2O_3 (peak A_3) and formation of more stable Fe(III) species (peak A_4) and the cathodic scan due to the reduction of species formed on the anodic scan.

Key Words: Iron, NaOH, Cyclic voltammograms, A.C. impedance.

Introduction

Iron is one of the metal used in several fields of industry. Iron and similar metals can be exposed to corrosion in connection with environmental conditions. The corrosion rate varies subject to structure of ions and molecules, kind and concentration of ion, kind of solution and kind of materials.

Oxidation and reduction process taking place on iron electrode in alkaline media are important from the point of view of alkaline accumulators, and many authors have dealt with the reaction mechanism, influence of additives, etc.

Extensive studies of the iron electrode in alkaline solution have been presented in numerous publications. Two main reasons of this great interest can be given: one hand, iron electrodes in alkaline solution could be appropriate for various accumulator applications (Fe/NiOOH, Fe/air etc). On the other hand, iron is one of the most important materials in modern technology. Arising corrosion problems are covering the whole range of pH in aqueous systems from acidic to basic, solutions.

Iron electrodes for batteries are normally placed in concentrated alkali solution 5M KOH. The charged state of the battery in Fe(O) gained by electrochemical reduction (discharge). The discharge reaction first leads to Fe(II), which is found to be $Fe(OH)_2$. Prolonged discharge leads to the formation of a sludge which was identified by *in situ* Mossbouer spectroscopy during cyclic galvanostatic oxidation-reduction of iron and found to be mainly FeOOH and unreacted $Fe(OH)_2$ on numerous occasions, it has been pointed out that the formation of oxides involves soluble Fe(II) and Fe(III) species.

Experimental

The test electrode was made of pure iron obtained from Saudi iron and steel company and having the following chemical compositions (wt%) (C.0.052, Mn 0.189, S0.011, P 0.008, Si 0.011, Al 0.039, N 0.001, Cr 0.012, Cu 0.04, Mo 0.024, Ni 0.029, and the remaining is iron). Acylindrical iron rod embedded in aralidite with exposed surface area of 0.5 cm^2. Prior to each experiment, the surface of iron specimen were mechanically polished with different grades of emery paper, degreased with acetone and rinsed by distilled water. No attempts were made to deareate them. The electrolytic cell was all pyrex and described elsewhere.

Cyclic voltammograms curves (CVs) were performed using auto lab (ECO Chemie) combined with the software package GPES (General Purpose Electrochemical System) was used. This is a computer controlled electrochemical measurements system. It consists of data acquisition system and potentiostat-galvanostat CVs were used to study the electrochemical behaviour of iron in different concentrations of NaOH solutions sweeping from hydrogen evolution to oxygen evaluation. All measurements were taken at 25 ± 1 °C.

The electrochemical impedance spectroscopy (EIS) was carried out in a conventional three electrodes electrochemical cell. The counter and reference electrodes were a platinum plate (2 cm^2) and saturated calomel electrode (SCE) respectively. The measurements were recorded using a voltalab PGZ 301. EIS voltammetry system with an accompanying PC and soft ware.

Results and Discussion

Cyclic Voltammogram Behaviour of Iron Electrode in NaOH Solutions

Figure represents the cyclic voltammograms of iron electrode in different concentrations of NaOH at a voltage scan rate 50 mV/s in the potential range -1300 to +600 mV. An inspection of this figure four anodic peaks (A_1-A_4) and two cathodic peaks (C_1 and C_2) are observed. Similar curves were obtained by Burke and Lyons.

The general shape of the cyclic voltammograms suggesting that the composition of the film both in the passive and in the active region. The peak A_o at the upper and of the potential corresponds to the oxygen gas evolution reaction and the peak C_0 at lower end of the potential corresponds to the hydrogen gas evolution reaction.

There are two anodic peaks or humps A_1 and A_2 at more cathodic potentials than A_3. From the curves in Fig. 13.48. suggest that the cathodic peak C_1 conjugated with the anodic peaks A_1 and A_2. This behaviour is in accord with MacDonald and Owen.

The hump A_2 which is next to the peak A_3 corresponds to the reaction of $Fe \rightarrow Fe(OH)_2$ only the cited authors [15] assumed the less probable reaction $Fe(OH)_2 \rightarrow Fe_3O_4$, hence the back reaction $Fe(OH)_2 \rightarrow Fe$ proceeds in the peak C_1. Confusion exists, however, regarding the hump A_1 (which is next to A_2) it has been attributed either to oxidation of adsorbed hydrogen or to oxidation of iron or to both. The first step in the oxidation of iron appears more probable than oxidation of hydrogen. This sep should be formulated as $Fe \rightarrow Fe(OH)_{ads}$, contrasting with $Fe \rightarrow Fe(OH)_2$ proceeding in peak A_2.

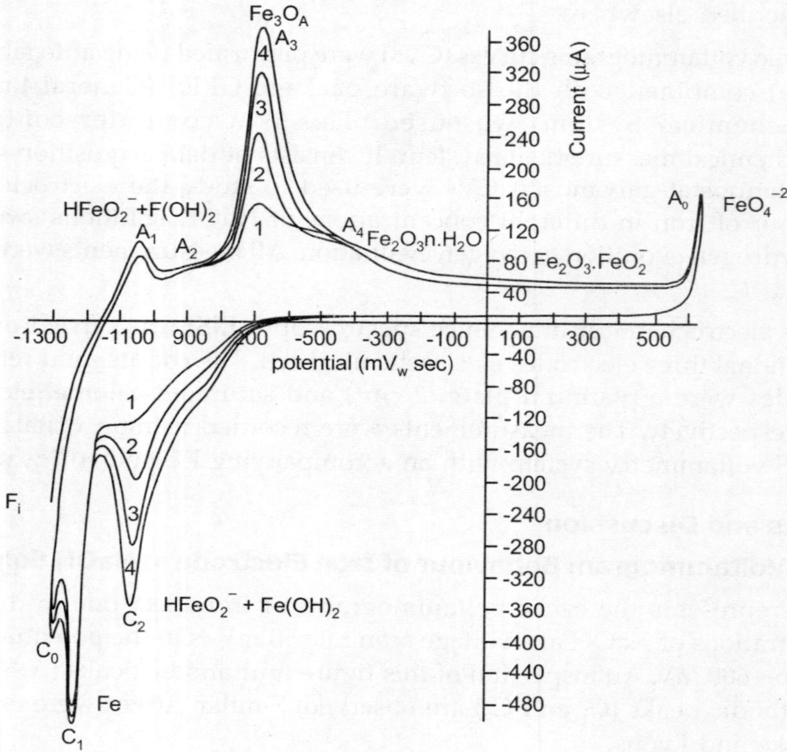

Fig. 13.48 : Cyclic Voltammetry of iron in different concentrations of NaOH solutions at 50mV/sec.

Further inspection in Fig. 13.48, it is clear that the peak A_2 and C_1 do not increase with the number of cycles distinguishes them well from the peaks A_3 and and C_2 and implies a passivity property of Fe(ll) hydroxide film formed. This probably has a low porosity and thus hinders the diffusion of ions necessary for its growth. The film is formed in NaOH solution-precipitation mechanism. By contrast, the "classical" passivity of iron occurs at more anodic potential and is due to the formation of non-porous film of Fe(III) oxides. Since the anodic charge corresponding to the humps A_1 and A_2 is considerably smaller than that corresponding to the peak A_3, it is obvious that the latter can not be due merely to one electron oxidation of the film formed is the proceeding sites as suggested by Burke it is much more probable that the peak A_3 involves oxidation of both $Fe(OH)_2$ and Fe tc Fe(III). Peak A_3 always lies in the region where oxidation of $Fe(OH)_2$ (either to Fe_3O_4 or to FeOOH) takes place. The conjugated peak C2 logically

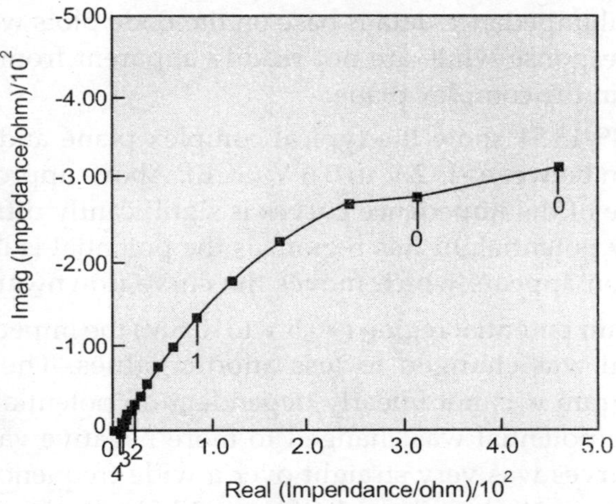

Fig. 13.49 : Complex plane of passive film on iron in 1M NaOH in low potential (-1.2V).

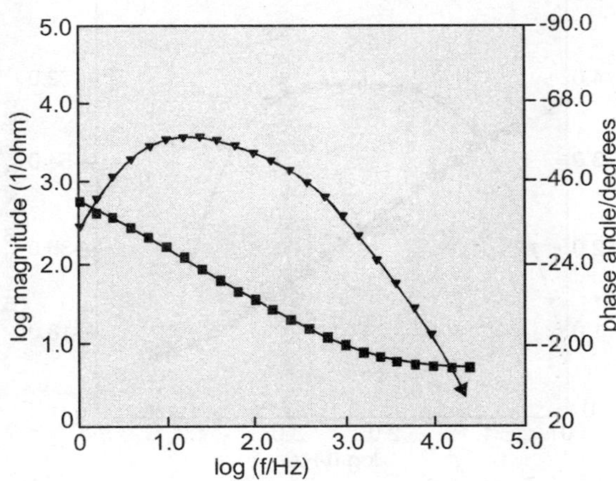

Fig. 13.50 : Bode plots of passive film on iron in 1m NaOH in low potential (-1.2V).

corresponds to the back reaction.The composition of the oxidation product may depend on the experimental conditions, the following compound have been considered by various authors, $Fe(OH)_3$ or FeOOH or Fe_2O_3 and Fe_3O_4. The peak at A, represents the formation of the magnetite or FeOOH.

The hump A_4, which is more anodic than the peak A_3, is observed it might correspond to the formation of more stable Fe(III) species than that formed in the peak A.

A.C. Impedance Behaviour of Iron in Alkaline Solutions

Impedance measurements were made of the passive film on pure iron from the dissolution potential to a potential of oxygen evolution. The analysis of the experimental impedance data is base on the Bode plots which emphasize aspects of the response while are not readily apparent from the analysis of the impedance in the complex plane.

Figures 13.49-13.51 show the typical complex plane and Bode plots for passive film iron between -1 .2 V to 0.6 V (SCE). Above approximately +0.6V (SCE), the shape of the impedance curves is significantly different from that observed of low potential. In this region, as the potential is increased a very definite inflection appears which moves the curve downward Fig. 13.50.

In the medium potential region (+0.5 V to -0.5 V) the impedance decreased as the potential was changed to less anodic values. The change of the impedance diagram was not linearly dependent on potential and this effect increased as the potential was changed to more negative values. The log Z versus log of curves was very straight over a wide frequency range but the slopes were apparently less than -1, (Figure 13.51). In the potential region

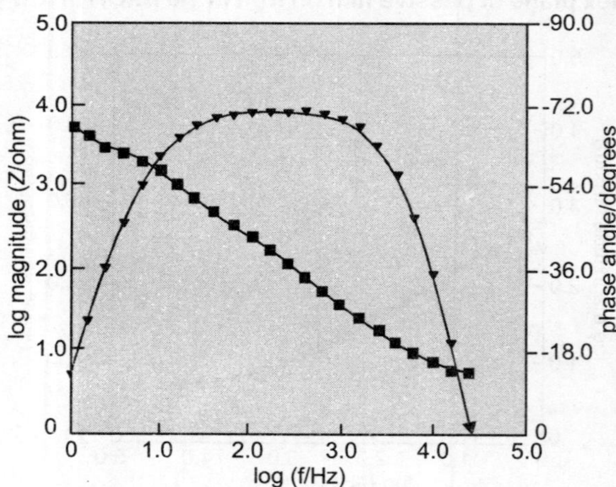

Fig. 13.51 : Bode plots of passive film on iron 1M *NaOH* in intermediate potential -0.5 to +0.5V

where the film starts to dissolve/there was a clear separation of the impedance curves at various potential values and the slope of these lines becomes significantly less than -1 accompanished by phase angle decreases (Fig. 13.50).

At low frequencies, the impedance showed a straight line with a slope close to -1 which corresponds to the capacitance. At high frequencies the curves become flat with a slope approaching zero which corresponds to a pure resistance. When the potential was removed from the rest potentials the log Z measured at low frequencies decreased linearly with potential, which means that the resistance decreased exponentially with the over potential increase.

In the impedance diagrams, the most sticking characteristic is the straightness of the log impedance versus log frequency curve and the fact that the slope of these lines deviate from -1. This important features precludes the possibility that the oxide can be represented by a pure capacitor, because in a Bode plot, the impedance of a "perfect capacitor" should be represented by a straight line with a slope of -1 and a phase angle of -90°.

REFERENCES

Anderson, B. and L. Ojefors: *J. Electrochem. Soc.* 123: 814 (1976).

Armstrong, R.D. and I. Baurhoo: *J, Electroanal. Chem.* 40: 325 (1972).

Beck, F., R. Kaus and M. Oberst: *Electrochim Acta* 30(2): 173 (1985).

Burke, Z.D. and M.E.G. Lyons: *J. Electroanal Chem.* 198: 347 (1986).

Burke, Z.D. and M.E.G. Lyons: *J. Electroanal. Chem.* 198: 347 (1986).

Burke, Z.D. and M.E.G. Lyons: *J. Electronal. Chem.* 198: 347 (1986).

Castro, E.B., *Electrochim. Acta,* 14: 2117 (1994).

Cerny , J. and K. Micka: *J. of Power Sources* 25: 111 (1989).

El-Sayed, A., *Revue Roumaine de chime:* 38(2): 139 (1993).

Geronov, Y., I. Tonov and S. Georgiev: *J. Appl. Electrochem.,* 5:351 (1974).

Hunny, Z.Q. and J.L. Ord. *J. Electrochem, Soc.* 132:24 (1985).

Hurlen, T., *Electrochim, Acta,* 8: 609 (1963).

Lorbeer, R and W.J. Lorenz: *Corros. Sci.* 21: 79 (1981).

Macdonald, D.D. and D. Owen: *J. Electrochem. Soc.,* 120: 317 (1973).

MacDonald, D.D. and Owne: *J. Appl. Electrochem.* 15: 675 (1985).

Muralidharan, V.S., *J. Appl. Electrochem.* 15: 675 (1985).

Ojefors, L., *J. Electrochem. Soc.* 123: 1891 (1976).

Shams, A.M. El-Din and S.M. Abd El-Haleem, Werkst. *Korros.,* 24: 389 (1973).

Silver, H. G. and E. Loaks: *J. Electrochem. Soc.,* 117: 5 (1970).

Stimming, U. and J.W. Schultze: *Electrochim Acta* 24:859 (1979).

Zor, S., B. Yazici and M. Erbil: *Corros. Sci.,* 47: 2700 (2005).

Zor, S., Turkish: *J. Chem.* 26: 403 (2002).

INHIBITING EFFECT OF CYTISINE DERIVATIVE ON THE CORROSION OF MILD STEEL IN ACIDIC MEDIUM

Wequar Ahmad Siddiqi,[1] Vishwa Mohan Chaubey[2] and M. Sharif Ahmad[1]

[1]*Department of Applied Sciences & Humanities. Faculty of Engineering and Technology, Jamia Millia Islamia, New Delhi-110025 (India)*

[2]*Department of Chemistry. Faculty of Natural Sciences, Jamia Millia Islamia, New Delhi-110025 (India)*

ABSTRACT

The inhibition effect of Cytisine derivative namely [N-(3- Methylthio-5-acetamido-1, 2, 4-thiadiazolyl) cytisine] on mild steel in 1M H_2SO_4 has been studied by using weight loss, electrochemical polarization and scanning electron microscopic (SEM) techniques. It has been concluded that percentage inhibition increases with increase in concentration of inhibitor. The adsorption of [N-(3-Methylthio-5-acetamido-1, 2, 4-thiadiazolyl) cytisine] on mild steel surface in 1M H_2SO_4 obeys Langumir adsorption isotherm, surface analysis studies are carried out to establish the mechanism of corrosion inhibition. The polarization data indicate that this compound act as very good cathodic inhibitors for mild steel in 1M H_2SO_4 and its inhibition efficiency increases with concentration and the highest value obtained is around 92 per cent.

Key words: Corrosion, Inhibition, mild steel, H_2SO_4, [N-(3- Methylthio-5-acetamido-1, 2, 4-thiadiazolyl) cytisine].

Introduction

Corrosion is destructive attack of metal by its environment. One of the methods used to reduce the rate of metals corrosion is the addition of inhibitors. Many metals and alloys which used in different human activities are susceptible to different mechanisms of corrosion due to their exposure to different corrosive media. Many studies have been carried out to find suitable compounds to be used as corrosion inhibitors for different metals and alloys in different aqueous solution. These studies reported that there are a number of organic and inorganic compounds which can do that for the corrosion of mild steel. Many organic compounds containing oxygen, nitrogen and sulphur have been used as corrosion inhibitor for metal. Amines are effective inhibitors for steel corrosion in acidic solution. The present paper deals with the study of inhibiting action of [N-(3-Methylthio-5-acetamido-1, 2, 4-thiadiazolyl) cytisine] on mild steel in acidic media. The electrochemical behaviour of mild steel in H_2SO_4 media in absence and presence of different concentration of inhibitor has been studied by galvanostatic polarization and SEM method.

Experimental

Specimens

The mild steel coupons of composition(C = 0.16%, Mn = 0.035%, Si = 0.05%, S = 0.025%, P = 0.25% and balance Fe) and have been used for weight loss measurements. These coupons were mechanically polished with emery papers of 1/0, 2/0, 3/0 and 4/0 grade and degreased with acetone before use.

Electrolyte

The aggressive solutions used were made of AR grade of H_2SO_4 acids. Appropriate concentrations of acid were prepared using double distilled water. The concentration range of inhibitor employed was 100 ppm to 1000 ppm in acidic solutions.

Weight Loss Studies

The mild steel strips of size *i.e.* (1 cm × 1cm × 3 cm) were used for weight loss measurement studies. All the weight loss experiments were carried out at 298 to 328k temperatures and immersion time 6, 12 and 24 hour. The experiments were performed as per ASTM G31-72 method. The percentage inhibition efficiency was calculated using the following equation:

$$I\% = \frac{Wo - Wi}{Wo} \times 100$$

where, Wo and Wi are weight losses in the absence and presence of inhibitor respectively.

Electrochemical Studies

For potentiodynamic polarization studies, mild steel strips of above mentioned composition were used and the experiments were carried out at different temperatures and time period, up to 24 hours in the absence and presence of inhibitor. For polarization studies a cylindrical mild steel rod of the same composition, as that of weight loss, coated with araldite (exposed area of 1 cm^2) was used. The electrodes were polished with emery papers and degreased with acetone before used. For accurate measurements of potential and current densities, galvanostatic polarization studies were carried out at different temperatures. A platinum foil and saturated calomel electrode were used as counter and reference electrode respectively. Polarization studies were carried out in 1M H_2SO_4 in the absence and presence of inhibitor of varying concentrations and temperatures.

Scanning Electron Microscopy Studies

To know the surface morphology of mild steel, scanning electron microscopy technique using LEO 435 V. P. Scanning Electron Microscope is used. The polished specimens, which are used in this experiment, are examined to find out any surface defects by optical microscope. The specimens selected for study were having smooth surfaces. After this the specimens were washed with double distilled water and dried in desiccators. These specimens were then dipped in the solutions of 1000 ppm and 100 ppm concentration for the inhibitor in 1M sulphuric acid for 24 hours at room temperature.

These specimens were then washed with distilled] water and dried in desiccators. The SEMI photographs were recorded of these corroded as well as uncorrode mild steel specimens.

Results and Discussion

Weight Loss Measurement

The corrosion inhibition efficiency (%I) of [N-(3- Methylthio-5-acetamido-1, 2, 4-thiadiazolyl) cytisine] for corrosion of mild steel is calculated using the

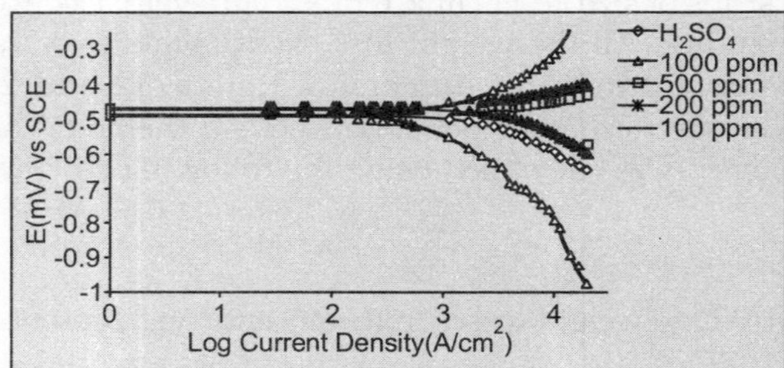

Fig. 13.52 : Galvanostatic Polarization Curves of Mild Steel in 1M H_2SO_4 solution in presence of different concentrations of [N-(3-Methylthio-5-acetamido-1,2,4-thiadiazolyl) cystisine] at 298K.

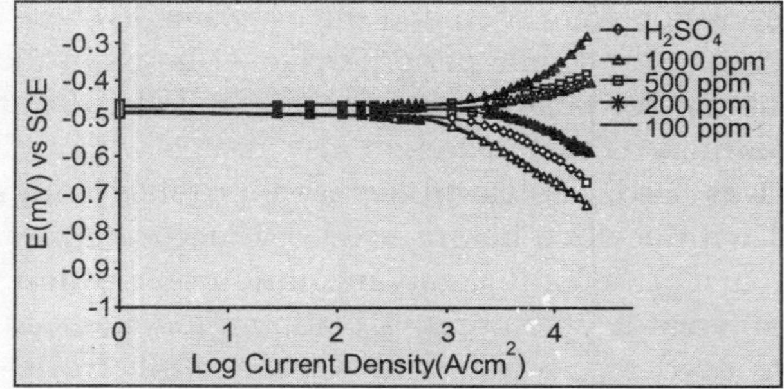

Fig. 13.53 : Galvanostatic Polarization Curves of Mild Steel in 1M H_2SO_4 solution in presence of different concentrations of [N-(3-Methylthio-5-acetamido-1,2,4-thiadiazolyl) cytisine] I at 308 K.

above mentioned equation. Table gives the value of inhibition efficiencies obtained from weight loss study for various concentrations and temperatures. It has been observed that the inhibition efficiencies slightly decrease at the temperature increases from 298 K to 328 K for all inhibitor concentrations. The changes in inhibition efficiencies are quite less for all concentrations *viz.* 1000 ppm, 500 ppm, 200 ppm and 100 ppm at temperature 298 K. While changes in inhibition efficiencies are more as the temperature increases from 308 K to 328 K for all concentrations.

Galavonstatic Polarization Measurement

Figures 13.54 and 13.55 show the anodic and cathodic polarization curves (Tafel's plot) of mild steel in 1M H_2SO_4 solution with and without the addition of various concentration of [N-(3-Methio-5-acetamido-1,2,4-thiadizoyl) cytisine) at different temperatures *i.e.* 298 K, 308 K, 318 K and 328 K. The various electrochemical parameters corrosion current density (I_{corr}) corrosion potential (E_{coor}), Tafel's value b_a and b_c for different concentrations are given in Table 13.6.

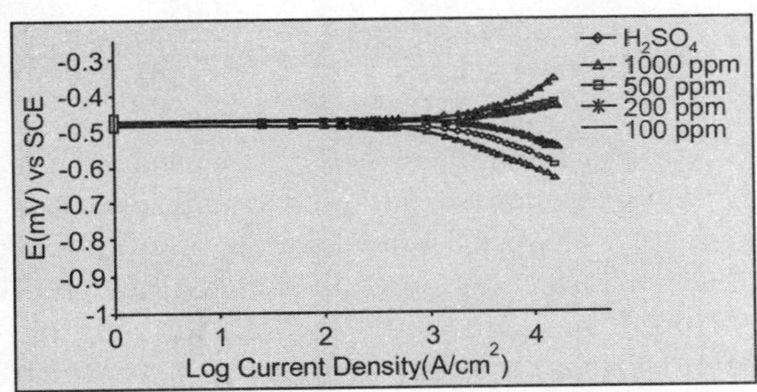

Fig. 13.54 : Galvanostatic Polarization Curves of Mild Steel in 1M H_2SO_4 solution in presence of different concentrations of [N-(3-methythio-5-acetamido-1,2,4-thiadiazolyl) cytisine] at 318 K.

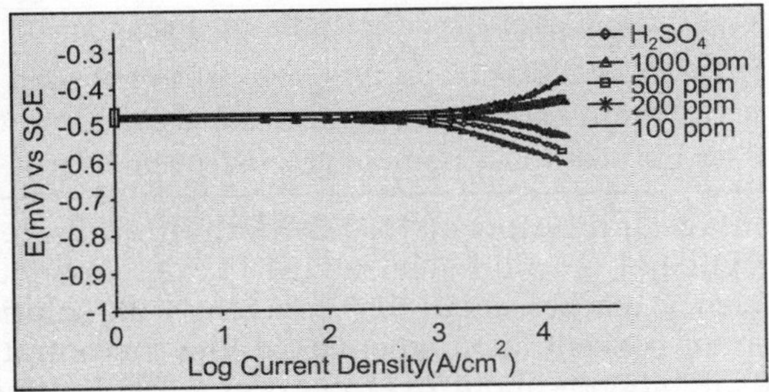

Fig. 13.55 : Galvanostatic Polarization Curves of Mild Steel in 1M H_2SO_4 solution in presence of different concentrations of [N-(3-methylthio-5-acetamido-1,2,4-thiadiazolyl) cytisine] at 328K.

The corrosion current densities are calculated by extra plotting the tangents of anodic and cathodic curves and their intersection with corrosion potential. These curves explain that the corrosion current densities decrease with increase in concentration of inhibitor. The percentage inhibition of each inhibitor at various concentrations in 1M H_2SO_4 is shown is Table 13.6 after being calculated from the expression:

$$\%\text{Inhibition} = \frac{I_{(corr)uninh} - 1_{(corr)inh}}{I_{(corr)uninh}}$$

Table 13.6 : Inhibition Efficiency of [N-(3-Methylthio-5-acetamido-1,2,4-thiadiazolyl) cytisine]

Temperature	Solution in ppm	Weight loss/gram	%I
298K	1M H_2SO_4	0.0786	—
	100	0.0099	69.39
	200	0.0073	80.71
	500	0.0041	94.78
	1000	0.0035	92.54
308K	1M H_2SO_4	0.1568	—
1.	100	0.0715	54.40
1.	200	0.0598	61.86
1.	500	0.0179	88.58
1.	1000	0.0071	95.47
328K	1M H_2SO_4	0.5468	—
1.	100	0.3454	36.83
1.	200	0.2374	56.58
1.	500	0.1675	69.36
1.	1000	0.0260	95.24
328K	1M H_2SO_4	1.1891	—
1.	100	0.8028	32.48
1.	200	0.6849	42.40
1.	500	0.2349	80.24
1.	1000	0.0683	94.25

The percentage inhibition of [N-(3-Methylthio-5-acetamido-1,2,4-thiadiazolyl) cytisine] on mild steel in 1M H_2SO_4 shows that corrosion inhibition efficiency reaches about 92.5 per cent with solution containing 1000 ppm inhibitor concentration where as at low concentration (100 ppm) the percentage inhibition is about 73.41 per cent at 298 K. While at 328K the corrosion inhibition efficiency reaches 90.8 per cent with solution containing 1000 ppm inhibitor. On the other hand the percentage inhibition efficiency is about 33.93 per cent containing solution 100 ppm concentration. This effect could be attributed to the fact that inhibition increases due to large alkyl chain group, which cause enough coverage on the metal surface. In this way small area of surface is left uncovered, which produces less corrosion on mild steel. The trend in the values of b_a and b_c suggest that many inhibitor processes are participated in corrosion inhibition.

From the experimental method, it is concluded that inhibition effect is anodic at temperature 298K rather than cathodic except 1000 ppm. At higher temperature the inhibitor [N-(3-Methylthio-5-acetamido-1,2,4-thiadiazolyl) cytisine] is anodic type.

Adsorption Kinetics

With high concentration of inhibitor a protective inhibitor layer formed on the mild steel surface which reduces the chemical attack on metal. The surface coverage θ values have been obtained from electrochemical measurements

Table 13.7 : Corrosion parameters of Mild Steel in 1M H_2SO_4 in presence of [N-(3-Methylthio-5-acetamido-1,2, 4-thiadiazolyl) cytisine] as additive

Temp.	Inhi. conc. in ppm.	E_{corr} mV μA/cm²	Log I_{corr}	b_c mV/dec	b_a mV/dec	%I
298K	0	512	3-45	99	141	—
	10^{-7}	482	2-55	91	161	87.41
	10^{-5}	463	2.43	81	179	90.45
	10^{-3}	485	2.20	100	168	94.30
	10^{-1}	541	2.13	241	349	95.20
308K	0	522	3.38	111	151	—
	10^{-7}	482	3.05	91	133	53.22
	10^{-5}	453	2.95	78	248	62.84
	10^{-3}	495	2.48	85	100	87.40
	10^{-1}	525	1.99	163	457	95.50
318K	0	500	3.35	75	73	—
	10^{-7}	485	3.15	40	98	36.90
	10^{-5}	455	2.99	93	204	56.34
	10^{-3}	482	2.83	81	159	80.80
	10^{-1}	480	2.03	168	432	95.21
328K	0	480	3.29	41	93	—
	10^{-7}	482	3.11	81	91	33.93
	10^{-5}	462	3.05	76	173	42.45
	10^{-3}	462	2.60	43	120	79.58
	10^{-1}	440	2.00	117	432	94.87

for various concentrations. There are many adsorption isotherms to study the adsorption process. Here, Langumir adsorption isotherm is tested. Fig. 13.57 shows the plot of log θ/1-θ v. log C graph, a straight line with approximately unit slope. The value of heat of adsorption can be calculated from the formula

$$\log\frac{\theta}{1-\theta} = \log A + \log C - \frac{Q_{ads}}{2.3RT}$$

where, A is Arrhenius constant, C is inhibitor concentration and Q is heat of adsorption.

The value of heat of adsorption for [N-(3-Methylthio-5-acetamido-1,2,4-thiadiazolyl) cytisine] is 4.50 Kcal/mol.

To calculate the activation energy, the current densities are plotted against temperature in absence and presence of inhibitor. The value of activation energy can be finding out by Arrhenius equation.

$$\frac{\partial \log I_{corr}}{\partial T} = \frac{E_a}{RT^2}$$

where E_a is the activation energy. The value of activation energy of [N-(3-Methylthio-5-acetamido-1,2,4-thiadiazolyl) cytisine] is Kcal/mol.

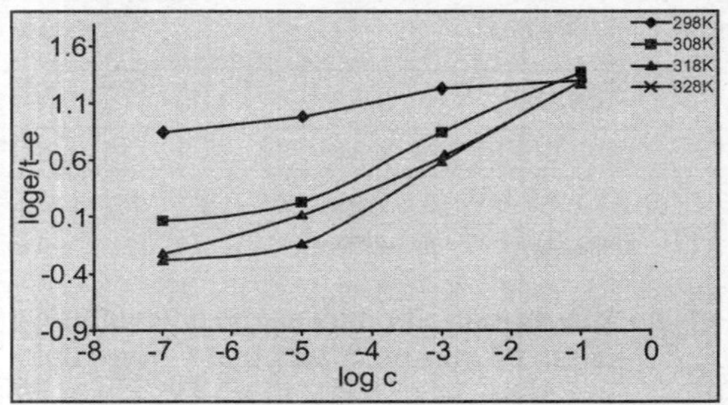

Fig. 13.56 : Variation of Surface coverage vs. concentration at different temperature of [N-(3-Methlythio-5-acetamido-1,2,4-thiadiazolyl) cytisine].

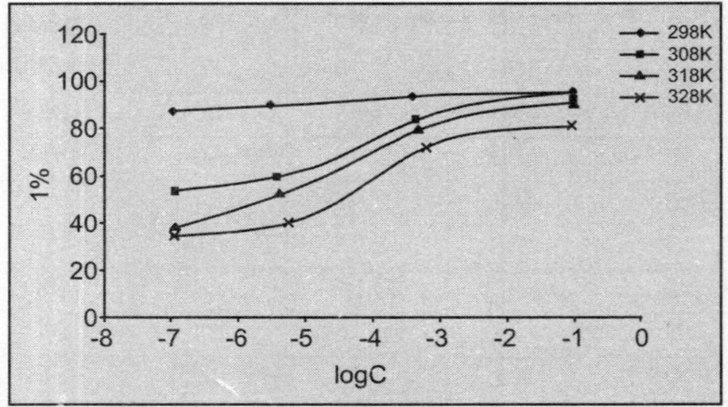

Fig. 13.57 : Inhibition efficiency vs. concentration of [N-(3-Methylthio-5-acetamido-1,2,4-iadiazolyl) cytisine] at different temperatures.

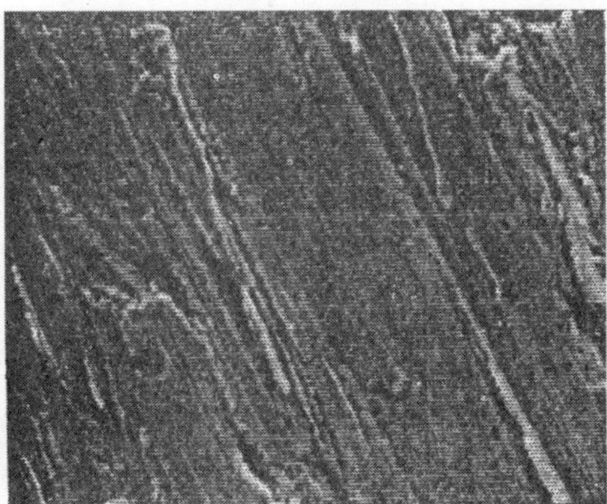

Fig. 13.58 : Scanning Electron Micrograph of plain Mild Steel at 2000 magnification.

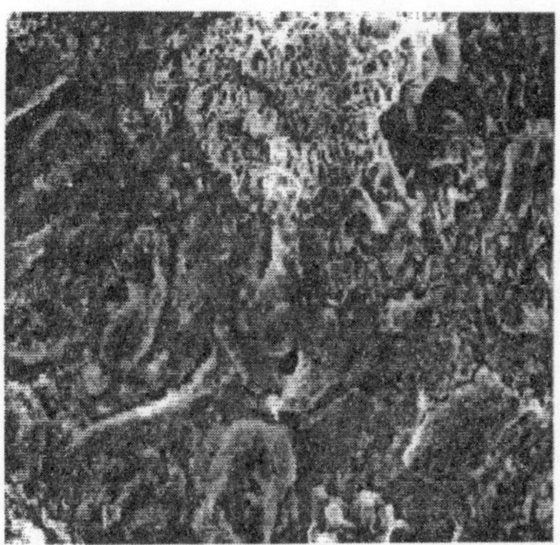

Fig. 13.59 : Scanning Electron Micrograph of Mild Steel in 1NH_2SO_4 at 2000 magnification.

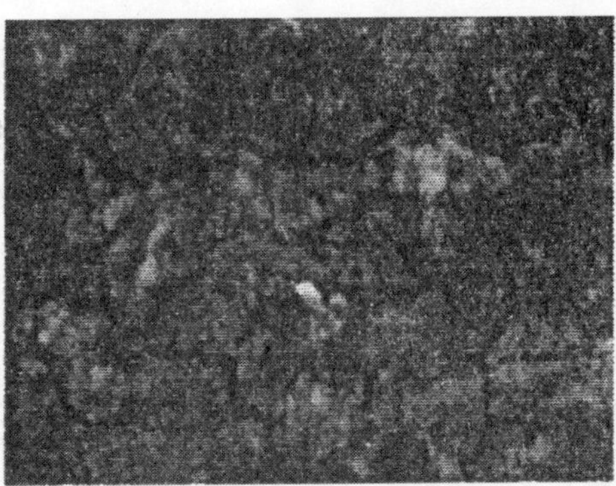

Fig. 13.60 : Scanning Electron Micrograph of Mild Steel in presence of 100 ppm of [N-(3-Methylthio-5-acetamido-1,2,4-thiadiazolyl) cytisine] in 1M H_2SO_4 at 2000 magnification.

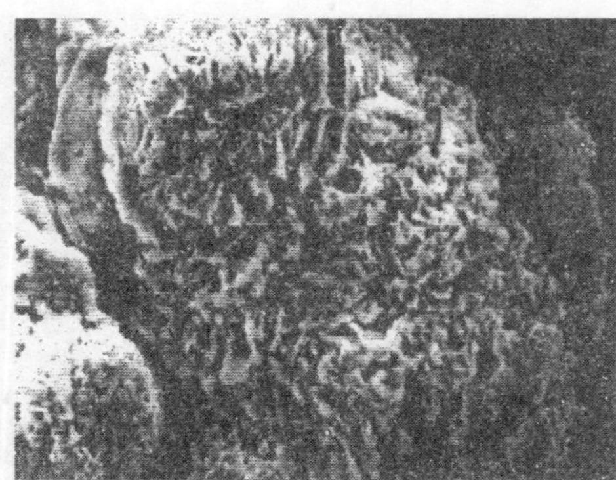

Fig. 13.61 : Scanning Electron Micrograph of Mild Steel in presence of 1000 ppm [N-3-Methylthio-5-acetamido-1,2,4-thiadiazolyl) cystine] in 1M H_2SO_4 at 2000.

Scanning Electron Microscopic Study

To study the surface morphology of mild steel coupons SEM techniques has been used. Figures 13.58 to 13.60 show the surface morphology of plain mild steel, in 1M H_2SO_4 and corroded surfaces after dipped in [N-(3-Methylthio-5-acetamido-1,2,4-thiadiazolyl) cytisine] inhibitor at 100 ppm and 1000 ppm. The micrograph obtained from different concentrations show that the surfaces are inhibited due to formation of insoluble stable film of mild steel surface. It proves that additive act as good inhibitor at higher concentration 1000 ppm.

REFERENCES

Abdel, S.S., H.H. Hassaan, M.A. Amin, *Journal of Mater. Chem.Phys.* 70 64 (2001).

Agrawal, Y.K., J.D. Talati, M.D. Shah, M.N. Desai and N.K. Shah, *Corrosion Science,* 46: 633 (2004).

Azhar, M. El, M. Traisnel, B.Mernari, L.Gengembre, F. Bentiss, M. Largrenee, *Journal of Applied Surface Science.* 185:197 14. (2002).

Chun, C.M. and T.A. Ramanarayanan, *Oxide. Met.* 62: 71 (2004).

El Azhar, M., B. Mernari, M. Traisnel, F.Bentiss, M.Lagrene, *Corrosion Science.* 43: 11. 2229 (2001).

Fan, H-B., C.-Y. Fu, H.-L Wang, X.-P. Guo and J.-S. Zheng, *Brit. Corros. J.,* 122: 37-2 (2002).

Founda, A.S., A.A. El-Bindary, A.A.Ai-Sarawy, *E.E.El-Katori, Bulletin of Electrochemistry.* 21: 481 (2005).

Garcia-Alonso, M.C., G.Macchi, C.Brugnoni, *M.F. Stroosnijder, Corrosion Science.* 44:129 (2002).

Grabke, H.J., *Mater, Corroc.* 54: 736 (2003).

Manivel, P. and G. Venktachari. *Journal of Metallurgy and Materials Science.,* 46(4): 263-270 (2004).

Osman, M.M., M.N. Shalaby, *Mater. Chem. Phys.* ***77:*** (2002).

Popova, A., E Sokolova, S Raicheva, M. 16. Christov, *Corrosion Science.* 45: 33 (2003).

Ramanathan, Lalgudi V Corrosion Prevention and Control Augus (1999).

Shetty, S.D., Prakash Shetty, H.V.S. Nayak, *Indian Journal of Chemical Technology.* 12: 462 (2005).

Standard, A.S.T.M, Practice for Laboratory Immersion Corrosion Testing of Metals, *Annual Book of Standards,* G 31-72, 3.02 (1990).

Takeuchi, K., A. Nishijima, K. Ui, N. Koura and C.K. Loong, *Journal of The Electrochemical Society,* 152(9) B: 364-B368. (2005).

Xiao-Ci, Y., Z.Hong, L.Ming-Dao, R. Hong- Xuan, Y. Lu-An, *Corrosion Scinece.* 42: 645 10. (2000).

INHIBITION OF ACID CORROSION ON MILD STEEL WITH AGAR IN HYDROCHLORIC ACID MEDIUM AT DIFFERENT TEMPERATURES

WEQUAR AHMAD SIDDIQUI[1], VISHWA MOHAN CHAUBEY[2] and M. SHARIF AHMAD[1]

Department of Applied Sciences & Humanities, Faculty of Engineering & Technology

Jamia Millia Islamia, New Delhi-110 025 (India)

Department of Chemistry, Faculty of Natural Sciences, Jamia Millia Islamia New Delhi-110 025 (India)

ABSTRACT

The inhibitive effect of (agar) on the corrosion of mild steel in 1M HCl has been investigated using gravimetric and electrochemical techniques. The percentage inhibition efficiency was found to increase with increasing the concentration of inhibitor and wtth decreasing temperature. From both gravimetric and electrochemical experiments, the inhibition efficiency of the agar was found to be in the 92-98 per cent range for 1M HCl medium. Galvanostatic study indicates that this compound act as a mixed type corrosion inhibitor. The rate of corrosion of mild steel rapidly increases with temperature over the temperature range of 30°C to 60°C, both in absence and presence of inhibitor. Thermodynamic parameters for adsorption process have been calculated using the Langmuir's adsorption isotherm.

Key words: Corrosion, Inhibition, agar, HCl, Mild steel.

Introduction

Due to the wide use of acidic media in many industrial fields, several researchers devoted their attention to develop more effective and non toxic inhibitors to reduce both acid attack and protection aspects. Organic inhibitor are applied extensively to protect metals from corrosion in many aggressive acidic media (*e.g.* in the acid pickling and cleaning processes of metals). The chemical components of agar had been analyzed from 1859 to 1938 by many scientists, and verified to consist of D-galactose, 3, 6-anhydro-L-galactose and sulphate. From the 1940's to 1950's the substituted galactose such as methylated, sulphated and pyruvated galactoses were proved to be the constituents of the agar molecule as well. Araki (1956) offered the evidence proving the heterogeneity of the agar by separating the agar into two different polysaccharides named agarose and aparopectin using the acetylation method. The agarose is a virtually neutral polymer, while the agaropectin is an acidic polymer. Later, Araki *et. al.*, and other scientists—

by acid hydrolysis and enzymic degradation of agar—isolated the agarobiose and neoagarobiose, respectively, and revealed that the agarose is composed of agarobiose repeating disaccharide units alternating with 1, 3-linked-β-D-galactopyranose and 1, 4-linked-3, 6-anhydro-α-L-galactopyranose. The agaropectin seems to have the same backbone as the agarose, but contains considerable amount of acid groups such as sulphate, pyruvate and glucuronate groups.

It is partially soluble in water at lower temperature but soluble in water above 30°C, it is rich in hydroxyl group and carboxyl group. Thus it is likely to be one of the good inhibitors. There are several ways to prevent atmospheric corrosion. Among the available methods of preventing corrosion, the use of inhibitor is the most promising method particularly for closed systems. The inhibitors find wide applications in the industrial field. The inhibition by organic additives on metals in acids has been studied. The organic substances belonging to this group contain mainly oxygen, sulphur, nitrogen and multiple bonds in the molecules that facilitate the adsorption on the metal surface are strongly polar. According to ref sulphur compounds such as thiourea are very effective corrosion inhibitor for steel in acidic condition because sulphur atom is easily protonated in acidic solution and a stronger electron donor than nitrogen. Therefore sulphur atom is more strongly absorbed to the metal surface. It has been observed that adsorption mainly depends on the presence of electrons and heteroatom, which induce greater adsorption of the inhibitor molecules on the surface of metal. The study of corrosion of iron is a matter of tremendous theoretical and practical concern and has received a considerable amount of interest. Iron is widely used as constructional material in many industries due to its excellent mechanical properties and low cost. The highly corrosive nature of aqueous mineral acids on most metal require degree of restraint to achieve economic maintenance and operation of equipment, minimum loss of chemical product and maximum safety condition.

The aim of this work is to study the effect of agar-agar as corrosion inhibitors for dissolution of mild steel in 1M concentration of HCl acid , by chemical and electrochemical technique. The effect of temperature on the dissolution of the mild steel in free and inhibited acid solution was also investigated.

Experimental

Electrolyte

The aggressive solutions used were made of AR grade of HCl acids Appropriate concentration of acid were prepared using double distilled water. The concentration range of inhibitor employed was 100 ppm to 1000 ppm .

Specimens

The mild steel coupons of composition (C=0.5%, Mn=0.5%, Si=0.05%, 3=0.025%, P=0.25% and balance Fe) and have been used for weight loss measurements. These coupons were mechanically polished with emery papers of 1/0, 2/0, 3/0 and 4/0 grade and degreased with acetone before use.

Weight Loss Studies

The mild steel strips of size (*i.e.* 1 × 1 × 3 cm) were used for weight loss measurement studies. All the weight loss experiments were carried out at 30°C to 60°C temperatures and immersion time 24-hour. The experiments were performed as per ASTM G31-72 method. The percentage inhibition efficiency was calculated using the following equation:

$$I\% = \frac{W_o - W_i}{Wo} \times 100$$

where W_o and W_i are weight losses in the absence and in the presence of inhibitor respectively.

Electrochemical Studies

For potentiodynamic polarization studies, mild steel strips of above mentioned composition were used and the experiments were carried out at different temperatures and time period, up to 6 hours in the absence and presence of inhibitor. For polarization studies a cylindrical mild steel rod of the same composition, as that of weight loss, coated with araldite (exposed area of 1 cm^2) was used. The electrodes were polished with emery papers and degreased with acetone before used. For accurate measurements of potential and current densities, galvanostatic polarization studies were carried out at different temperatures. A platinum foil and saturated calomel electrode were used as counter and reference electrode respectively. Polarization studies were carried out in 1M HCl in the absence and presence of inhibitor of varying concentrations and temperatures. The percentage inhibition efficiency was calculated using the following equation:

$$\text{I.E.}\% = \frac{\text{I}_{\text{corr}} - I_{\text{corr}'}}{I_{\text{corr}}} \times 100$$

where I_{corr} and $I_{corr'}$ are the corrosion current density of in the absence and in the presence of inhibitor respectively.

Results and Discussion

Weight Loss Measurements

Table 1 gives the values of inhibition efficiencies for different concentrations of (agar-agar) in 1M HCl medium obtained from weight loss measurements. The percentage inhibition was calculated using the above described equation. The results are listed in table 13.40. The results show that the inhibition efficiency increases with increasing the concentration of inhibitor at higher temperature. As the temperature increases the inhibition efficiency also increases because Agar-Agar formed a strong protective jell on alloys surrounding at studied temperature. The inhibition efficiency is appreciably higher *i.e.* HCl acid in presence of 1000 ppm of (agar-agar) concentration at 60°C temperature.

Table 13.8 : Inhibition Efficiency of Agar-Agar on Mild Steel In 1M HCl Medium from Weight Loss at various Temperatures

Temperature	Solution in pom	Weight loss/gram	%I
30°C	1M HCl	0.5457	---
	100	0.1334	75.7
	200	0.1118	79.5
	500	0.0835	84.7
	1000	0.0668	87.7
40°C	1M HCl	0.7935	—
	100	0.1695	78.6
	200	0.1445	81.7
	500	0.1175	85.1
	1000	0.0725	90.8
50°C	1M HCl	0.8350	—
	100	0.1445	82.7
	200	0.1235	85.2
	500	0.0885	89.4
	1000	0.0382	95.4
60 °C	1M HCl	0.8975	—
	100	0.1205	86.5
	200	0.0957	89.3
	500	0.0484	94.6
	1000	0.0175	98.0

Galvanostatic Polarization Measurements

The electrochemical parameters such as corrosion potential (E_{corr}), Tafel's slopes (b_a and b_c), corrosion current (I_{corr}) and inhibition efficiency (I.E%) for corrosion of mild steel in 1M HCl in absence and presence of gelatin (agar-agar) as inhibitor of different concentrations and temperatures are calculated using above mention equation and listed in Table 2. Figures 1 to 4 show the effect of inhibitor concentration on the current potential curves for both the cathodic and anodic reactions at different temperatures in 1M HCl. As the inhibitor concentration increases there is an increase in the values of both the Tafel's slopes in this acid solution. The values of Tafel's slopes (cathodic and anodic) are more in case of 1000 ppm concentration of inhibitor in 1M HCl. The percentage inhibition curve of agar-agar on mild steel in 1M HCl solution shows that the corrosion inhibition efficiency reached about 88 per cent with solution containing 1000 ppm of inhibitor where as at the lower concentration of 100 ppm, the percentage inhibition was about 75 per cent at temperature 30°C. The percentage inhibition of (agar-agar) in 1M HCl is about 98 per cent having concentration 1000 ppm while at lower concentration 100 ppm the percentage inhibition was about 86 per cent at 60°C temperature. The value of I_{corr} is found to be little more in case of lowest concentrations inhibitor compound in this medium. As the concentration increases there is a decrease in the values of I_{corr}. The inhibition efficiency of (agar-agar) depends on many factors including number of adsorption active center in the molecule and their charge density, which are affected by (–OH) group. The values of inhibition efficiency obtained by weight loss method and galvanostatic polarization studies show fairly good agreement.

Adsorption Isotherm

The adsorption isotherms were constructed by evaluating the Icorr value in the absence and presence of the inhibitor $I_{corr'}$. All measurements are carried out in normally oxygenated solutions without stirring at temperature 60° C. The Surface coverage values (θ) have been obtained from polarization measurements (inhibition efficiency), for various concentration of inhibitor (agar-agar). Thus on the basis of this consideration, the value of (θ) is calculated as:

$$(\theta) = 1 - (I_{corr'}/I_{corr})$$

where, $I_{corr'}$ = corrosion current in the presence of inhibitor. And Icorr = corrosion current in the absence of inhibitor. According to the literature the adsorption process of aromatic containing compounds on ferrous metals can obey Langmuir, Temkin or Frumkin isotherm. The data shown in 13.9 were tested graphically for fitting a suitable adsorption isotherm. A straight line is obtained by plotting a graph between tog $\theta/1 - \theta$ vs. $1/T$ (Fig. 13.66). This clearly proves that the adsorption of Agar on mild steel surface obey Langmuir's adsorption isotherm.

Table 13.9 : Electrochemical Parameters of Mild Steel in 1M HCl in Presence of Agar-agar as Additive

Temp.	Solution/ mol (L^{-1})	E_{corr} mV	Log I_{corr} $\mu A/cm^2$	b_cmV/ dec	b_cmV/ dec	% I
30°C	1M HCl	478	2.73	29	40	—
	100	451	2.15	21	29	75.1
	200	439	2.06	30	32	79.6
	500	390	1.99	20	20	83.0
	1000	485	1.82	75	45	88.45
40°C	1M HCl	462	2.98	21	22	—
	100	427	2.32	18	18	78.2
	200	437	2.25	16	17	81.3
	500	420	2.16	13	20	84.8
	1000	475	1.88	22	24	91.50
50°C	1M HCl	454	3.21	28	28	—
	100	451	2.44	14	16	82.9
	200	431	2.38	16	16	85.2
	500	420	2.26	20	20	89.6
	1000	468	1.98	25	20	94.75
60°C	1M HCl	456	3.54	20	11	—
	100	442	2.66	17	16	86.7
	200	441	2.57	12	12	89.2
	500	457	2.29	18	08	94.3
	1000	475	1.81	31	32	98.25

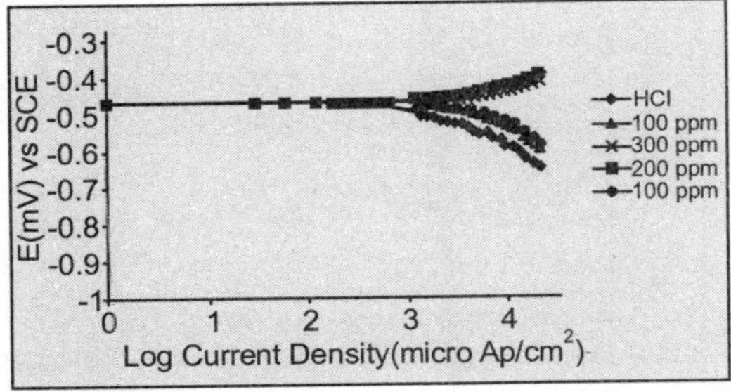

Fig. 13.62 : Galvanostatic Polarization curves of Mild Steel in 1M HCl solution Containing different concentrations of Agar-Agar at 30°C.

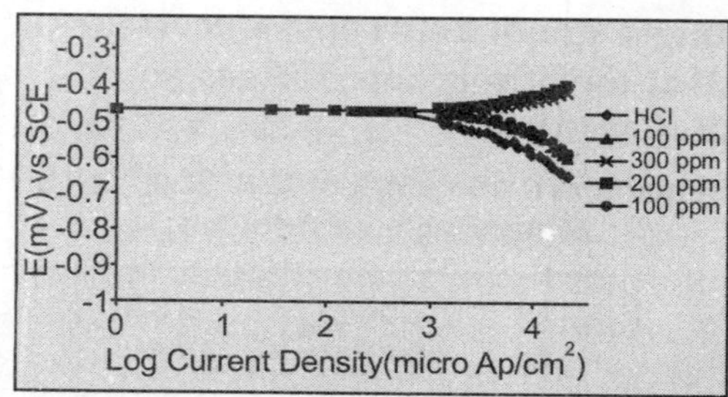

Fig. 13.63 : Galvanostatic Polarization curves of Mild Steel in 1M HCl solution Containing different concentrations of Agar-Agar.

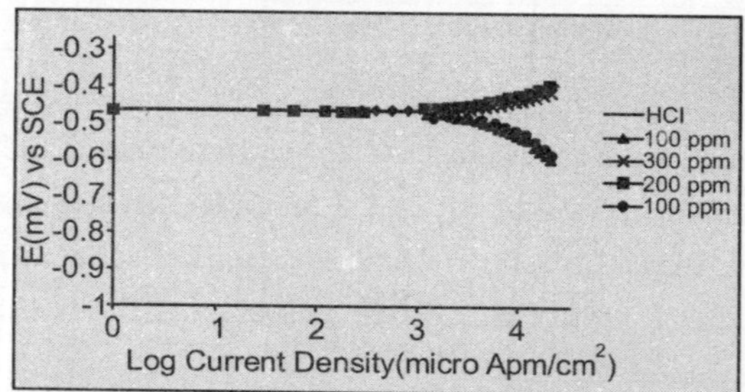

Fig. 13.64 : Garvanostatic Polarization curves of Mild Steel In 1M HCl solution Containing different concentrations of Agar-Agar at 50°C.

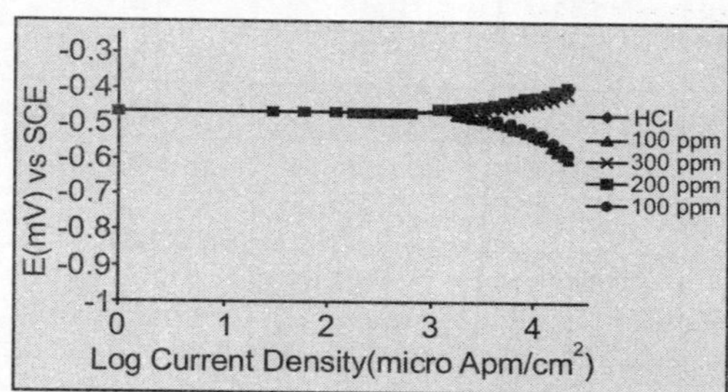

Fig. 13.65 : Galvanostatic Polarization curves of Mild Steel in 1M HCl solution Containing different concentrations of Agar-Agar at 60°C.

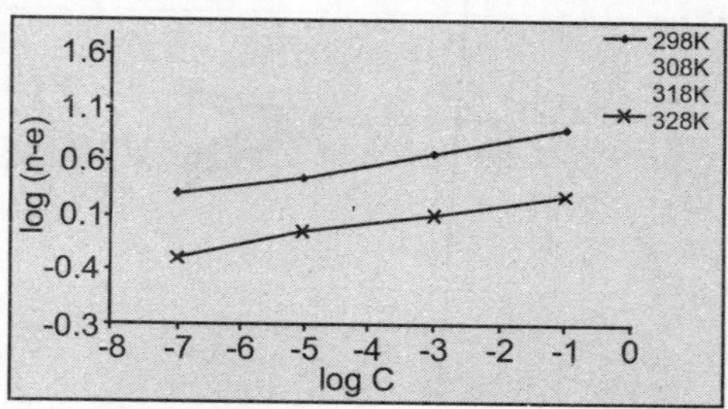

Fig. 13.66 : Variation of Surface coverage vs Concentration at Different temperatures of Agar-Agar in 1 M HCl.

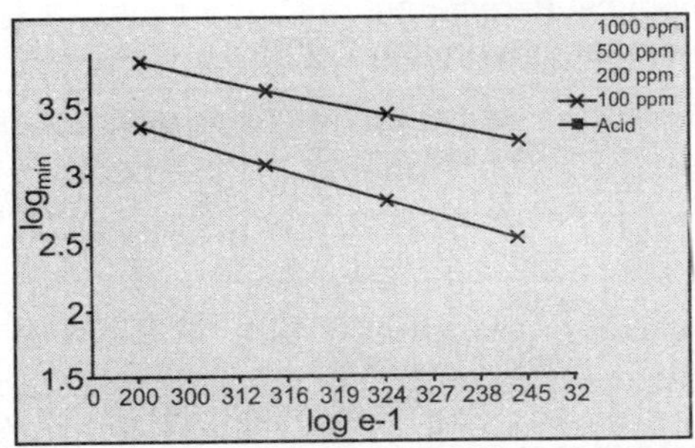

Fig. 13.67 : Arrhenius plots calculated from Corrosion current density foe Mild Steel 1M HCl and 1M HCl + different concentrations of Agar-Agar in 1M HCl.

Effect of Temperature

The change of the corrosion process rate with temperature increase was studied in 1M HCl, both in the absence and presence of inhibitor. We were interested in exploring the activation energy of the corrosion process and the thermodynamic of adsorption of Agar-Agar. This was accomplished by investigating the temperature dependence of the corrosion current, obtained using the Tafel Extrapolation method. Fig. 13.66 shows Tafel plots, for the mild steel electrode in, 1M HCl with addition of 100 ppm to 1000 ppm, in the temperature range 30°-60°C, it has been observed that the corrosion current density (I_{corr}) increased with increasing temperature. The Icorr increased with one order of magnitude with increase temperature, both in uninhibited and inhibited solutions. Corresponding data are given in Table 13.10, the result of the blank (1M HCl) in the temperature range 30°-60°C reported previously. It is seem that the Agar investigated have been inhibiting properties at all temperature studied and the values of inhibition efficiency of Agar increase with temperature increase. Thus, the Agar efficiencies were temperature-dependent.

The fact that (I.E.%) increases with temperature is explained by A.S. Founda *et al.*, as the likely specific interaction between the mild steel surface and the inhibitor. M. Lebrini considers the increase the (I.E.%) with temperature increase as the change in the nature of the adsorption mode, the inhibitor is being physically adsorbed at lower temperatures, while chemisorptions is favoured as temperature increases. The corrosion reaction can be regarded as an Arrhenius—type process, the rate is given by

$$Icorr = k \exp\left(-\frac{Ea}{RT}\right)$$

Table 13.10 : Electrochemical Parameters of Mild Steel in 1M H_2SO_4 in presence of N-(4,6-diphenylpyrlmidin-2-yl)thiourea as Additive

Temp.	Solution/ mol (L^{-1})	E_{corr} mV	Log i_{corr} $\mu A/cm^2$	%I	θ	θ/1-θ
30°C	1M HCl	478	2.73	—	—	—
	100	471	2.15	75.1	0.751	3.01
	200	453	2.06	79.6	0.796	3.90
	500	481	1.99	83.0	0.830	4.88
	1000	485	1.82	88.45	0.884	7.62
40°C	1M HCl	462	2.98	—	—	—
	100	478	2.32	78.2	0.782	3.58
	200	481	2.25	81.3	0.813	4.34
	500	472	2.16	84.8	0.848	5.57
	1000	475	1.88	91.50	0.915	10.76
50°C	1M HCl	454	3.21	—	—	—
	100	480	2.44	82.9	0.829	4.84
	200	464	2.38	85.2	0.852	5.75
	500	470	2.26	89.6	0.896	8.61
	1000	468	1.98	94.75	0.947	17.86
60°C	1M HCl	456	3.54	—	—	—
	100	471	2.66	86.7	0.867	6.51
	200	470	2.57	89.2	0.892	8.25
	500	472	2.29	94.3	0.943	6.54
	1000	475	1.81	98.25	0.982	54.55

Table 13.11 : The Influence of Temperature on the Electrochemical Parameters for Mild Steel Electrode Immersed in 1M HCl, 1MHCl + 1000 ppm of Agar.

Inhibitors	Temperature (°C)	Icorr (micro A/cm^2)	Erest. Pot (mV/SCE)	I.E. (%)
Blank	30	575	-478	—
	40	960	-462	—
	50	1635	-454	—
	60	3512	-456	—
Agar	30	66.45	-485	88.4
	40	79	-475	91.5
	50	97	-468	94.7
	60	65	-475	98.2

Where Ea is the apparent activation corrosion energy, T is the absolute temperature, k is the Arrhenius pre-exponential constant and R is the universal gas constant. This equation can be used to calculate the Ea values of the corrosion reaction without and with the inhibitor. Plotting the natural logarithm of the corrosion current density vs 1/T, the activation energy can be calculated from the slope.The temperature dependence of mild steel dissolution in deaerated 1M HCl and in the presence inhibitor is presented in Arrhenius co-ordinates in Fig. The calculated values of the apparent activation corrosion energy in the absence and presence of 1000 ppm if Agar is 49.54 and 34.37 KJ/mol. respectively. The lower values of the activation energy of the process in an inhibitor's presence when compared to that in its absence is attributed to the chemisorptions of inhibitor on mild steel surface. This conclusion was in accordance with findings of other researchers.

Conclusion

Agar inhibits the corrosion of mild steel in 1M HCl and its percentage inhibition efficiency increased with the inhibitor concentration, polarization studies showed that this inhibitor is mixed type inhibitor. The performance of this compound as an inhibitor in this acid is very much encouraging. The inhibition efficiency increases with increase in concentration, inhibition efficiency also increases with increase in temperature, which indicate that it is a good organic inhibitor at high temperatures. The adsorption of Agar on mild steel surfaces obey Langmuir's adsorption isotherm.

REFERENCES

A.S.T.M., Slandered Practice for Laboratory Immersion Corrosion Testing of Metals, Annual Book of Stan., G 31-72, 3.02 (1990).

Abdallah, M., E.A. Hetal and A.S. Fouda. *Corrosion Science.* 48, 1639-1654 (2006).

Agrawal, Y.K., J.D. Talati, M.D. Shah, M.N. Desai and N.K. Shah, *Corrosion Science,* 46, 633 (2004).

Agrawal, Y.K., J.D. Talati. M.D. Shah, M.N. Desai, N.K. Shah. *Corrosion Science* 46, 633(2004).

Ammar, I.A., F.M. El Khorafi, *Werkst. Korr.* 24 702 (1973).

Blustein, G., J. Rodriguez, R. Romanogli and C. F. Zinola, *Corrosion Science.* 47, 369-383 (2005).

Chun, C.M. and T.A. Ramanarayanan, *Oxide. Met.* 62. 71 (2004).

El Azhar, M., M. Traisnel, B.Mernari, L.Gengembre, F. Bentiss, M. Largrenee, *Journal of Applied Surface Science.* 185, 197 (2002).

Fan, H.-B., C.-Y. Fu, H.-L. Wang, X.-P Guo and J.-S. Zneng, *Brit. Corros. J.,* 37-2, 122 (2002).

Felhosi, Ilona, Erika Kalman *Corrosion Science,* 47, 695-708 (2005).

Founda, A.S., A.A. El-Sindary, A.A.Ai-Sarawy, E.E.El-Katori, *Bulletin of Electrochemistry. 21 (2005) 481.*

Garcia-Atonso, M.C., G.Macchi, C.Brugnoni, M.F. Stroosnijder, *Corrosion* Science. 44,129 (2002).

Grabke, H. J., Mater. *Corrosion*. 54, 736 (2003).

Lebrini, M., M.Lagrenee, H.Vezin, L.Gengenbre, F. Bentiss. *Corrosion Science*. 47, 485 (2005).

Manivel, P. and G. Venktachari. *Journal of Metallurgy and Materials Science* 46, No. 4 263-270 (2004).

Muller, B., *Corrosion Science,* 46,159-167 (2004).

Osman, M.M., M.N. Shalaby, *Mater. Chem. Phys.* 77 (2002).

Popova, A., E. Sokolova, S Raicheva, M. Christov, *Corrosion Science*. 45,33 (2003).

Quraishi, M.A. and S. KhanrIndian *Journal of Chemical, Technology*. 12, September, pp. 576-581 2005.

Scendo, M., *Corrosion Science*. 47, 2778 (2005).

Shetty, S.D., Prakash Shetty, H.V.S. Nayak, *Indian Journal of Chemical Technology*. 12, 462 (2005).

Takeuchi, K., A. Nishijima, K. Ui, N. Koura and C.K. Loong, *Journal of The Electrochemical Society* 152 (9)B 364-B368 (2005).

Xiao-Ci, Y., Z.Hong, L.Ming-Dao, R. Hong-Xuan, Y. Lu-An, *Corrosion Science*. 645 (2000).

CORROSION INHIBITION OF COPPER IN SULPHURIC ACID USING DIFFERENT SURFACTANTS

JITENDRA SINGH CHAUHAN and D.K. GUPTA

Government Motilal Vigyan Mahavidyalaya, Bhopal-462 003 (India).

ABSTRACT

Four commercial non-ionic surfactant compounds, namely *Bixin, Zenthoxylum almauta, Echitamin, Nyctanthin* were tested as inhibition for corrosion of Copper 0.5 M sulphuric acid solution. Weight loss measurements, potentiostatic polarizatiors and cyclic voltammetry techniques were used in this study. It was found that all the four used compounds act as good inhibitors for acid corrosion of Copper. The inhibition efficiencies obtained by the three techniques were almost the same, and increases with increasing the surfactant concentration. The polarization studies show that all used compounds act also mixed inhibitors. The inhibition action of these surfactants is interpreted in view of their adsorption on the metal surface making a barrier to mass and charge transfer. It was found that the adsorption of compounds follows Longmuir isotherm. The values of free energy of adsorption for them were calcopperlated. It was found that the adsorption process is spontaneous and increases, for different surfactants, in the same direction as inhibition efficiency. The cyclic voltammetry shows that there is only one anodic peak corresponding to the dissolution reaction of electrode. The copperrrent of this dissolution peak was used also for corrosion rate measurements and in evaluation of inhibition efficiencies of the used compounds.

Key words: Corrosion Inhibition, Surfactant, copper and sulphuric acid.

Introduction

Copper and aluminum is one of the most important metals and is used in a large number of applications. The pure copper has good corrosion resistance and is frequently used as protective coat for metals and alloys. For the same reason, copper used as alloying elements, copper based alloys shows considerable resistance against different type of corrosion. Even the addition of small quantity of copper to an alloy improves its corrosion resistance character. The corrosion resistance of copper is due to the formation of passive film on its surface upon exposure to the corrosive media. Nevertheless, copper could be attacked by acidic media in a considerable rate. Many workers conducted to study the passivation of copper in different acidic media. It was reported that the passive film formed on copper surface in low concentration of sulphuric acid. However, it obtained results showed that copper establishes a kind of passivity in which the corrosion current, in the passive potential range, is somewhat higher than those recorded by other passive metals. Because copper is frequently used in contact with acidic solutions, its corrosion rate must be controlled. One of the useful methods of controlling the corrosion process is the addition of corrosion inhibitors.

Many researchers were published in the literature concerning the usage of inhibitors for copper in acidic solution. Most of inhibitors are organic compounds containing sulfur or nitrogen in their chemical structures. It was found that this kind of compounds is chemically adsorbed on the copper surface forming a barrier for mass and charge transfer who consequently decreases the rate of corrosion. Unfortunately, most of these compounds are harmful for human health and for the environment. Therefore, additional work should be conducted to find safe and cheap corrosion inhibitors for copper in acidic solutions. This work devoted to test a series of organic compounds as inhibitor for the copper in sulphuric acid solution. These compounds can be easily synthesized from relative cheap materials. In addition, these compounds are non toxic and have surface active property. Weight loss measurement, cyclic voltammetry techniques were used in the study to evaluate the inhibition efficiency of the tested compounds.

Experimental

Coupons of pure copper with dimensions of 1 × 2 × 0.5 cm were used in weight loss experiments. For potentiostatic polarization technique a cylindrical rod of copper embedded in araldite with an exposed bottom area of 0.5 cm^2 was used. Before each experiment, the electrode was polished to a mirror finish with different grades of emery papers, degreased with acetone and finally rinsed with distilled water. BDH grade sulphuric acid was used for the preparation of the test solution. Weight loss measurements were carried out by the same method as described elsewhere. Each of the copper was immersed, for 24 hours, in 50 ml of 0.5 M sulphuric acid solution containing of surfactants, at 30°C. All electrode cells, with saturated calomel reference electrode and platinum foil counter electrode was used in polarization experiments. Both potentiostatic polarizations a cyclic voltammetry technique were carried out using a PS remote potentiostat with zum PS-6 software for calculation of electrochemical parameters.

Results and Discussion

Weight Loss Measurements

The losses of weight of copper sheets due to their immersion in solution of 0.5 M sulphuric acid containing different concentrations of the inhibitors were measured. It was found that the addition of any the used all compounds lowers the weight loss of the copper sheet than its value in the acid solution. This result indicates the all the natural products act as inhibitor for the corrosion of metals in acidic solution. The inhibitive action could be attributed to the adsorption of their molecules on the copper surface, forming a barrier between the bar metal and the corrosive environment. The surface activity of natural compounds as well as the presence of function group, in their structures facilitates such adsorption. The surfactant molecules adsorb on the surface via their functional group. Since the compounds mixed in to the solution they repel aggressive anions away from the metal surface and therefore inhibit the corrosion reaction. The inhibition efficiencies of different concentrations of the compounds are given in Table 13.12. The inhibition efficiency was calculated using the following equation:

$$IE\% = [(w_f - w_i) / w_f] \times 100$$

Where w_f and w_i are weight loss of metals in free and inhibited acid media respectively.

Inspection of Table 13.12 reveals that the inhibition efficiency increases as the inhibitor concentration is increased. This behaviour could be attributed to the increases of the metal surface area covered by the adsorbed inhibitor molecules with the increasing inhibitor concentration. Furthermore, data of Table 13.12 shows that the extent of inhibition of different compounds on their structures. The inhibition efficiency increases in the following order.

Table 13.12 : Dependence of IE% of the Inhibitors of their Concentration as Revealed from Weight Loss Measurements

Concentration of inhibitor	Bixin	Zentheloxylum almauta	Echitamine	Nyctanthin
50 ppm	49.58	57.43	78.9	82.9
100 ppm	68.9	71.6	84.32	90.67
200 ppm	80.21	81.65	94.1	95.34
300 ppm	88.123	90.24	95.7	98.10
400 ppm	92.30	94.6	96.12	98.673

Bixin < Zenthoxium almauta < Echitamine < Nyctanthin

This sequence reflects the effect of type of the unit present in the compound and their inhibitive action.

Potentiostatic Polarization

Figure 13.68 represents the anodic and cathodic polarization curves of copper electrode in 0.5 M sulphuric acid solution containing different concentrations of inhibitor. Similar curves were also obtained for the other inhibitors.

Table 13.13 : Electrochemical Parameters of Cu Corrosion in Free and Inhibited 0.5 M Sulfuric Acid Solutions

Inhibitor Concen-tration/ ppm	E_{corr} Mv	I_{corr} mA/cm²	(β_q)	$-(\beta_c)$	IE%	Θ
0.0 Bixin	–280	12.89	296	768	—	—
50	–80	6.56	199	546	49.1	0.49
100	–61	4.123	199	505	68	0.68
200	–52	2.68	167	398	79.2	0.79
300	–48	1.123	156	368	91.2	0.912
400	–29	1.124	178	340	91.5	91.5
600	–18	1.124	159	329	91.5	91.5
1.0 Zenthoxylum Alatuma	–280	12.89	296	768	—	—
50	–98	5.432	165	498	57.8	0.57
100	–84	3.4325	145	476	73.4	0.73
200	–76	2.1678	133	450	83.2	0.83
300	–69	1.3980	121	405	89.1	0.89
400	–63	0.9867	120	401	92.3	0.92
600	–54	0.9861	116	389	92.3	0.92
2.0 Echitamine	–280	12.80	296	768	—	—
50	–100	3.45	153	410	73.2	0.73
100	–92	2.912	146	356	77.4	0.77
200	–82	1.8970	157	342	85.5	0.85
300	–62	1.2180	169	322	90.5	0.90
400	–54	0.8189	168	301	90.7	0.907
600	–44	0.6231	162	289	95.1	0.95
4.0 Nyctanthin	–280	12.89	296	768	—	—
50	–108	3.0237	142	410	76.5	0.76
100	–98	1.1876	144	356	90.7	0.90
200	–89	1.0970	158	342	91.4	0.91
300	–68	1.0180	169	322	92.1	0.92
400	–54	0.6142	171	301	95.2	0.95
600	–45	0.4123	171	289	96.8	0.96

Analysis of Fig. 13.68 find that both the anodic and cathodic polarization curves are shifted to less current density values in the presence of inhibitors. This behaviour suggests that the inhibition action of the compounds. The extant of the shift in current density increases with increasing of the concentration of compounds.

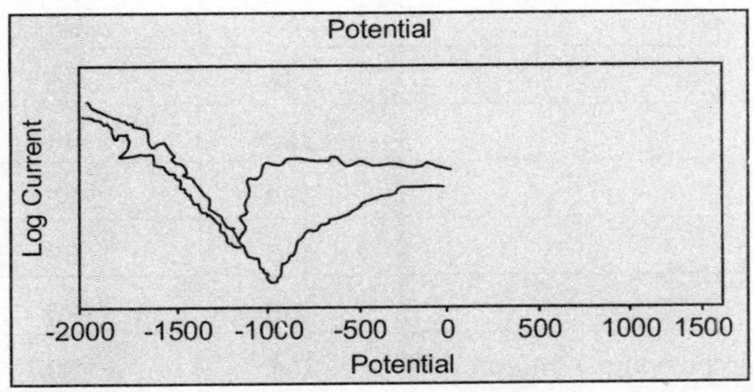

Fig. 13.68 : Polarization curves of Copper in 0.5 M Sulphuric acid containing different concentration of Surfactants.

The value of corrosion current density (I_{corr}), corrosion potential (E_{corr}), anodic Tafel constant (β_a) and cathodic constant (β_c), exclude from polarization curves. Inspection of Table 13.13 given an idea that the corrosion potential of copper and aluminium in acidic solution is largely shifted to less negative values upon addition of the compounds. The magnitude of this shift increases with increasing of the association of natural product like Bixin, Zenthoxylum almatum, echitamine and Nyctanthin, and with the increasing of the additives concentration.

On the other hand current density is greatly reduced upon addition of any of the four inhibitors. These results suggest the inhibitive effects of the tested compounds. The data in Table 13.14 reveals that the values of inhibition efficiency obtained by polarization technique are comparable to those obtained by weight loss measurements. The inhibition efficiency increases with increasing of concentration of compounds. The efficiency could be recognized Table 13.14 that the inhibition efficiency of the compounds increases in the following order:

Bixin < Zenthoxlum Almauta < Echitamine < Nyctanthin

It is of interest to note that this sequence is the same like that obtained by weight loss measurements. Further, inspection of Table 13.13 reveals that the addition of increasing concentration of compounds decreases both the anodic and cathodic Tafel constants. This result indicates that the non ionic surfactants act as mixed inhibitors. This means that the surfactant molecules are adsorbed on both the anodic and cathodic sites resulting in an inhibition of both anodic dissolution and cathodic reduction reactions. The greater

Table 13.14 : Cyclic Voltammetry of Cu in 0.5 M Sulphuric Acid Solutions containing Different Natural Products. V = 10 mv/sec

Inhibitor concentration/ppm		E_pMv	I_pmA	IE%
00	Bixin	256	160	—
50		288	88	45
100		346	56	65
200		350	44	72
300		388	38	76
400		405	32	80
600		458	26	83
0.0	Zenthoxylum Alatuma	256	160	—
50		300	78	51
100		340	45	71.8
200		366	36	77.5
300		398	28	82.5
400		422	22	86.25
600		470	18	88.7
0.0	Echitamine	256	160	—
50		305	64	60
100		376	40	75
200		401	30	81.25
300		430	22	86.25
400		468	18	88.7
600		479	14	91.25
0.0	Nyctanthin	256	160	—
50		312	50	68
100		390	28	82.5
200		426	22	86.25
300		468	16	90
400		488	08	95
600		494	04	97.5

the metal surface area occupied by adsorbed molecules, the higher the inhibition efficiency. A parameter (e) which represents the fraction of the metal surface covered by adsorbed using the following equation:

$$\Theta = [(I_f - I_i) / I_f]$$

Where I_t and I_i are the corrosion currents in free and inhibited acid solutions, the values of *e* corresponding to different concentrations of natural products.

Plotting of log θ/(1-θ) versus logarithm of concentration of natural products give straight lines with the slop the value close to unity for the compounds, but the values are deviated from unity.

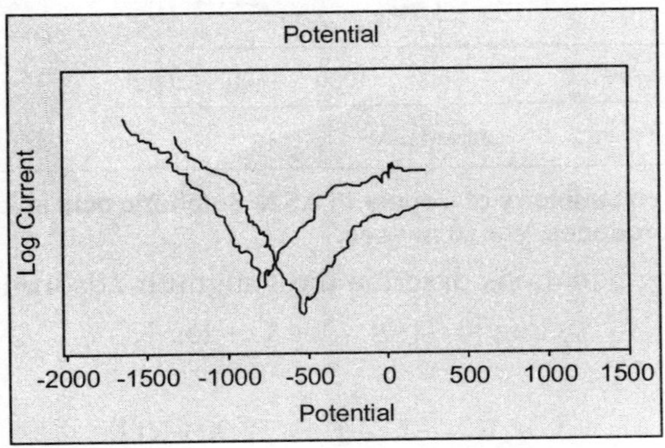

Fig. 13.69 : Polarization curves of Al in 0.5 M Sulphuric acid containing different concentration of surfactant.

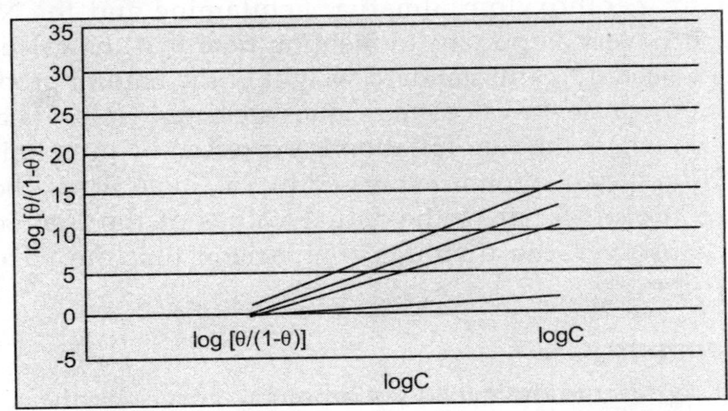

Fig. 13.70 : Isotherms of different Natural Products.

These results suggest that the adsorption of the compounds on Copper surface follows Longmuir adsorption isotherm. This isotherm postulates that there is no kind of interaction force that could arise between the molecules adsorbed at metal surface. Thus, the free energy of adsorption of the molecule is independent on the value of θ.

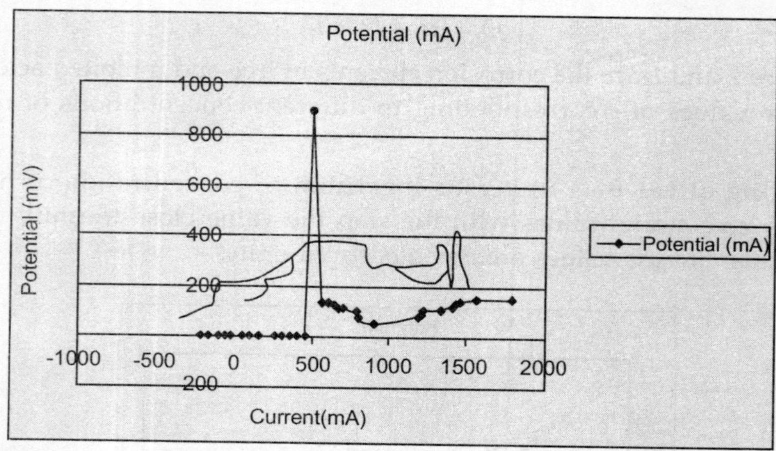

Fig. 13.71 : Cyclic voltammetry of Copper in 0.5 M Sulphuric acid solutions containing different Natural produces. V = 10 mv/sec.

The following equations describe the Langmuir adsorption isotherm:

$$\text{Log } [\theta/(1\text{-}\theta) = \log C + \log K$$

where

$$\text{Log } K = -1.74\text{-}[\Delta G°/2.303 \text{ RT}]$$

Thus, the values of free energy of adsorption (ΔG°) are calculated using these equations. It was found that ΔG° values are –198, –209, –1004, –1200 joule for Bixin, Zenthoxylum almatua, Echitamine and for Nyctanthin respectively. It is very important to mention here that the calculated AG° values are not related to any standard weight of the natural products, such as mole. This is because the calculated values are based on the data extracted from Fig. 13.68, where the concentration is expressed by ppm unit, whereas the value of R in the equation is expressed by cal/mole. Thus, the obtained values of ΔG° do not refer to the actual values of the free energies of adsorption. However, these values comparison that the adsorption is spontaneous process.

Cyclic Voltammetry

Figure 13.69 represents the cyclic voltammetry curves analysis of copper corrosion in 0.5 M on sulphuric acid solution containing different concentration of natural products, traced at scanning rate of 10 mv/sec, between hydrogen and oxygen evolution potentials. Similarly curves also obtained for different more compounds but not shown here. Inspection of

Figure 13.69 reveals that there is only one large anodic peak and no peaks for cathodic loop. Some authors reported that copper gives a small anodic peak in addition to large one and other recorded a very small cathodic peak. However, we determine the appearance of a small anodic peak by using voltage scanning rate smaller than the 10 mv/sec. It was determine that the large anodic peak obtained due to the formation of oxide of cooper. Thus, this peak is responsible for the passivation of copper in sulphuric acid solution. So, the dissolution of copper take place at its potential and analysis in the formation of passive layer, which retards the rate of copper corrosion in sulphuric acid solution. The presence of such type of dissolution peak makes it possible to use its current to represent the corrosion rate of copper, and its potential as the corrosion potential. With the analysis of Figure 13.69 is found that in acidic media the anodic peak current largely decreased. This behaviour is in contrast with the other recorded inhibitor, which increases anodic peak current upon their addition. It was observed that the all compounds enhance the passivation and consequently lead to more saving of copper against the corrosion peak. However, it could be observed that the addition of compounds decreases both the current of the passive current. This behaviour 16 conclude that the adsorptions of molecules of inhibitors prevent the dissolution of copper and act as passive layer better than the oxide film. That mean, other compounds act through enhancement of copper dissolution and produces a thick layer of passive oxide, the natural compounds act through adsorption on the cooper surface preventing directly dissolution of copper. This is the reason of the observe higher inhibition efficiency of natural products.

Potentials and current of anodic peak, in 0.5 M solution containing different concentration of natural plant extracts, as well as the inhibition efficiencies calculated from the peak current reveals that the peak potential, which refers to corrosion potential, is shifted toward more noble direction in the presence of natural products. The magnitude of potential shift increases as the concentration of inhibitor is increased. This behaviour is in agreement with that observed in the potentiostatic technique, although the difference in the absolute values of the potential. On the other hand, the peak current is greatly reduced as a result of addition of extract of natural products, indicating the inhibition efficiencies calculated from the cyclic voltammetry technique, are comparable with those calculating by weight loss and potentiostatic techniques.

Conclusions

- The tested compounds established a very good inhibition for copper corrosion in sulphuric acid.
- These compounds inhibit the copper corrosion by adsorption on its surface and act better than passive oxide film.

REFERENCES

Aksut, A.A., Bilgic, S., *Corros. Sci.* 33: 379 (1992).

Borea, P., Zucchi, F., Trabanelli, G., *Corros Sci.* 13:858(1973).

Keddam, M., Takenouti, H., Yu, N., *J. Electrochem Soc.* 132: 2561 (1985).

Kish, J.R., Ives, M.B., Kodda, J.R., *J. Electrochem. Soc.* 147: 3637 (2000).

Ohtsuka, T., Husler, K.E., *J. Electro anal, Chem.* 102: 175(1979).

Sato, N., Kudo, K., *Electrochim. Acta* 19:461 (1974).

Index

A

Ahmad, M. Sharif, 208
ALWC, 84
Anaerobic corrosion, 56-57
Anodic protection, 109
Anodization, 85
ANOVA, 139

B

Beromunster Reserve Broadcasting Tower, 21
Boller, H., 195

C

Chaubey, Vishwa Mohan, 208
Chauhan, Jitendra Singh, 229
Consequence of corrosion, 13-21
    biohazard symbol used since 1966, 18-19
    chemical hazard, 20
    corrosion challenge, 14-15
    early radioactive trefoil, 17
    European hazard symbols, 20
    hazard symbols, 16
    importance of corrosion studies, 14
    nature and extent of the corrosion problem, 15-16
    new ISO 21482 radiation symbol, 18
    non-standard warning signs, 21
    poison sign, 19
    types of hazard symbols, 17
    warning sign, 20
Corrosion, 2
Corrosion in non-metals, 76-87
    corrosion in passivated materials, 81-82
    corrosion of glasses, 77-78
    corrosion removal, 80
    crevice corrosion, 83
    galvanic corrosion, 79-80
    galvanic series, 80
    glass corrosion tests, 78-79
    high temperature corrosion, 83-84
    intrinsic chemistry, 81
    microbial corrosion, 83
    passivation, 81
    pitting corrosion, 82
    resistance to corrosion, 80
    weld decay and knifeline attack, 82
Corrosion inhibition of copper in sulphuric acid using different surfactants, 229-238
Corrosion testing, 147-154
    base case, 147-149
    coated case, 149-150
    design issues, 151-152
    lessons learned-review questions, 151
    material issues, 151
    processing issues, 152
    testing/environmental exposure issues, 152-153
Cyclic volatammetric behaviour of
    copper electrode in sodium sulfide solutions, 195-201
    iron electrode in sodium hydroxide solutions, 178-187

D

Dow Chemical Company, 18

E

Electrochemical behaviour of iron electrode in
 NaOH solutions, 202-207
 sodium sulphide solutions, 188-194

G

GDP, 14
Generals Purpose Electrochemical System, 196
Gupta, D.K., 229

I

ICCP, 86
India, 2
Inhibiting effect of cytosine derivative on the corrosion of mild steel in acidic medium, 208-217
Inhibition of acid corrosion on mild steel with agar in hydrochloric acid medium at different temperatures, 218-228
Inhibitors, 121-131
 adsorption isotherms, 129-130
 classification of inhibitors, 122-125
 effect of adsorption inhibitors on cathodic and anodic partial processes, 129
 inhibitor in acid solution, 125-126
 interaction between organic inhibitor and metal surface, 126-129
 Langmuir adsorption isotherm, 130-131
 thermodynamic and corrosion kinetics in the presence of inhibitors, 129
International Organization for Standardization, 18
Introduction, 1-3

K

Khairou, K.S., 155

L

Langmuir adsorption isotherm, 130-131
Leptospririllum ferrooxidants, 58-59
Literature survey and scope of the work, 4-12
 scope of the work, 8-10
 survey of the earlier work, 4-8

M

Metallic corrosion, 48-75
 anaerobic corrosion, 56-57
 bacteria known to feed on iron are *Thiobacillus ferrooxidants* and *Leptospririllum ferrooxidants*, 58-59
 bacterial anaerobic corrosion, 56
 binary compounds, 66-69
 biotribocorrosion, 51
 concrete, 73-74
 control, 60-61
 copper band corrosion, 62-64
 crack growth, 54-55
 electrical resistivity measurement of concrete, 74-75
 environmental stress cracking, 71-73
 environmental stress fracture, 69-70
 examples, 55
 fracture, 71
 hydrogen embrittlement, 70-71
 iron bacteria, 58
 isotopes, 64-66
 metals attacked, 53
 nominally anaerobic corrosion of carbon steel in near
 neutral pH saline environments, 57-58
 passive metals, 51-52
 phenomena in different engineering fields, 51
 polymers attacked, 53-54
 possible indicators, 59-60
 prevention, 55, 60
 shock chlorination, 61-62
 stress corrosion cracking, 52-53
 transformation of ferrous hydroxide into magnetic, 57
 tribocorrosion, 50-51
 zinc pest, 69
Methods of corrosion control, 107-120
 adsorption and its influence on inhibition of corrosion, 111-113
 adsorption isotherms, 114-115

anodic protection, 109
cathodic protection, 108
classification of inhibitors, 109-111
correlation between adsorption and inhibition of corrosion, 113-114
corrosion inhibitors, 109
methods of evaluation of inhibitors, 115-116
modification of metal, 108
other methods, 116-117
Methods of protection from corrosion, 84
anodic protection, 86
anodization, 85
biofilm, coatings, 85
cathodic protection, 85
controlled permeability formwork, 85
economic impact, 86-87
impressed current cathodic protection, 86
reactive coatings, 84-85
sacrificial protection, 86
surface treatments, 84

N

National Bureau of Standards, 47
NTP, 9

P

Pitting Corrosion of pure iron electrode in OH/CL solutions and its inhibition by sulphated water soluble natural polymer, 163-168
Potential-modulated reflectance study of the iron in alkaline solution, 169-177

S

Sample research work on corrosion, 155-162
adsorption isotherms, 159-161
carrageenans compounds, 156
experimental, 157
introduction, 156
results and discussion, 157-159
SCPL, 3
SEM, 10
Siddiqi, Wequar Ahmad, 208
Synthesis of the inhibitors, 132-146
techniques adopted, 134-140

T

Theories of corrosion, 88-94
corrosion monitoring techniques, 89
electrochemical methods, 90-94
expressions for corrosion rate, 89
heterogeneous theory, 88
homogeneous theory, 88-89
non-electrochemical methods, 90
Theory of atmospheric corrosion, 95-106
experimental procedure, 97-100
results and discussion, 100-105
Thiobacillus ferrooxidants, 58-59
Types of corrosion, 22-47
bimetallic corrosion, 37-38
coatings, 32-37
cosmetic corrosion, 27-29
crevice corrosion, 37
definition of basic corrosion conditions, 23-27
electrochemical theory of corrosion, 44-47
introduction and definition of basic corrosion conditions, 22-23
losses due to corrosion, 47
pitting corrosion, 37
steel materials, 29-32
stress corrosion, 38-44

U

United States, 47
US Federal Highways Administration, 86

W

World War II, 69

Z

Zaafarany, I., 155
Zinc pest, 69